# Meeting the Challenge

## of Learning Disabilities in Adulthood

The reviews are in—**Meeting the Challenge** is a "winner":

"This much awaited book shares an honest and intimate journey through the public and private lives of adults with LD...their stories offer a window of understanding into the complex world of adults with LD."

**Anne Ford, Chairman**
**The National Center for Learning Disabilities**

"This book expands understanding of the total impact of learning disabilities and can be used as a supplement to traditional textbooks so that a deeper understanding can be developed...it explores previously unexplored areas and it does so with adult case studies which show the life-long challenges that individuals with learning disabilities must resolve."

**Esther Minskoff, Ph.D.**
**Professor of Special Education**
**James Madison University**

"Dr. Roffman has given us a remarkable book about the learning disabled adult experience. From the words of 13 adults with learning disabilities, she conveys their trials, triumphs, and tribulations in a revealing, yet sensitive manner. Her book is rich with quotes, insights, wisdom, and experience. With this book Dr. Roffman has set a new standard. We now see the faces and understand the lives of adults with learning disabilities. This book is a gift to the learning disabilities community."

**Paul J. Gerber, Ph.D.**
**Professor of Education**
**Virginia Commonwealth University**

"An excellent overview of the field of LD and ADHD written in non-technical language, this book makes complex concepts readily understandable. Arlyn Roffman speaks to the reader from her wealth of professional knowledge and experience and also speaks from the heart about what matters the most to those with LD and/or ADHD."

**Susan A. Vogel, Ph.D.**
**Author of *Learning Disabilities, Literacy, and Adult Education***

"This work is a unique and valuable contribution to the literature in this field, especially the extensive, practical guidance offered by individuals who have coped with learning disabilities in their own lives."

**Patricia Horan Latham, J.D.**
**Attorney and co-author of *Learning Disabilities and the Law***

# Meeting the Challenge of Learning Disabilities in Adulthood

by

**Arlyn J. Roffman, Ph.D.**
Lesley College
Cambridge, Massachusetts

·P A U L·H·
BROOKES
PUBLISHING C&#809;

Baltimore • London • Toronto • Sydney

**Paul H. Brookes Publishing Co.**
Post Office Box 10624
Baltimore, Maryland 21285-0624

www.brookespublishing.com

Typeset by Eastern Composition, Binghamton, New York.
Manufactured in the United States of America by
Versa Press, East Peoria, Illinois.

All stories in this book are based on the author's actual experiences and appear
herein with permission. Some names and identifying details have been altered to
protect confidentiality.

**Library of Congress Cataloging-in-Publication Data**

Roffman, Arlyn J.
   Meeting the challenge of learning disabilities in adulthood / by Arlyn J.
Roffman.
        p.    cm.
   Includes bibliographical references and index.
   ISBN 1-55766-430-7
   1. Learning disabilities.   2. Learning disabled.   3. Attention-deficit
disordered adults.   4. Attention-deficit hyperactivity disorder.   I. Title.
LC4818.5 .R64    2000
371.93—dc21                                                99-086790

British Library Cataloguing in Publication data are available from the British Library.

# Contents

# About the Author

**Arlyn J. Roffman, Ph.D.,** Lesley College, 29 Everett Street, Cambridge, Massachusetts 02138-2790

Dr. Roffman is Professor of Special Education at Lesley College, where she currently teaches graduate-level courses in psychology and special education. She also served at Lesley College as the founding director of the Threshold Program (for young adults with learning disabilities [LD]) from 1981 to 1996. Her research interests include social skills development and adolescents and adults with LD.

Dr. Roffman is the author of numerous articles and chapters on LD, a book entitled *The Classroom Teacher's Guide to Mainstreaming* (Charles C Thomas, 1983), and a spelling game, *Rule-ette* (Educators Publishing Service). She has served on the editorial boards of the *Journal of Postsecondary Education and Disability* and *LD Research and Practice* and on the professional advisory boards of the National Center for Learning Disabilities, the National Center for Adult Literacy and Learning Disabilities, the Learning Disability Research and Training Center, the National Network of Learning Disabled Adults, and the Boston University Learning Disabilities Program. She has served as a trustee of Riverview School and the Anchor to Windward Program.

Dr. Roffman has presented and consulted on issues related to special education throughout the United States and abroad. A licensed psychologist, she also maintains a private practice, primarily focusing on adolescents and adults with LD/ADHD. She lives in the Boston area with her husband and daughter.

Readers are invited to e-mail their comments, experiences, and strategies to aroffman@mail.lesley.edu, with CHALLENGE in the subject field. Readers can also mail their comments to Dr. Roffman at Lesley College.

# Foreword

Learning disabilities (LD) are a lifetime disability. A child with LD will become an adult with LD. About 50% of children with attention-deficit/hyperactivity disorder (ADHD) will become adults with this disorder. Thus, it is critical to help adults with LD and ADHD understand their difficulties and learn how to overcome or compensate for them.

To become a successful adult, it is necessary to master several psychological and social tasks. Simply put, an adult must feel like an adult, live like an adult, work like an adult, and relate to others as an adult. Having LD or ADHD, or both, creates a special challenge when trying to master each of these tasks.

To feel like an adult, it is necessary for individuals to feel good about themselves (self-esteem) and to believe that others feel positively about them (self-image). These feelings are based on a lifetime of experiences with family, school, and peers. For an adult with LD/ADHD to have a positive self-image and self-esteem, it is important that he or she experiences success. To do this requires understanding, accepting, and compensating for one's disabilities and knowing how to maximize one's strengths.

To live like an adult means living independently. It is necessary to handle the daily tasks of independent living, from getting up on time and handling personal hygiene issues to managing money, shopping, and eating properly. These and so many other daily challenges are affected by LD/ADHD. The adult with these disabilities must learn how to succeed by understanding and dealing with his or her disabilities.

To work like an adult is essential to earning a living. Each work setting has its own demands for work skills as well as personal, inter-personal, and social skills. Of equal importance is having a positive attitude and a good work ethic. It is important that adults with LD/ADHD understand the possible effect each problem might have on these work-related requirements if they are to develop strategies for being successful.

To relate to others as an adult requires feeling good about oneself. It means learning to trust others. It means understanding others. The ultimate form of relationship, intimacy, requires great risk taking. Each adult in the relationship must feel safe being close to the other. And each must be open and comfortable enough to feel safe being himself or herself and caring enough to accept the other as he or she truly is.

Dr. Arlyn Roffman's book is a positive "you can do it" guide for adults with LD/ADHD. She offers understanding, stressing the positive message that by understanding and learning to accommodate or cope, you can succeed. Personal stories of adults with these problems make the material real and vivid for readers. Readers can identify with these people. They have been there, too. Or, they are there now. Readers can identify with the ways these adults coped and see possibilities for themselves.

Whether writing about personal life, the work place, the family, or daily tasks, Dr. Roffman offers understanding, sensitivity, and positive ways for maximizing strengths, compensating for weaknesses, and, if needed, seeking professional help.

This is a no-nonsense book that is full of compassion for and understanding of the life issues of adults with LD/ADHD. But, much more, it is a positive, "You can take control of your life. You can succeed" book. It is a must-read for adults with these special challenges. It is also a useful book for families and professionals who are part of the lives of these adults.

*Larry B. Silver, M.D.*
*Clinical Professor of Psychiatry*
*Georgetown University Medical Center*

# Acknowledgments

I am extraordinarily grateful to the many people who so generously provided assistance as I prepared and wrote this book. I certainly want to extend my gratitude to all of the individuals who revealed so much of themselves in their interviews and to the Kissires and Sylvesters for granting permission to share their stories as well.

A number of professional colleagues helped in a variety of ways. I thank Craig Michaels, with whom I initially conceptualized an outline and designed the interview questionnaire. Craig conducted several of the interviews. I want to extend sincere thanks to the several others who provided moral support and acted as readers, including Pat Anderson, Cynthia Bioteau, and Rosalie Fink. Paul Gerber, one of the great experts on adults with LD and a dear friend, gave generously of his time to read the manuscript and to encourage my efforts at many critical stages of the writing process.

My editor, Elaine Niefeld, her assistant, Lisa Yurwit, and my book production editor, Kimberly Murphy, cheered me on when the work seemed overwhelming and offered valuable suggestions that improved the final product.

And finally, I am deeply grateful to my family, in particular to my late mother, Beatrice Roffman, who was my cheerleader, but who, sadly, did not live to see the finished product; to my mother-in-law, Bayle Greenberg, who generously shared her journalist's wisdom; and to my dear husband, Bill Greenberg, and my wonderful author daughter, Alissa Greenberg, who sustained me with their love and encouragement throughout more than 2 years of research and writing.

*For Bill and Alissa with love*

# Introduction

## More Than an Academic Matter

Learning disabilities (LD) do not go away. Although the effects of symptoms may be felt in different ways and in varying degrees over time and across situations, research and clinical evidence suggest that LD is broadly felt throughout the lifespan. The symptoms of LD surface most predominantly in the classroom during childhood and the years of formal education, but by adulthood it becomes evident that LD is much more than an academic matter as symptoms rise to the surface in all areas of an individual's life.

This book explores the impact of LD within the many domains of adult life and offers strategies for management of many of the challenges that arise. Through a combination of interviews with a group of adults with LD, a review of the related literature, and my own observations, it is meant to provide a portrayal of the many strengths and challenges individuals with LD typically carry into the adult world.

In an effort to understand the experiences and to capture some of the voices of a cross-section of adults with learning disabilities, interviews were conducted with 13 individuals diverse in a variety of dimensions, including age, gender, religion, ethnicity, socioeconomic status, educational achievement, vocational experience, marital status, and age at time of diagnosis. I chose to interview several adults whom I knew through professional channels as well as others who were referred by colleagues assisting me in my efforts to achieve diversity. Thus, in addition to interviewing people who had earned advanced degrees and held prestigious positions in their places of employment, I spoke with some who, for a time, had been on public assistance, one who was working with great determination to achieve literacy and to earn a general educational development (GED) diploma; one who spent time in a juvenile detention center during her turbulent youth; several who contemplated suicide—at least one of whom has made a serious attempt; and many who had experienced divorce. The people interviewed—married, single, Caucasian, African American, Hispanic, Jewish, Christian—ranged in age from 22 years old to more than 65 years old at the time of our interview.

Time constraints limited the number of interviews, which, in turn, limits the extent to which the results can be generalized. But the goal was never quantitative, and I do believe readers will find that the comments of the individuals who were interviewed provide valuable insights into the experience of living with LD.

In a semi-structured interview that was several hours in duration, each individual was asked a series of open-ended questions about his or her experiences of living with LD. Questions addressed such varied domains as

- *Mental health*: "If you have ever had psychological support, describe the format you have found particularly helpful. What are some things you feel a therapist should know in order to help people with LD?"
- *Day-to-day life*: "How (if at all) does your LD affect your day-to-day life in areas such as shopping, cleaning, organizing, driving, getting to new places on time, or managing money? What strategies have helped you manage in these areas?"
- *Education*: "Describe any formal learning experiences you have had since high school and how (if at all) they have been affected by your LD."
- *Employment*: "Describe your employment history. What effect, if any, have the laws protecting the civil rights of people with disabilities—including the Americans with Disabilities Act (ADA) of 1990 and Section 504 of the Rehabilitation Act of 1973—had on you? What accommodations, if any, have you needed?"
- *Family of origin*: "Describe how (if at all) your relationships with your family members—parents, grandparents, siblings—have been affected by your LD."

- *Friendships*: "How (if at all) have your friendships been affected by your LD?"
- *Romantic partnerships and marriages*: "How (if at all) has your romantic life been affected by your LD? How have you handled disclosure of your LD with new partners? How (if at all) has your married life been affected by your LD?"
- *The parenting experience*: "How (if at all) has your experience as a parent been affected by your LD?"
- *Spirituality*: "How (if at all) has your LD affected your spirituality and/or your involvement in religion? And what impact, if any, has spirituality had on your life with LD?"
- *Quality of life*: "What does the term *quality of life* mean to you? How would you describe your own quality of life at this point? Which quality of life areas, if any, have been affected by your LD?"

Although a set array of questions was posed, all responses were welcome, even when they fell outside the parameters of the planned focus of the interview. This flexibility resulted in an invaluable richness of response and in poignant reflections that are peppered throughout the book. It also resulted in more extensive responses in certain areas by some of the individuals, which is why they may be more heavily quoted in some chapters.

Each taped interview was transcribed. Quotes were selected and were then sorted loosely into topical chapters to focus on particular life issues. An outline emerged somewhat organically through careful study of points made in the interviews and through an extensive literature review pertaining to the issues of adults with LD.

Because several of the people interviewed had been diagnosed with attention-deficit/hyperactivity disorder (ADHD) along with their LD, and because these disabilities often appear in tandem, the literature review was extended to include issues of adults with ADHD as well. Indeed, many references will be made throughout the book to LD/ADHD, which should be interpreted as either LD alone or both LD *and* ADHD. For the particular issues of adults with ADHD alone, readers are referred to the many fine books that focus on that topic.

In addition to the interviews, the transcript of a 3-hour taped session of a Learning Disabilities of America (LDA) conference presentation provided insight into relationship issues experienced by two couples within which one of the partners had a diagnosed learning disability. This information was further supplemented by an exploration of the many articles and books written by Dale Brown, a leader in the LD self-help movement and a prolific writer, who has poignantly described many of the challenges faced by adults with LD in social and employment settings.

My own observations rounded out the data collected. These were accumulated over a period of nearly 20 years of extensive involvement with adults with LD. During that time, I served for 15 years as the founding director of Threshold, a life skills–oriented, nondegree program for young adults with severe LD/ADHD at Lesley College in Cambridge, Massachusetts. I concurrently maintained a private practice in psychology, largely focusing on the adjustment and social skills issues of adolescents and adults with LD and ADHD. References to clients are made throughout the text, although never by name and, on occasion, as a composite of several individuals. Identifying details have been changed to protect their privacy.

## INTRODUCTION TO THE INDIVIDUALS QUOTED IN THIS BOOK

**Terry Bromfield**, 43 years old, resides in Newton, Massachusetts, with her husband and two children. She has a master's degree in education from Lesley College, where she is on the faculty of the Threshold program. Terry has been active in the Newton school community as a resource person for the LD unit of a curriculum entitled, "Understanding Disabilities." She has also acted as a PTA president and representative and was president of the Albemarle Playground Project. Terry struggled in school as a child; she was diagnosed with LD as an adult.

**Andre Fulton**, the father of three children, is in his forties. Separated from his second wife since the time of his interview for this book, Andre lives in Atlanta, Georgia and attends college part time. He has had employment difficulties since he was fired from his job as a police officer for using Ritalin. Andre was not diagnosed with ADHD and did not discover his LD until he was in his thirties. He would like to be an agent or liaison for directing other adults with LD/ADHD to different resources where they can go to get help.

**Jo Ann Haseltine**, a single woman in her fifties, founded and began acting as administrator of Puzzle People, an agency in Marin County, California, that provided a variety of social opportunities for adults with LD for 20 years. Puzzle People closed shortly after Jo Ann's interview due to funding problems. As of this writing, she finds herself "working to the bones to stay alive" with a combination of part-time jobs in dog care, child care, elder care, and housecleaning. She is also working as a paraprofessional in a local school district. Jo Ann lives in California, where she shares a home with her much-loved dog, Marshall Tucker.

**Pat and Weldon Kissire** are heard on the Learning Disabilities Association of America (LDA) conference tape. Pat Kissire learned to comprehend reading only after she was in college. With the help and encouragement of her husband, Weldon, she received her doctorate after she was 50 years old. Together, Pat and Weldon make a team and help other married couples in which one of the spouses has LD. Pat works in Arkansas as a Special Education Coordinator, helping students with behavior problems.

**Lilia,** a woman in her early forties who requested that only her first name be used, is the mother of four children and is raising two other children as well. Having dropped out of school at the age of 14, she has struggled to help her children with their homework but has been better able to help them due to her participation over the past 5 years in the Dorca's Place Parent Literacy Program in Providence, Rhode Island.

**Jule** (a pseudonym) is divorced with no children and lives in the Southeast United States. A psychologist in her early fifties, she is the director of a mental health center for children and families. Jule earned a master's degree in LD and a doctorate in developmental psychology from rigorous academic programs at two prestigious universities. She wants readers to know that, despite her professional competence and accomplishments, she continues to have problems with basic skills. Jule was 35 when she realized she had LD/ADHD and reports, "It was sort of a shock but only to me."

**Nancie Payne**, in her forties, is the mother of two grown children. She resides in Olympia, Washington, with her second husband.

Diagnosed as a hyperactive child, Nancie did not find out about her LD and ADHD until her late twenties. She owns two businesses, a consulting service that helps organizations understand how to more effectively serve people with LD, ADHD, and other disabilities, and a community rehabilitation program that assists people (again, primarily with LD, ADHD, or both) in employment, education, training, counseling, and assessment. She sings and collects antiques. Her passion—believing everyone can learn—keeps her always asking, "Why not?"

**Betty Pike**, a social worker living and working in Howard County, Maryland, is in her early fifties. From 1976 to 1984 she was a commissioner on the Maryland Commission for Women, where she was a catalyst in starting most of the shelters for battered women in Maryland. She received a master's degree in social work from the University of Pennsylvania in 1990. Betty began having significant problems in school at the age of 9 but was not formally diagnosed with both LD and ADHD until the age of 42.

**Rich**, who requested that his last name not be used, was diagnosed with LD as a child in the 1950s, when he attended the Orton Clinic at the Massachusetts General Hospital in Boston for 3 years. He received his doctorate from St. Louis University and completed postdoctoral work in administration at Boston College and Southern Illinois University. In his early fifties, Rich is married and the father of two adult daughters. He and his wife live in the Midwest, where he is the Executive Director of a boarding school for students with LD and ADHD. Rich is a consultant in the area of program development and good teaching practices and currently sits on the boards of several national organizations.

**Nonnie Star**, widowed more than 15 years ago at age 50, has two adult children and two grandchildren, all of whom have LD. A psychiatric social worker, specializing for more than 30 years in LD/ADHD, Nonnie originated the college program for students with LD at Adelphi University and served as the Program Coordinator of the Social Service Center. A columnist, Nonnie has written numerous articles related to LD and is the co-author of a book, *Understanding Learning Disabilities and Substance Abuse,* published by Haseldon. She maintains a private practice in Woodmere, New York, where she resides with Mickey Goldstone, her partner of several years.

**Harry and Janet Sylvester** are heard on the LDA conference tape. They have been married for more than 46 years and live in Maine, where Janet served until recently as executive director of the Maine chapter of LDA. As of this writing, Harry, the partner with LD, has retired from his boat-building business and is the national president of LDA.

**Nina Vansuch**, in her late forties, is the divorced mother of one teenage son and a performance artist. For 25 years she has worked in arts organizations and social service organizations with children and adults, including her current position as director of an after-school program for elementary and middle school children in the Boston area. Nina was one of the 35 performers chosen nationally as a 1999 Fellow in the Cabaret Symposium in the Eugene O'Neill Theater Center in Connecticut.

**Glenn Young** is the divorced father of an adult daughter. Now in his late forties, Glenn was not diagnosed with LD until age 30, when he was still reading and writing on a second-grade level. After interventions, he entered college and rapidly achieved an associate's degree, a bachelor's degree, and a master's degree in public administration from the University of Washington. Glenn has been working for the federal government for the last several years, formerly as an LD specialist with the U.S. Department of Health and Human Services and the National Institute for Literacy, and currently as Disabilities and Adult Literacy Specialist with the U.S. Department of Education, Office of Vocational and Adult Education. He provides further support for the Department of Labor in its efforts around welfare reform. Glenn serves as a board member of LDA.

**Allyssa**, who requested that her last name not be used, is a single woman in her early twenties who works with individuals with disabilities in New York City. She was diagnosed with LD in the fourth grade. In a letter to the author after her interview, she wrote, "I feel as though I have overcome so much in my life and I have a lot of hope for my future. I don't feel like I have any disably, only great ableties" (sic).

The final interviewee, a full-time student, chose not to be quoted in the book.

Throughout this book the effects of LD/ADHD on adults are discussed, and practical strategies are presented. Chapter 1 sets the stage, with definitions and examples of the various characteristics along with a description of the diagnostic process. Mental health concerns are featured in Chapter 2, along with a model of psychological service delivery. Several chapters that focus on relationships follow: Chapter 3 on relationships within the family of origin; Chapter 4 on friendships and dating; Chapter 5 on long-term partnerships and marriages; and Chapter 6 on parenting. Chapter 7 delves into the effects of LD/ADHD on daily life, particularly on self-care, housekeeping, money management, and "getting around." Continued learning opportunities for adults are discussed in Chapter 8, along with the effects of LD/ADHD on adults in academic environments. The effects of LD/ADHD on work are explored in Chapter 9. The book concludes with a final chapter on quality of life. To help the adult with LD/ADHD successfully adapt in the various contexts of adulthood, practical suggestions are provided in Chapters 2–10.

# Defining and Diagnosing LD/ADHD

## WHAT IS A LEARNING DISABILITY?

There is no universal definition for *learning disability* (LD), but it is widely agreed that it is a neurological disorder, a dysfunction of the central nervous system that affects an individual's ability to store, effectively process, and/or transmit information to others. Individuals with LD have deficits in one or more of the following areas (Rehabilitation Services Administration, 1985):

- Attention
- Reasoning
- Processing
- Memory
- Communication
- Reading
- Writing
- Spelling
- Calculation
- Coordination
- Social competence
- Emotional maturity

As implied by the name, a learning disability interferes with the ability to learn and often results in a person's performing below his or her ability level.

## WHAT IS ATTENTION-DEFICIT/HYPERACTIVITY DISORDER?

Attention-deficit/hyperactivity disorder (ADHD) is also a neuro-physiological disorder; however, while individuals with LD have difficulty with processing information, those with ADHD have difficulty gaining access to and focusing on the information at hand (Barkley, 1998). ADHD involves "a persistent pattern of inattention and/or hyperactivity that is more frequent and severe than is typically observed in individuals at a comparable level of development" (Silver, 1999, p. 41). According to the *Diagnostic and Statistical Manual of Mental Disorders, Fourth Edition* (DSM-IV; American Psychological Association, 1994), these problems must be chronic, having surfaced by age 7; be pervasive, occurring in two or more environments, such as work and home; and impair social, academic, or occupational functioning.

One common misconception is that hyperactivity is an essential feature of ADHD; however, even a *hypo*active (underactive) person can be diagnosed with a subtype of ADHD if he or she is inattentive or distractible. The individual in this category, quite unobtrusive, is often viewed by others as somewhat of a "space cadet."

Many people have both LD and ADHD. Although this book focuses on adults with LD, in acknowledgement of the significant number of adults who also have ADHD, the term *LD/ADHD* is used to refer to those who have LD alone or LD and ADHD; however, those who have ADHD alone do not fall under this umbrella term.

### CAUSES OF LD

No one knows the exact cause of LD. Generally, both biological and psychosocial factors come into play. One possible factor is genetics. There is often a family history of LD/ADHD among those who are diagnosed. As Betty Osman wrote, "Just as artistic talent and athletic ability seem to run in families, so do learning problems" (1997, p. 25). This is certainly true among the adults interviewed for this book. Terry, for example, notes the uncanny similarities in the challenges with which she and her father live:

> I think my father has the same exact issues. He certainly has it with the auditory discrimination stuff. He and I mispronounce the

same words almost exactly, and he has a lot of trouble with spelling. Just recently, I started to talk to my father about having a learning disability. I tried to explain to him about what it was that was hard for him to do, and he was looking at me like, "My God, how do you know this stuff?" And I said, "Because it's hard for me. I totally understand it."

LD has been associated with pre- and postnatal trauma as well as difficulties related to birth itself. Poor prenatal care, alcohol or other drug use, untreated Rh factor blood incompatibility, prolonged labor, premature delivery, low birth weight, and oxygen deprivation either during or after delivery have all been cited as possible causal factors, as have brain injury, poor nutrition, child abuse, and exposure to lead and other toxins (e.g., Osman, 1997).

## CHALLENGES OF LD/ADHD: THE YIN

I think that there's a yin and yang in everything. What appears to be a deficit can also be a strength and vice versa.

Glenn Young

Challenges that the characteristics of LD/ADHD create are often offset by considerable strengths and talents. These are the yin and yang of LD/ADHD. The yin will be explored on the following pages through discussion of the characteristics of the disability. Individuals typically exhibit several, but not all, of the many characteristics of LD. Just as no two people have the same fingerprints, no two bear the same set of symptoms. Glenn describes his own particular collection of LD- and ADHD-related issues:

I have mild classic dyslexia in which I reverse words and letters when I see them. I have somewhat more severe oral dyslexia, where I often say the opposite of what I'm meaning, saying "yes" for "no" or "left" for "right." I also have anomia, which is where I often cannot recall the label or word or title of an object or cannot recall the name of the person standing in front of me, even though they may be my next-door neighbor. There are moderate to severe recall issues. I am severely dysgraphic, which basically means that

I cannot transform thought into written form and have severe handwriting problems. I also have classical left–right hemispheric conflict, where I don't always know left from right. I get lost in space. I have poor depth perception.

In addition to that, I have attention-deficit disorder. LD tends to be more defined and is a neurological issue, whereas ADHD is more described as a neurochemical issue. So you have different manifestations as a result of different issues. I've worked very hard to control the manifestations of ADHD. If you knew me 10 years ago, the manifestations were much more out of control— extreme hyperactivity; flitting from thing to thing; constantly appearing to be in chaos; an inability to focus in for a long period of time or becoming absolutely hyperfocused on something and not being able to break from it; extreme levels of energy and then extreme collapses. I could be completely on for something for days and then have to go into hyper-space for days or hours on end, often [with] a very severe lack of perception of what is going on around me socially and mechanically, often missing a lot of cues of how people are responding to me and not understanding their response.

## CHARACTERISTICS OF LD

Characteristics of LD include several different kinds of perceptual impairments, difficulties with time and space, communication problems related to language disorders, and social skills difficulties.

### Perceptual Impairments

Individuals with LD often struggle with problems of perception. As Dale Brown aptly noted:

> LD adults receive inaccurate information through their senses and/or have trouble processing that information. Like static on the radio or a bad TV picture, the information becomes garbled as it travels from the eye, ear, or skin to the brain. (1981, p. 2)

There are several kinds of perceptual difficulties.

*Auditory Discrimination Deficit*    Auditory discrimination involves differentiating between similar sounds. Many people even without disabilities experience a problem in this particular area when they are on the telephone and, for whatever reason, must distinguish between the sounds of the letters *f* and *s*. For example, the last name *Roffman* invariably sounds like *Rossman* over the telephone wires, and it is generally necessary to spell it out, explicitly noting that the middle letters are "double-F, as in Frank." Brown offered another example; she once heard, "Go to the wall and turn on the light," when the person had really said, "Go to the hall and turn to the right" (1981, p. 2). This auditory confusion led her quite literally in the wrong direction.

People with auditory discrimination problems may have trouble with rhythm and rhyme and often have difficulty pronouncing and spelling polysyllabic words. Finding it challenging to hear the separate sounds within words, they are likely to be poor spellers and have difficulty learning to speak foreign languages. Indeed, even in English many struggle to learn new terminology or names and often mispronounce words, as Terry describes:

> I have a lot of problems with auditory discrimination, especially with long words and the sounds in the middle of words. There are just a lot of cases where I don't even know the right words. An example was when my son was studying for a history test, and he asked what Little Big Horn was. I said, "Well, that was Custard's last stand," and my husband laughed, "It's not custard—it's not a dessert!" Whatever the words are, they just are what they are to me—probably even if I saw it written on a piece of paper, I would say custard. I don't have a phonics base. I don't understand how the sounds of letters relate to the spoken language. I don't have a clue. Also, I don't have a strong visual memory for the words I do know that I can actually draw upon. I can't figure it out by listening or visualization; it kind of compounds the problem of not being able to write my thoughts or get things out in a fluid way.

*Auditory Figure–Ground Problems*   Some people with LD have an auditory figure–ground problem, which is the inability to pick out necessary and relevant sounds from incidental background noises. Individuals with auditory figure–ground difficulties are distracted by sounds that would be considered subtle for others, such as the ticking of a clock, noises produced by a heating system, or the rush of traffic on faraway streets. Many people with trouble in this area stop listening as a defense against "auditory overload." Frustrated that they cannot readily pay attention to any one sound, they tune out altogether in noisy environments. This is true for Rich, who reports, "I don't make small talk. I have difficulty with auditory processing, so if I'm in a crowd of people, I have a real difficult time staying focused."

*Auditory Memory Deficit* A third auditory perceptual impairment involves memory. An auditory memory deficit is the inability to store and retrieve upon demand what has been heard, such as telephone numbers, song lyrics, and new terminology. As Betty recalls, problems in this area plagued her even when she was at church: "As a child, I never memorized prayers because with my disability I can't memorize. The expectations on me were phenomenal; and with my LD I couldn't meet those expectations."

Individuals with auditory memory problems are apt to remember some but not all elements of a set of instructions and frequently must ask for oral directions to be repeated. One person notes an associated social problem:

> People tend to get ticked off, like I'm being defiant or lazy, when I don't follow through on a set of instructions they've just whipped through in what sounds to me like a jumble of words. But it's just that I can't remember all the things that I was supposed to do.

In addition to having difficulty remembering each step of the directions, they may struggle to remember the sequence. This leads to everyday nuisances, such as getting lost on the way to new destinations. As one individual explains, "It's impossible for me to follow oral directions. I can never remember if I'm supposed to go left-left-right or right-right-left."

*Visual Discrimination Problems* Weak visual discrimination is the inability to visually distinguish one object from another. People who have difficulty in this area often struggle with differentiating sizes and shapes and with the process of comparing and contrasting similar items, such as the letters *p*, *b*, and *q* or the numbers 6 and 9. Because visual information is inaccurately processed, they have trouble accurately copying words, numbers, or figures from text or off a backboard or wall posting. One person bemoans:

> I wrote down the time the movie began, picked up my friend, and proudly arrived in plenty of time to get popcorn and good seats.

Unfortunately, I had done one of those 6/9 inversion things, so we arrived at 9:30, when the show we'd hoped to see had run only at 6:30 that night. What a drag!

*Visual Figure–Ground Deficit*    Visual figure–ground perception is the ability to focus on one figure from a visual background. People with difficulties in this area have trouble using dictionaries, telephone books, and maps; reading the stock pages; checking movie times in the newspaper; and reading charts and diagrams. Another woman with a movie-related problem explains:

> I can't use the newspaper to figure out what time a movie begins. I just look at the zillions of numbers on the page and, for the life of me, I cannot pull out the one that tells me when I should show up for the film. So I always use the telephone to get that particular information.

*Visual Memory Deficit*    Visual memory is the ability to store and retrieve on demand what has been seen. Those adults who struggle in this third visual perceptual area cannot readily recall television shows, movies, or presentations that were primarily visual in format. They also find the process of visualizing and revisualizing a challenge and generally have trouble spelling sight words, often writing the correct letters, but in the wrong sequence (e.g., *said* becomes *siad*). Terry provides another example of how her difficulty with conjuring up images from memory translates into day-to-day reality:

> I basically can't type. Forget it—I took typing three times. I really wanted to learn how to type, but I can't visualize what the keyboard looks like. I don't know where the letters are. So, what I do is I pick and peck. I look at the keyboard, and after I get a complete thought out, I then look back at the screen and read it and sort of rearrange the words.

*Visual-Motor Impairment*    The inability to coordinate vision with the movements of the body or parts of the body is called visual-motor impairment. People with visual-motor problems often have poor eye–hand coordination. This causes them to have difficulty with handwriting, which may be illegible or composed of a mix of cursive and printed letters. Additional challenges include sewing, cutting, sweeping, and copying. Those who have problems in this area tend to have difficulty in many athletic activities and may be somewhat awkward on the dance floor as well, appearing clumsy because they cannot readily replicate demonstrated dance steps. They are frequently aware of their mistakes and experience frustration with their inability to correct their errors.

*Tactile Differential Impairments*    A further perceptual difficulty associated with LD is tactile differential impairment, difficulty interpreting perceptions through touch. Individuals with problems in this area may use either too light or too tight a grip when they shake hands with others. They also may be hypersensitive to touch.

### Temporal Problems

Temporal problems involve difficulty understanding the concept of time. Because adults with temporal issues lack a sense of how much time it takes to complete tasks, many procrastinate or miscalculate work time and, subsequently, often miss deadlines. Nancie describes her difficulty with time concepts:

> I get terribly overwhelmed if I have too many things going on. I don't manage time well at all. I don't understand how long it takes to do a process, even though I might have done it three or four times. I believe that I'm part procrastinator, but part of the problem is just kind of a reasoning and problem-solving deficit. It may be that reasoning and problem solving are deficits because I procrastinate; however, I don't really think I understand the intensiveness of what needs to be done and how long it takes until I actually do it. Then I realize it, and then I get overwhelmed.

### Spatial Problems

The inability to relate oneself to space and subsequent inability to relate sets of objects in space to each other indicate spatial problems. Those who have spatial difficulties frequently lose their way and/or their belongings. Confusion about direction and a deficient sense of self-in-space contribute to an individual's tendency to become disoriented, even in familiar surroundings. A student who used the same subway stop twice a day on her way to and from work reports an example of this phenomenon:

*One day a construction crew blocked off the steps I usually take back up to the street level, and I had to use a different stairway on the other side of the station. When I got up to the street, I had no idea at all which way I should walk, even though I was just across the street from where I usually come out. I was completely befuddled.*

Many people who have spatial problems also struggle with handwriting; their letters and words are often poorly organized on the paper, spaced either too far apart or too tightly crowded on each line. Some have difficulty using a telephone; they "dial" inaccurately and frequently connect with wrong numbers. Some struggle with depth perception and are in some degree of danger when they drive or navigate steep stairways.

### Communication Problems

Communication problems challenge many individuals with LD. The difficulty may be with input (understanding the meaning of verbal and nonverbal messages) or with output (expression of thoughts and feelings to others).

*Receptive Language Difficulties*   Receptive language involves understanding language that is spoken or written by others and relating speech and words to meaning. People with receptive language problems tend to have a limited vocabulary and often fail to understand the subtleties of figurative speech. Slow to respond to verbal stimuli and requiring extra time to process verbal input, they frequently appear puzzled when given oral instructions and may need directions repeated several times before they are able to grasp what it is that they are being asked to do. These individuals are often challenged when expected to learn the rules of a new game or to understand explanations of new procedures. Some cannot follow conversations with frequent shifts in topics. One person complains, "I simply cannot track the fast banter of my friends, particularly when they are excited about something. The words seem to just fly by, and I can't reach up and grab them. I just sit there, lost."

*Expressive Language Disorder*   Difficulty producing language by speaking or writing is known as, expressive language disorder. Adults with problems in this area may appear nonfluent at times as they stammer, stutter, or use "uh" excessively. They may omit, substitute, distort, or add sounds in words. Further, they often search for words and may refer to "whatchamacallit" and "whoosit" on a fairly regular basis, or they may use definitions for objects whose names they cannot recall, avoiding the word "sweater," for example, by referring to "that wool thing you wear over a shirt when it's cold outside." As a defense mechanism, they may have developed shyness, marked by a reluctance to speak.

### Skills Deficits

Skills deficits are common among individuals with LD. For many, the process of **reading** and sounding out (decoding) words is not automatic; it is a rather laborious task. They read very slowly, or they skip words, or they decode well but have difficulty with comprehension. In his personal account of life as an adult with LD, Christopher Lee shared an insight: "I feel like I am a prisoner of the written word. If I lived in a society in which the printed word were not important, I would have no learning disability" (Lee & Jackson, 1992, p. 40).

Many adults with decoding problems have trouble handling everyday tasks, such as reading signs at the grocery store or laundromat or important notices in the newspaper. Jo Ann snickers as she recalls:

> I had to laugh when one organization for LD started looking for interview subjects to gather data on learning disability adults— they put a little box on the front page of our local paper to get interviewees. Know how many responses they got? One. And it was probably mine.

Terry describes her difficulties in reading:

> I was tested recently; my reading speed is sixth grade; my reading comprehension level topped out at 15 or whatever the top level is. I'm a slow reader for a very specific reason—I do not read the words I don't know. I actually don't read them since I don't have knowledge about how to attack them. So I have to step back and think about the context, and that takes time.

Difficulties with reading can be very limiting. Glenn describes dramatic limitations on the types of reading he can tackle. Although he is able to do quite well with linear material, such as history, he cannot read a Brontë novel or poetry by Shelley because the subtlety and flow of the language are lost on him. Reading difficulties cause a different type of problem for a man who recently confessed that he is very reluctant to try to use the Internet; while he realizes he is limiting himself by refusing to use this tool, he reports that he finds the amount of text on the screen too daunting to approach. Nonnie recognizes the limitations caused by her own reading problems, particularly on her general fund of knowledge: "I feel badly that I don't know the classics or the things that most people seem to. There's a bank of information that's lost because I had a learning disability. You can't backtrack that. So you lose."

In addition to decoding and comprehension limitations, people with LD may have weak **writing**, also known as encoding ability. Writing is closely tied to reading, and issues with one are likely to be linked to the other. Lee commented, "I still struggle so much with reading individual words that I don't see where sentences or paragraphs begin or end. I never see any structure when reading; therefore, I don't know how to use it when I am writing" (Lee & Jackson, 1992, p. 29).

Difficulties with language often translate into challenges in the writing process. Nancie describes the link:

> My understanding of my learning disability is that it's language-based and affects the way I write. It sometimes affects the way I talk and think, although I think I have pretty good strategies to keep organized. It affects the way I read—I can read, but I don't read fast, and I don't comprehend what I read the first time. The writing piece is really the biggest part that's affected. It takes me hours and hours and hours to write one or two sentences even. But that's the composition part, not the penmanship part. Also, the grammar's bad. For some reason, spelling never was affected too much.

Harry finds that his LD has significantly limited his ability in written expression. Despite his concerted efforts to improve this area, his difficulties persist:

> My disability comes in language. I have had verbal expression problems. I am reading at the 30th percentile, I am spelling at the 7th percentile. My written expression is virtually zero, even today with as much schooling as I have had, as hard as I have tried to do something about that.

Like Nancie and Harry, a significant number of other individuals with LD have difficulty committing words to paper, organizing their thoughts, sequencing their ideas, and proofreading effectively to prevent mechanical issues from compromising strong content. Poor spelling is the characteristic of LD that is, perhaps, most obvious to others. A very significant issue for most people with LD, difficulty with spelling is evident in inconsistencies (e.g., spelling the same words different ways), rotated letters (e.g., *b/q; m/w*), omitted or added letters, and letters out of sequence. Poor spelling may be the by-product of a visual memory impairment, which makes it difficult for the person to remember what the word looks like; of an auditory discrimination deficit, which makes it difficult for the person to hear and identify the sounds to represent phonetically; or of a conceptual failure to understand spelling rules and basic phonetic principles. Poor spelling may even be a byproduct of impulsivity, the end result of an individual's failure to pause and take the time to accurately use the skills that he or she has developed.

**Math difficulties** may be conceptual, spatial, or tied to an inability to make the basic number facts automatic in one's mind. In the case of word problems, difficulties may be tied to reading issues, with the individual losing the meaning of the problem itself as he or she struggles to decipher the words on the page. Difficulty with math is evident in

- Reversal of digits (e.g., *15* for *51*)
- Omission of steps in a math sequence
- Careless errors
- Failure to line up the digits properly
- Confusion with vocabulary words that refer to math concepts

Nancie has always been challenged by math and money matters:

> I have trouble with math, any kind of higher-order math numbers—things like checkbooks, all that stuff—although I can add, subtract, multiply, and divide. If I think about it and

remember all the steps, I can get there, but I just have to kind of prep myself.

## Social Imperception

Although social imperception is not generally included among the basic characteristics of LD, it is indeed a concern. Social skills deficits are evident in individuals with LD when they have poor eye contact; when they lack sensitivity to the thoughts, feelings, and need for personal space of others; when they interrupt; when they have difficulty making social inferences; and when they find it difficult to shift their behaviors according to varying social situations.

## CHARACTERISTICS OF ADHD

Distractibility, impulsivity, and hyperactivity are core characteristics of ADHD but may also be experienced by individuals with LD.

### Distractibility

Distractibility is supersensitivity and limited ability to "tune out" both internal stimuli (e.g., thoughts, pain, hunger, sex drive) and environmental stimuli (e.g., noise, movement). Silver described two types of internal distractibility: 1) *drifting*, which involves the mind wandering, commonly referred to as "daydreaming"; and 2) *jumping*, which involves "not being able to block unwanted thoughts . . . trying to listen or do something and thinking of two or three other things at the same time" (1999, p. 43). Individuals who are distractible are troubled by drifting and jumping, making it difficult for them to plan ahead and think through consequences. They may have difficulty sustaining effort and often exhibit a pattern of starting projects that they lose interest in and fail to complete. With their tendency toward flight from idea to idea, they often tackle several challenges at once, which can be viewed as both a strength and a weakness, as the multiple-balls-in-the-air approach can be rather overwhelming to others. Jule describes her own style and its effect on those with whom she works:

> I can assimilate information very quickly, and I can do more than two, three, four things at once. I can be talking to one person in my

office and sometimes turn to somebody else and say, "Now don't forget about such and such." It drives people crazy.

### Impulsivity

Impulsivity is a lack of restraint that leads to reacting immediately, without thinking ahead. Because adults who are impulsive do not stop to consider past experiences, they often make judgment errors. One person reports:

> I don't stop to think through the consequences of my actions. I have an understanding of this, but that doesn't stop me from barreling ahead the next time. I do things like write a check for something when I know full well that there's nothing in my account. I hate bouncing checks, but at the moment of the purchase, I just have to have the T-shirt or CD or whatever.

Impulsive people frequently have trouble delaying gratification and typically get angry if they are expected to wait, often interrupting others and blurting out whatever is on their mind. They tend to offer quick responses to sensitive issues and inappropriate expressions of anger and hurt, which they later regret.

### Hyperactivity

Hyperactivity is persistent, heightened, and sustained activity levels that are situationally and/or socially inappropriate. By adulthood, hyperactivity often appears as a general restlessness that is evident even when the individual is interested in the subject at hand. Describing himself, one client comments:

> I drive people nuts because I fidget, tap pens, jiggle my knees, and pace, all of which feels entirely involuntary. It's not that I'm not paying attention; it's just that I can't seem to do it without moving some part of my body.

Such constant body movement can be problematic in a variety of situations. Nina finds that her restlessness even interferes with her spiritual pursuits:

> It's hard to go to church and sit still. I think sometimes about going. My fantasy is to join the Quaker Church—because their

> services are quieter—and I thought I would just go take my Ritalin
> and sit there. That would actually be a wonderful thing for me to
> have people only talk if they feel like talking. And some days I'd go
> without my Ritalin and shake them up!

Despite good intentions, the hyperactive adult may embark on projects but become waylaid by a surplus of energy and a frustrating lack of self-control. When this occurs, motivation diminishes, and the individual is unlikely to follow through, which further erodes self-esteem and makes him or her feel like a failure.

### Hypoactivity

Hypoactivity, the other extreme, is insufficient motor activity. Like individuals who are hyperactive, those who are hypoactive are often inattentive. Reacting and working slowly and seeming unemotional, hypoactive people appear lethargic and "spacy" and are often accused of being lazy.

## GIFTS AND TALENTS COMMON TO LD/ADHD: THE YANG

Despite the daily challenges, individuals with LD/ADHD also enjoy many gifts and talents. Recognition of this balance of yin and yang can change an individual's outlook, leading to a far healthier self-concept and increased potential for success (Gerber, Ginsberg, & Reiff, 1992). This recognition has provided a boost to Allyssa's self-concept. Although she at one time focused on and mourned her weaknesses, her perspective has changed, and she is now able to view herself in a far more positive light:

> I have respect for myself today, and I feel good about myself. I
> know I'm blessed, and I know that I have gifts. I'd rather talk to you
> about the gifts that I have than my weaknesses, because my
> weaknesses aren't even weaknesses anymore—they're strengths.

### EMPATHY

Because of their own longstanding difficulties, many people with LD/ADHD have an extraordinary empathy for the struggles of others. Allyssa believes her compassion is a divine gift that enables her to offer a rare level of understanding to the clients with whom she works:

> Because I have a learning disability, I look at people with compassion. I know that God gave me a learning disability because he knew I could overcome it and touch people. And that's what I do every day. I took jobs where I could help people and where I know you would totally need a lot of patience. I worked in group homes and had to change diapers for handicapped adults, give them showers. [People] say, "Oh, wow, how could you do that?" I tell them, "God has given me compassion. I can do that stuff."
>
> Those choices that I made for those jobs are only because I've been hurt by society, and I know what it feels like to feel different, to feel "less than," to feel like garbage. The handicapped children I worked with, they couldn't sit still for half a second. I viewed them as myself when I was little. All I wanted was somebody to sit down with me and not get frustrated when I didn't understand and tell me that they're proud of me and I was doing a good job. That's all I wanted my whole life, and I didn't get it. And that's all they want. That's why I love working with handicapped [children and] adults.

Jule, too, believes that her own problems have enhanced her professional sensitivity:

> I've had a children's clinic, primarily for assessment and intervention. In reflecting back, I realized that a lot of the difficulties I had were in some ways similar to the ones of the children that I saw. I got into [focusing on] attention–deficit [in my practice] and started looking at histories that I would take. I would see myself in them. And it wasn't that it was an excuse. I mean you are what you are, and you just deal with what you've got. But I think it's made me a better professional.

Rich agrees that this empathy is a professional bonus and notes that he is able to respond to the students in his school in a manner that could not be replicated by most headmasters without LD/ADHD:

> It's very easy for me to really pinpoint for the kids [at my school
> for LD students] what's going on for them, particularly if they
> don't have the language to do it themselves, and eliminate that
> sense of isolation which they may have in relation to their LD.

Lilia reports that her volunteer activities have been enhanced by the
empathy she has developed as a result of her LD. She has been
volunteering to work with children for the last several years and
feels she understands what they are going through when they
"can see a person's mouth move and hear words being said, but
cannot find meaning in those words."

### INTERPERSONAL STRENGTHS

Although some adults with LD/ADHD struggle socially, many find
strength in their connection with others and engage in social
networking that results in friendly support from a variety of people.
Finding and taking advantage of a friendship circle serves to lay a
foundation for success within a number of areas of adult life (Reiff,
Gerber, & Ginsberg, 1997).

Andre speaks proudly of his interpersonal flexibility, noting that
he gets along with people very well and can adjust to almost any
situation. Terry, too, finds strength in her interpersonal skills and
notes that her best learning occurs through interpersonal experiences
with others. Relative to Howard Gardner's (1993) theory of multiple
intelligences, which breaks IQ into eight different domains, she
explains:

> If you were to ask, "Well, what's the way that you're the most
> smart?" I would say, "Interpersonal." That would be the thing that
> I get the most. If I'm learning something about how people interact
> with each other, I can think about it in terms of something that I
> know that's happened or that I've been involved in, and then it
> makes sense to me. If it's something that I've not experienced or
> that I only have a little bit of a sense of, it's harder.

Christopher Lee, who also considers himself to be strong interper-
sonally, noted the contrast between his grasp of verbal versus
nonverbal communication: "If verbal communication is my dragon,

nonverbal communication is my sword. I understand its importance, and I know how to use it. Basically, I am good at reading people" (Lee & Jackson, 1992, p. 75).

## DRIVE

Gerber et al. (1992) noted that a key characteristic of the successful adults whom they studied was a strong desire or drive to move ahead. Several of the adults interviewed for this book demonstrate considerable drive. Some, like Nonnie, are driven to provide help to others who have similarly struggled:

> I was in my thirties when my daughter was called retarded. I didn't have denial, but I just didn't believe it. When she was diagnosed with minimal brain dysfunction, which is what they called LD when she was young, and they asked, "Who has it in your family?" I was so happy that there was a label, a name for what I was feeling all my life. I was happy with the label. When I heard that there was a real reason for all my sadness and all my crying secretly and all the hurts I'd felt, and all the lack of understanding, I decided my mission was to try to teach other people—professionals—what to do with their own clients.

## FOCUS AND RESOLVE

Many find that when they are interested in something or someone, resolve sets in, and they are able to hyperfocus. Silver (1999) noted that hyperfocusing can be a coping strategy for individuals who struggle with distractibility; in order to attend to activities they find enjoyable, they tune out all other stimuli, sometimes to the extent that they appear to go into a trance. Rich describes his own ability to stick with projects, despite his ADHD:

> Once I get focused on something, I could stay on it and stay with it, come hell or high water, which is an advantage for me. I just work my tail off until it's accomplished. And the stuff I'm not interested in, well, I'm not interested in.

Nonnie suggests that with resolve comes a fighting spirit:

I always had a spirit, felt you should put the most into each day. People have always seen me as up in a ring, and if the count was 9 1/2, by 10 I'd be up on my feet. The mistake I might make 10 times might be rectified by trying it yet another way.

Jule agrees and exhibits this same attitude. She describes how her ADHD energizes her:

With ADHD, when you go for something, you go for it. When others would stop and others would get discouraged or when you're told "no," you just keep going—you just figure out the other way to get there. If you get to a cabin and there are no matches and it's raining outside, you still figure out how to light the fire.

### TENACITY ("STICK-TO-IT-IVENESS")

Tenacity is a close cousin to resolve, and many adults with LD/ADHD are quite extraordinarily tenacious. For example, over the course of 2 decades, as Jo Ann Haseltine developed and oversaw Puzzle People, an organization for adults with LD, she demonstrated remarkable tenacity. Her journey began one day during her college years, when she despondently remarked to the late John Arena, who had arranged for her to be tested, counseled, and tutored, that there was no one else like her anywhere. He consoled her and introduced her to a few other young adults who similarly felt unique and isolated. She recounts a story of profound determination:

John got a couple of us together, and we sat down and had coffee and shared war stories. After a while that was boring, and I said, "What else do you want to do?" And so, we started Puzzle People, literally on a shoestring—no money, no nothing. It was done at my folks' home. We started out with a one-page letter that was saying, "This month, we're going to go roller skating and dah, dah, dah, dah." And that started it. I was 30. We got the group together, and the turn-outs were pretty good. In November there was very low attendance, and I thought, "Oh, why am I doing this? I'm not getting anywhere." Then Christmas I had over 15 people at my folks' house, and it was wonderful! So I said, "Oh, I've got to keep going with this!"

Our newsletter grew to a one-page legal sheet. In 1980, Betty Lou Kratoville came out with her son, and she thought this was wonderful, what I was doing. With her help, we were able to get incorporated. Betty Lou helped me write a grant, and we got $143,000 for 3 years. It was wonderful. In retrospect, I look back at that now—I had no administrative skills or anything—I was running everything in the dark, with no technical systems person. You can't just lean back on money like that forever. There were just a lot of holes, and, of course, that showed up. We were also tied in with what was called the Learning Difficulties Institute—in my vision it was going to have a huge extensive library on learning disabilities, services for children, adult tutoring, counseling. The whole 9 yards was all going to be under one roof. Well, this particular woman who was in charge of it had different ideas, and she was going to take my project and throw the baby or the founder out of the project. Fortunately, we were free-standing in the sense that we had a Board and could say, "Oh, no, you're not." But by doing that, we severed any other funding. So, from 1986, we just struggled along on our own. And we did okay.

Jo Ann worked for years with no salary, supported by her parents, who worried how she would manage once they were gone. Despite the financial hardship, she was buoyed by the accomplishments of this grassroots effort for local adults with severe LD, whom she describes as "not the ones who went off to college."

At the time of our interview, Jo Ann was grappling with funding problems and the unknown future of Puzzle People, yet she was tenaciously holding on to her dream:

If I had dropped it last year and said, "Well, I give up"—it would have folded then, and I would have felt like I was a failure, even though I'd done everything I possibly could. I will just give anything if somebody's out there, somebody big enough that could make a [financial] difference. I just want [a salary] that I can survive on and do something that I love to do, which is being in touch with other LD's and talking and being able to finish my life off with Puzzle People.

## CREATIVITY

The creativity demonstrated by Jo Ann in establishing the Puzzle People seems characteristic of many people with LD/ADHD.

Although research is scant on the topic, many people are convinced that creativity is somehow tied to these disabilities. But what is the connection? Is it a correlated talent, or is it a coping mechanism? Nancie speaks proudly of her strength in the arts, which helps her cope, fortifying her as she contends with the day-to-day challenges of life with LD: "The strengths and talents are probably the part that help me get through life with LD, actually. I'm extremely musical and artistic. My original goals in high school were to be a stage performer in piano and voice."

Gerber et al. (1992) coined the term *learned creativity* to refer to the unconventional ways adults with LD devise strategies or adapt methods to master a new task. They list this type of problem solving as one of the factors prevalent in the lives of successful adults with LD. Indeed, Betty often tells people she thinks the greatest strengths and positive aspects of having LD are the wonderful creativity and energy that make it possible to generate new ideas and put things together.

Glenn agrees that there is creative thinking among some adults with LD/ADHD; however, he questions crediting the population as a whole with the ability to make unique connections in their thinking:

> One of the classic concepts about [people] with LD and ADHD is that they see things differently than other people. Because of that ability to perceive things differently, you can often make connections, perceptions, and relationships that have never been thought of and that manifest into wonderful things. I do that a lot. The question is, do I do that because of who I am—or am I who I am because I am LD and ADHD? The fact is that so many people who are LD and ADHD don't appear to have that capacity. It's kind of a "super crip" myth that all people with LD tend to have it. Let me put it this way, I tend to think that the hyperenergy level that is there because of the ADHD heightens my capacity to do those things and make the connections, rather than being totally responsible.

## LEADERSHIP SKILLS

Many adults with LD/ADHD have strong leadership skills. Terry's vision and take-charge attitude make her a natural leader. She is able to see "the big picture" and oversee large projects that might easily be overwhelming to others. Her ability to think long-range and see everything that needs to be done was evident on a relatively small scale when she remodeled her kitchen. Acting as her own general contractor, she created a major plan and organized all the workmen so that the bulk of the job was completed in a mere 12 days. This ability was evident on a larger scale when she led a 3-year project building a community playground. She was involved in every phase from fundraising to designing to purchasing to construction. She comments, "People talk about me as a person that can make things happen. And, in fact, that's one of the things that I enjoy the most." Terry attributes some of her success in this regard to her strong delegation skills:

> [On the playground project] I was able to bring up that skill of finding the right people. I really viewed myself as the hub of something with many, many spokes off of it. If you don't have a hub, it's just a bunch of sticks laying on the ground. If you have a hub, you've got spokes that can become a wheel and make something happen. I kind of joke that getting other people to do work for me—one of my coping skills—has really been basically what you call cheating when you're a kid. When you're an adult, it's called leadership and delegating. You get to take this thing that maybe is not that positive in your life—I've sort of turned it around to be very positive.

Terry credits her early involvement in weaving fabrics with her ability to see all the parts of a whole issue or task. At the beginning of each project, she would have to break her imagined product down to the actual strings in order to know how to proceed in weaving. She describes it as a way of thinking, a type of problem solving that has served her well. She goes on to explain that once she has seen all the parts of a whole, she is able to synthesize. She describes chairing meetings, focusing closely on what is happening, and being able to see clearly what needs to be done. She reports, "I often end a meeting by saying, 'Okay, this is what I think we decided and this is what everybody said they're going to do between now and the next time we're going to meet.' "

Betty notes that being a team player is another quality essential to good leadership:

I'm a natural community organizer. I've always had leadership skills, even in high school. People have asked, "How did you do it?" and I said, "It was easy, I didn't have to read books." The energy from being an unmedicated ADHD helped. I could be pretty scattered, but at the same time I teamed up with a good friend who had a wonderful eye for details, where I could see the broad things. I'm very much a team person. We could draw on everyone's strengths.

## VISION

Associated with creativity, many adults with LD/ADHD have vision. Nina's was apparent from a young age:

When I was 19, I was a whipper-snapper. I actually developed an arts program for disturbed teenagers. When I was writing the grant, it was fairly well known that if you needed to have something done, I could do it. I said, "I have a very clear idea about how this program should work and can work but I'm going to have to walk around the room and talk to you, and somebody else will have to take my notes. I'll tell you what to write, but you have to write it." And people were very often happy to because I had good ideas.

## PROBLEM-SOLVING ABILITY

Unfiltered ideas frequently flood people with LD/ADHD when they think about possible solutions to issues at hand; as a result, they often exhibit strong problem-solving ability. Rich describes the process of generating multiple solutions:

I think I'm very bright. I've been able to use my ADHD issues to an advantage. Because of the way you're firing in your head, when somebody presents a problem, there's no one solution. For any one question, there's 10 different answers which automatically pop up. The filtering system that you go through makes you become much more analytical as to what's going on. Part of that analysis is a function of how fast the brain is firing at any particular point in time. Oftentimes, you'll come up with more than one solution to the problem, and all of them are of equal value. This sucks when you're trying to do a multiple-choice test, but in life it's more to your advantage.

Nonnie counts problem solving among her greatest gifts: "I think my strength is being street-smart, more my survival skills over my academic skills. There are some people that are brilliant academically, but they don't know how to problem-solve creatively. And that *is* my definite strength."

Nancie considers herself a good problem-solver and prides herself in her ability to take complex, higher-order ideas and translate them into practical action steps. Betty sees this as an area of strength as well and describes her contribution to the teams with which she has worked:

> My strength was this innovative, creative way of looking at things that nobody else had ever thought of, seeing things from a unique point of view. I'm an auditory learner, so what people say is something that kind of clicks, and I have a gift for pulling different, divergent ideas together. I look at life as a chocolate chip cookie. I make excellent chocolate chip cookies where you take the virgin elements together with a catalyst and create something new and good. I was introduced one day at a meeting, a conference, as a constructive catalyst, and I thought, "Here I am, a chemical reaction standing before you."

Weldon recognizes this strength in his wife, Pat, who regularly manages to come up with sound ideas. He notes that she "can reach and pluck an answer out of the sky" when presented with a problem, and the answer will be legitimate, although she often lacks awareness as to how she has arrived at it. It takes more than problem-solving to accomplish great things, however; a good bit of energy is needed as well. As Jule notes, fortunately, both are often available among adults with LD/ADHD:

> I think once you make up your mind to do something, you can generate an energy to do it and create ways of getting where you need to go that most people wouldn't even think of. When I finally decided at boarding school that I wanted to take overnights [off campus] but knew I'd have to get my grades up in order to earn that privilege, then I was able to figure out a way. Later, in college, when I had trouble taking notes or understanding stuff, I was able to figure out what to do to get where I needed to go. For example, I did laundry for people in college, and I went out on dates with

people I never would have gone out with because they were willing to tutor me.

## HIGH ENERGY

Most adults who have ADHD along with LD exhibit an extremely high energy level. Glenn says:

> I have an enormous energy level. I have an enormous capacity to do a lot of things and often take on tasks people seem to think are extremely daunting and way beyond their capacity, and for me it's normal rule of fit. I can take on major tasks and issues and put in all the energy and do all the work that needs to get this stuff done.

Betty recognizes the benefits of her high energy at her current job in social work as she notes, "Having ADHD is probably an asset because the phone rings off the hook all the time, and there's always 500 things to do." Rich, too, recognizes the advantages of having excess energy and likens himself to the "Energizer Bunny" that keeps on going and going and going.

> My ADHD, focus, drive, that type-A stuff—every employer likes it, because once you get turned on to the situation and you work, you're untiring in what you can do and will do. So part of the benefit to an employer is that you don't put limits on yourself— you just do what needs to be done. Your ADHD is an advantage because you don't just tire out.

## QUICK RESPONSE TIME

The flip side of hyperactivity and impulsivity is that many adults with LD/ADHD are able to respond quickly in stressful situations. Andre describes:

> My career choice [as a police officer] was greatly affected by my ADHD. Had it not been for the disability, I wouldn't have ever known the talent I had in the military organization. I'm no different from any other person with ADHD. They shine above other people in stressful situations. When the wheels come off and the bullets are flying everywhere, a person with ADHD is at home in that

environment because his mind works like that and goes that fast. To him, that's a normal thing. He can function well when "normal" people cannot stay up at that level very long and cannot take that stress.

## INTUITION

There is some speculation about whether individuals with LD/ADHD have higher than average levels of intuition. Many of the adults whom I interviewed reported that they indeed have finely tuned intuition. Jule feels intuition helps her understand her clients more fully. Nonnie feels the same. Andre attributes his uncanny intuition to his ADHD:

> When I was a police officer, I would go right to people [being searched for] when others couldn't find them. And in a criminal's case, sometimes I could *feel* where they were. It was like something inside me said, "Hey, go this way!" Sometimes I got in trouble because I was told to stay with everybody. I don't want to downplay that side of a person with ADHD, because I think some of that is a gift.

## ATTENTION TO DETAIL

Related to intuition is the ability to pick up subtleties in a variety of environments and perceive nuances and innuendoes that others might miss. Rich reports this as part of the upside of having ADHD—nothing goes unnoticed:

> There are definite benefits to my ADHD. As a teacher, because I don't filter out, I was able to pick up on all sorts of stuff going on in the classroom. Because I was able to pick up on the rattle or the noise or the whisper or the under-the-breath cursing, I could direct my attention to it immediately.
>
> You can train yourself so that all the filters are off and you're picking up everything at the same time, all the nuances which occur within that environment. You become very analytical as to what's going on, which allows you to pick up on cues—whether visual or auditory—from kids. That allows you to pick up on specific behaviors that occur. That's really an advantage, partic-

ularly if you're trying to deal with kids clinically or are trying to be sensitive to their needs or their responses.

## DIAGNOSIS:
## RECOGNIZING THE LD/ADHD THAT HAS ALWAYS EXISTED

Many of the individuals interviewed for this book were raised in the years before the widespread recognition of LD/ADHD. Thus, most discovered their own LD relatively late in life via an unconventional path of clinical diagnosis.

Nancie's discovery came through self-exploration during her college years, when readings for an education class about the symptoms of ADHD sounded oddly familiar. She recollects checking her impression with her husband, saying, "You need to read this and tell me if I just put myself in the book or if it's really who I am." Harry, too, found himself in books. His suspicion of having the disability himself was validated through reading Eileen Simpson's (1979) book entitled, *Reversals: A Personal Account of Victory Over Dyslexia*, which detailed difficulties in school that were very similar to his own.

Glenn remembers that the circumstances of his learning about his own LD, although ultimately through a diagnostician, initially came as an unintentional result of exploring his daughter's giftedness:

There are a whole lot of fortunate circumstances behind my being diagnosed. One has to do with my daughter, who was a very gifted child. [When she reached] age 4, we decided that we had to get her into a private school. We went to one of the several in the Seattle area designed for kids who are gifted and took her in for diagnostic testing for giftedness, not for disability. She was taken off into a room with a psychologist who was going to give her the exam. The head of the school sat down with her mother and me to show us what the exam was and what they were going to do—pretty standard format for entry into this type of school. When she got to a certain point, I said that a certain section of this test was the part that I always seemed to mess up on. She didn't say anything, just kept on going and I said, "That's the other part of the test I always seem to mess up on." She stopped and said, "I bet you can't spell too well. I bet you can't read very well. I bet you have. . . ." and she listed off about half a dozen things which were the deep dark secrets that I'd always tried to hide from everyone. All of sudden this woman was sitting there, having met me 10 minutes before, knowing all my deep dark secrets. How did she know this? She said, "If you're weak in these two sections of this test, it is a traditional sign of learning disabilities." Basically, I said, "Learning disability, what is that?" So that day it was confirmed that my daughter was a genius; it was also confirmed for the first time that I was not an idiot. . . . So that's how, at 30, I got diagnosed.

Terry's realization that there was something different about her approach to learning was confirmed during a conversation with a colleague during her practice teaching experience in college:

The crystallizing moment was when I was student teaching during my senior year. That particular school happened to be where the learning center was for the town. One day I said to one of the teachers, "You know, all my life I've had trouble learning stuff. I've had trouble mainly in spelling and being able to decode any words that I don't know and that aren't familiar to me in phonics. I have no idea why." She sat down and said, "Well, I have some time. Why don't you tell me more about it? Maybe I can do a little bit of testing." We didn't really do anything formal, but what she said to me was, "Well, you know how when you see words in your mind . . . ?" And I said, "No, I've never seen a word in my mind. I don't know what you mean by that." "Well," she said, "When you visualize the letters and kind of spell in the air, it's like you can see it," and I said, "No, I've never even heard of that. No one ever said that to me. People do that?" That was just such an amazing concept to me, because I'd never ever experienced that in my entire life. I think even now that I know about it, 20-something years later, I probably can do that with words that I'm extremely familiar with, but I don't really visualize things. I can't visualize a picture of something either. I really don't have a visual memory, which I guess is how people spell.

Jule became aware of her ADHD through informal conversations with professional contacts in the field of LD. She chuckles as she recalls:

I was probably 35 when I realized I had ADHD, and then it was sort of a shock. Larry Silver and I were walking one day at an LDA conference, and he asked me if I'd ever tried Ritalin. I was appalled and asked why he was asking. Of course, I had taken Black Diamonds or Black Gold in college to stay up and it had just evened me out, but I never thought of that. And he said, "Because you're ADHD." I said, "This is crazy." So, I started asking people that I knew at the conference as we walked around, "Do you think I'm ADHD?" and everybody went, "Oh, God, yeah." And I was just mortified.

Today adults who suspect they have a learning disability may research the matter by reading related articles, books, and newsletters; watching relevant videos; attending associated lectures and conferences; and joining organizations focusing on LD. A great deal can be learned via such informal means. However, individuals who seek greater understanding and suspect they may need accommodations in postsecondary learning or employment settings must also seek a professional diagnosis, because official documentation is required in order to access their civil right protections as people with disabilities (see Chapters 8 & 9).

## THE FORMAL ASSESSMENT PROCESS

A good formal assessment involves evaluation of strengths and weaknesses through fact-finding; testing and precise diagnosis; and the provision of recommendations.

### Evaluation Through Fact-Finding

During the fact-finding phase of the assessment process, the diagnostician takes a detailed case history, gathering extensive background information. Among areas explored are prenatal development, maturation milestones, and a full educational history, including grades earned, comments made by teachers, and the effectiveness of any implemented educational interventions. Through a detailed clinical interview, the diagnostician seeks information regarding problems that have come up on the job, within the family, and within the individual's social environment. Information is gathered about the learning patterns of other family members and about any history of psychiatric conditions, such as depression, anxiety, obsessive-compulsive disorder, or conduct disorder.

A full medical history is taken, including any current or past serious illness and any medications taken over the years. Medical problems must be ruled out as a cause for learning difficulties; thus, a full medical checkup is often required as an auxiliary element of the diagnostic process.

The experienced clinician can discover a great deal about a person through observation during the assessment process. For example, much can be learned by noting the individual's approach to each of the tests, along with his or her ability to sit and focus for extended periods of time and relate to the tester.

In addition to fact-finding through a clinical interview, the diagnostician may ask the individual to fill out a self-report rating scale or inventory. Because of the questionable reliability of such instruments, on which many people exaggerate or under-report their symptoms, the experienced diagnostician also collects observations from others who are familiar with the behavior and history of the person being assessed.

### Tests and Diagnosis

If the individual is seeking accommodations, a battery of neuro-psychological and educational tests must be administered to assess intellectual functioning, oral language, written language, cognitive processing, and educational achievement. Such testing often includes the Wechsler Adult Intelligence Scale, Third Edition (Wechsler, 1997), the Woodcock-Johnson Psycho-Educational Battery (Woodcock & Johnson, 1989), and the Nelson-Denny Reading Test (Brown, Fishco, & Hannah, 1993). From the results of this comprehensive assessment, a diagnosis may be made and reported in language that is as jargon-free as possible to allow the individual to acquire essential knowledge about his or her own strengths and weaknesses as a learner. Ultimately, it is this knowledge and the self-understanding that grows from it that set the stage for self-advocacy skills to develop.

### Providing Recommendations

The final step in the assessment process is the recommendation of strategies for capitalizing on identified strengths and for coping with identified weaknesses. Specific suggestions are made about instructional strategies and accommodations that are useful in continued schooling; employment strategies and accommodations that facilitate the individual's success on the job; and social strategies that could be useful in all arenas of the individual's interpersonal life. It should be noted, however, that although these recommendations are written in the official documentation, there are no guarantees that the exact accommodations listed will be provided in all environments. Indeed, another modification could be suggested as reasonable by an educational institution or workplace. Thus, it is essential that the person with LD/ADHD understand the purpose of the suggested strategies to enable him or her to participate actively in future discussions about modifying the strategies for particular learning or employment settings.

Although recommendations are made available in writing as part of an assessment report, the clinician should schedule a post-assessment interview with the individual to review and explain the findings and to give him or her an opportunity to ask questions or express feelings associated with the new label for long-experienced symptoms (see Chapter 2).

## THE DIAGNOSTICIAN

Who is an appropriate diagnostician? Good diagnosticians are professionals with a sophisticated level of understanding of LD. Their knowledge and experience make it possible for them to differentiate LD from other disabilities, such as mental retardation, that also lead to academic challenges, social problems, and limitations of day-to-day skills central to adult functioning (Brinkerhoff, Shaw, & McGuire, 1993). While many postsecondary schools state specifically from which fields they will accept diagnostic reports, diagnosticians come with diverse backgrounds in such areas as education, educational therapy, psychology, counseling psychology, rehabilitation, special education, or reading. Brinkerhoff and colleagues (1993) noted that the problem with this wide variation in background of those who test and diagnose is that their diagnostic reports may be skewed in the direction of their specialization. Testers may have

> Little practical experience with this distinct population as a whole. This raises serious concerns about interpretation of diagnostic results as well as about application of those results to recom-

mendations that bear relevance across a wide variety of settings in which they must function. (1993, p. 98)

Betty's story illustrates the problems and frustrations that can arise when working with a clinician who, despite an appropriate professional license, is unqualified to make a responsible diagnosis of LD. In the process of suing her employer for denying her needed accommodations, Betty sought a formal diagnosis for what she had recognized for quite some time as a significant learning disability. As she explains, her own understanding of LD was both an asset and a detriment in the diagnostic process:

I had to get a diagnosis quick, within about 2 weeks. I told this guy, "Look, I'm extremely bright, I am very successful, but I need a diagnosis of an LD. Can you do it?" He reassured me he could. This was a whole new experience [for me]. I took 3 days of testing. I'm a social worker, used to writing case studies, so I had written a case history. They gave me a written thing, they gave me memory things, they gave me the achievement tests I had taken in high school. And then they wanted to give the Minnesota Multiphasic Personality Inventory. I asked why—I was not asking for a diagnosis of mental illness, only for a diagnosis of LD. They said, "It will help us, and it won't cost any more money. We can bill it on your mental health benefit, but we'll have to put the diagnosis as Transitional Stress Disorder." I said, "I don't want to collect on my mental health benefits for Transitional Stress Disorder. I don't have that. Either you let my insurance company pay for it as a diagnosis of a learning disability, or I'm going to pay you cash because I don't want to collect on mental health records for something I don't have." I ended up giving him my MasterCard.

This Ph.D. psychologist gave me the results verbally, and he said, "Well, you have no abstract thinking ability and no concrete thinking ability." I said, "How did you figure that?" He said, "You were very slow with blocks and puzzles." He had my case history and my résumé—I had started umpteen programs and graduated from a masters program at a prestigious university, and he sat there with a straight face and said I had no abstract and no concrete thinking ability. He said, "You have no writing ability." I had written all my case history! He said, "You have no social skills." I said, "How did you figure that?" He said, "We talked to your supervisor." I said, "The gentle lady against whom I have nine grievances filed?" And finally, he screamed at me, "You have to accept that you have an IQ of 94. Stop overachieving!" I said, "How did you get the 94?" and he replied, "Well, you were in the 98th percentile in knowledge and use of words, but you're low average in reading, writing, math, spelling, memory." I said, "If I remember correctly, you just described a learning disability. You did not describe an IQ of 94. There's nothing wrong with an IQ of 94, but do you want to explain how I scored in the 98th percentile on knowledge and use of words with a 94 IQ?"

When the psychologist finally gave me the diagnosis in writing, he had addressed the concerns that I raised. When the written diagnosis came, it said that I had a very superior intelligence, but that was mitigated in the testing in terms of reading, writing, math, spelling. He took the statement that I had made and put it into the evaluation. Re: reading retention, I needed to hear recordings. Re: spelling, I needed accommodations because neurologically I couldn't spell. Re: writing, I needed to have access to a computer and an editor. He empirically validated every one of the deficiencies and stated clearly the need for accommodations that I had been stating all the way along from day one.

Betty's self-knowledge and self-understanding both served her well in the diagnostic process, which generally is a more positive experience for adults when they seek the services of a diagnostician who has a solid understanding of LD.

## SUMMARY

There is no universal definition of learning disabilities; however, it is widely accepted that individuals with LD have difficulties in one or more of the following: attention, reasoning, processing, memory, communication, reading, writing, spelling, math, coordination, social skills, and emotional development. Many who have LD also have ADHD, a problem of inattention, hyperactivity, or both. The cause of LD may be related to genetics, prenatal problems, difficulties with birth, or postbirth problems. Although people with LD typically exhibit significant weaknesses in a variety of areas, they are also likely to demonstrate numerous gifts and talents, including empathy, drive, tenacity, creativity, and problem-solving ability.

Older adults with LD/ADHD were raised at a time when these disabilities were largely unrecognized, but today comprehensive assessments are widely available. Through fact-finding, diagnosis, and provision of recommendations, qualified diagnosticians are able to help individuals with LD understand their strengths and weaknesses and provide official documentation necessary for gaining access to accommodations in postsecondary and work environments.

# Mental Health

The daily struggles of living with LD and coping with its symptoms often result in a variety of psychological concerns. For this reason, a full exploration of the effects of LD/ADHD on the lives of adults must include a discussion of impacts on mental health.

Because it is generally more straightforward and less threatening to focus on math difficulties or a reading disorder than it is to delve into psychological issues, many people with LD/ADHD choose to devote their energy to improving their skills rather than addressing mental health concerns. Janet Sylvester, the former executive director of the LDA (Learning Disabilities Association) of Maine, reports that in her dealings with a large number of adults with LD:

> It is my experience that very few people choose recovery. It is more comfortable to stay in the misery. You can't force anybody to look at the issues. They have to decide that it is more comfortable [to recover] than to stay where they are.

In order to tackle mental health concerns, adults with LD/ADHD need to make a conscious commitment to examining what is going on in their psychological lives and overcoming any embarrassment they may feel about asking for psychological help. Of course, not all will require formal mental health services, but those who do may have a negative mindset about therapy and may need to give themselves *permission* to seek the help that they need. Nancie explains that this was true in her case:

> I come from a family background on my father's side where going to
> see a psychiatrist means you're insane. It's not a derogatory
> statement on his part—it's just the way that we used to think
> about seeing mental health professionals.

Many adults find that addressing their mental health issues helps
them to develop strategies for coping with more technical symptoms,
such as difficulties with reading and writing. Thus, to truly help those
with LD/ADHD become fully functional in day-to-day life, it is critical
to expand the scope of treatment beyond the academic realm. Glenn
describes the importance of this element of treatment:

> I personally think that the mental health issue may be equal in
> importance to the technical issues. I guess my journey to being a
> functional person has as much or more to do with my journey in
> the mental health world as it does with my journey in the literacy
> world. If you continue to be severely stuck in negative images, severely
> stuck with inability to contact people, severely stuck in your own
> depression and around mental health issues in general, you may
> eventually learn to read and write but you will still fail miserably. I
> would say the mental health issue is the number one thing that
> needs to be addressed.

## MENTAL HEALTH–RELATED SYMPTOMS OF LD AND LD/ADHD

It is difficult to grow up with LD and experience repeated failure
and relentless taunting from peers without developing secondary
psychological issues, often referred to as *emotional overlay*. Emotional
overlay does not always develop into diagnosable mental health
problems, according to the *Diagnostic and Statistical Manual of
Mental Disorders, Fourth Edition* (DSM-IV; APA, 1994), but the
symptoms can be quite debilitating nonetheless. Particularly at risk
are those adults who were diagnosed late and never had an official
label to explain the many frustrating symptoms that they lived with
throughout their lives. With each year that those individuals went
undiagnosed, difficulties "compounded, resulting in secondary
emotional effects that continue[d] to grow and take on a life of their
own" (Solden, 1995, p. 49). Several of the secondary emotional
effects are discussed below.

## IRRITABILITY AND MOOD SWINGS

There are a variety of reasons why many adults with LD/ADHD experience mood swings and irritability. For example, impulsivity is at the root of many outbursts of anger. In *Driven to Distraction*, Hallowell and Ratey noted that the tendency for people with ADHD to flare up can be more readily understood as a problem of inhibition. "They lack the little pause between impulse and action that allows most people to be able to stop and think" (1994, p. 15). Andre admits with regret that this was true for him. He reports, "I had a very short temper, very low frustration tolerance," which he feels significantly interfered in his work life and in his first marriage. Nina, too, attributes her moodiness to impulsivity, which she describes as a response to frustration, beginning in her early years when she would "short out." As she reports, "I still do this today. I arrive at a point where I can't do anything anymore, and I just walk away."

A second reason for moodiness and irritability is the discomfort that comes with being overwhelmed, an all-too-familiar feeling among adults with LD/ADHD. Nancie explains why, despite her best efforts to control angry reactions, she still lashes out: "The anger outbursts come about when there's too many things going on, and it's too overwhelming. I've learned some of the triggers, and I've tried to walk away from them, but they're still there."

For some adults with LD/ADHD, a further reason for angry outbursts is their grief and disappointment with "the system" that let them flounder for so long without recognizing their problems and without providing the services they so needed. Many were treated poorly by educators, ill advised by teachers and counselors alike to let go of their dreams of applying for postsecondary schooling. These individuals may feel angry that they were born with LD and cheated that they are unable to learn as much as they would have liked. Many have become embittered, feeling entitled to a level of understanding from society that is not generally forthcoming.

Some individuals hide their vulnerability behind a mask of anger. In her insightful book, *Succeeding Against the Odds*, Sally Smith described this important defense mechanism:

> People who are continually labeled or categorized often react to others' rigid view of them by constructing a different but equally rigid and destructive face to present to the world. I call these

constructions masks. Adopting a mask and wearing it constantly can be very manipulative. The mask allows a person to control a situation to some extent. He decides to distract others so they won't focus on his inability to do a task or to read or write. (1991, pp. 43–44)

Although masks may also be at play among those who act clownish, outrageous, seductive, bored, or helpless, it was the mask of "the angry young man" behind which Rich chose to hide:

[My knowledge] didn't come out of writing, and the only way they measured you was by that medium. After frustrating many tutors, I was walking around with a chip on my shoulder, resisting help because I preferred to be called a bad-ass than a dummy. There was just a lot of residual anger associated with that—having kids make fun of you and then beating the hell out of them after school. You kind of learned that your anger protected you.

Nancie, too, wore a mask of defiance. She describes how she generally acted as if she "didn't care" during her turbulent youth, when she most certainly did care that she was different:

I got kicked out of one high school in my freshman year and went to another through my sophomore year and then went to a public school. At each one of those junctures, I had a lot of self-esteem issues. While I don't really think I felt at the bottom of the pile, I had an inferiority complex. I knew that I was different, and I knew that I couldn't do things, and I thought people talked about me a lot. The way I dealt with that was to get real verbal, not worry about it, and just kind of be who I was going to be and tell everybody I didn't care. I was pretty obnoxious. Had I been diagnosed at that point in time, I think it probably would have been with oppositional defiant behaviors. I was always in trouble. I transitioned from high school to being in a juvenile detention center for about 8 months, going to a group home, getting pregnant, being married long enough to have two children, and being on public assistance for 6 or 8 years.

In Nancie's case, her mask of not caring was directly tied to self-esteem issues that she now recognizes were behind much of her antisocial behavior.

## Low Self-Esteem

Feelings of inadequacy often arise out of a long pattern of repeated failure and misunderstanding by others. After years of hearing others label them "lazy," "retarded," or "stupid," some adults with LD/ADHD lash out; they react to these negative attributes and, like Nancie, become defiant, bossy, or pushy. Others internalize these messages, bowing to the power of negative reactions of others and coming to believe that they *are* somehow less worthy. Maladaptive behavior and beliefs can develop as a result of low self-esteem and low self-confidence. One common maladaptive belief is described by Barton and Fuhrmann, who noted:

> Successful learners view appropriate reliance on others (e.g., an editor) and on mechanical devices (e.g., a calculator) as a means to an end. In contrast, adults with LD often view such reliance as one more indicator of incompetence. An inappropriate belief that everyone else is self-reliant is reinforced. (1994, p. 82)

Procrastination may be a byproduct of low self-confidence; the individual who expects failure postpones starting a task, perhaps indefinitely, to avoid what seems an inevitable disappointment in his performance.

Harry and others interviewed for this book struggled for much of their lives with low self-esteem. Harry reports that it took him decades to recognize that he had strengths to offset his significant weaknesses in language processing. After years of failure in school, he recalls that it was not until he got to Algebra I in high school that he finally found he could excel in academics. His areas of strength were advanced math and the sciences. Although he eventually became a successful mechanical engineer, Harry recalls that it took him a very long time "to discover that I am not dumb." Allyssa's self-esteem, too, suffered the ill effects of negativity. She vividly recalls:

> I looked up to people. I said, "Wow, I want to be like that," and people would put me down, and it would just crush me. I always felt "less than." I was told from the time I was a little kid that I was stupid, that I was retarded, that I would never be anything. I've been told that a lot, my whole life really. If I'm going to point at anybody, it's society that says because I had trouble reading

and writing and all that stuff that I'm stupid. The fact is I was only different.

In some cases, feelings of inadequacy are so deep-rooted that the individual not only becomes demoralized and sad but also comes to expect failure, even when others see his or her potential. Glenn poignantly explains how, at one time, he devalued the opinions of anyone who believed in him:

> One of the truisms about my early life is that I was absolutely convinced that everybody in the world was stupid because they thought I was smart. Anyone who considered me smart when I was a kid or a young adult before I was identified had to be a jerk because I knew that I couldn't read, I couldn't write, I was really not very functional, I couldn't hold jobs. When they said I was smart, I thought, "I fooled another one."

## DEPRESSION

Depression may be biological in nature, a matter of internal chemistry, or reactive in nature, resulting from distressing life events. The chronic difficulties that accompany LD lead some adults to experience a reactive depression with symptoms that include difficulty concentrating, lethargy, diminished interest in almost all activities, a change in appetite, fatigue, and restlessness or agitation. "For some adults with LD, a seeming inability to understand why life continues to be a struggle creates a tragic and self-perpetuating cycle of loneliness and despair" (Reiff & Gerber, 1994, p. 72). Indeed, the sheer day-to-day effort required of individuals with LD can be exhausting and dispiriting.

Just as irritability can arise out of chronic overload, so, too, can depression. Rich explains:

> I think there are times when you can get overwhelmed by the struggle, by the persistence of the issues which you have. Even though you have all sorts of strategies to cope, every once in a while it does catch up. At that point, I think you get depressed or you feel sorry for yourself. Oftentimes that occurs when I'm not taking care of business, not focusing on getting life organized in the areas that need to be organized. Or when I'm not saying no. I keep on saying

*yes, yes, yes, and all of a sudden, there's too many yeses and I don't
have the time, the wherewithal, and the energy to do it all. The
areas in which you can get depressed are the areas in which you can
tend to procrastinate, and usually they are your deficit areas.*

Depression may also generate from low self-esteem and feelings
of worthlessness, often as a result of negative feedback from others.
Dale Brown described how she felt upon hearing her diagnosis as an
adult:

*I always thought of myself as insensitive, untactful, and rude. Now
it was clear that if I wasn't hearing right, I wasn't responding right.
Emotionally, it was a lot to absorb. I was depressed, full of self-
pity, and angry for weeks. (1981, p. 2)*

### STRESS AND ANXIETY

With LD as a source of regular frustration in so many aspects of life,
individuals with LD commonly experience stress and anxiety. Smith
noted, "People with LD become consumed by fears of being inadequate,
by anger at being born LD, and by guilt over their own inabilities
and over the problems that they cause for those around them"
(1991, p. 148). She quoted one woman who articulated what she
perceived as the pervasive negative effect her emotional life had on
others: "I sprinkled anxiety wherever I went. Calm people became
nervous, and nervous people fell apart. I couldn't get out the right
words. I trembled, and my insides writhed" (p. 148).

Adults with LD/ADHD often experience pressure as they work
to cope with their symptoms. Anxiety develops out of such day-to-
day occurrences as the loss of yet another set of keys or their inability
to take an accurate telephone message. Some adults find that, in
their efforts to cope, they psychologically "organize around worry"
(Hallowell & Ratey, 1994, p. 27), unconsciously deploying an internal
radar that continually scans their mental horizon for potential problems.
Many cope by establishing tight routines that give them a sense of
control. They cannot tolerate shifting or breaking these routines, as
the associated loss of control is distressing and may lead to frightening
reactions, such as panic.

Anxiety may also surface in less apparent ways, such as in sleep
disturbances—some find they have difficulty falling asleep; others

wake up in the middle of the night and find that they are unable to doze off again. Andre explains how a combination of stress and ADHD contributed to his sleep disorder:

> Sometimes, I just plain could not go to sleep because of so much adrenaline, especially the night before a math test. My wife tried to tell me, "You run in your sleep." I told her she'd lost her mind. My daughter said, "Daddy, your legs—you run in your sleep!" I had to go to a sleep clinic. When they hooked me up to all these electrodes, they said that I had a lot of leg movement. They put me on meds to help with the adrenaline rush at night so I could go to sleep.

Nightmares may be a by-product of the stress as well. One of Glenn's nightmares, apparently shared by others with LD, is a variation on a classic anxiety dream:

> I used to have nightmares whenever I'd go near an educational setting. It was a recurring nightmare, a classic one. I've told the story in speeches, and people have come up to me and said, "You stole my dreams!" This dream was that I was in a hallway filled with lockers stacked on top of lockers, endless rows of them. One of those lockers was mine, and what I needed in order to be functional for the day was in that locker. I had no idea which number locker it was, because I couldn't keep the numbers straight. There was an underlying sense of relief, because even if I could figure out which one of the lockers was mine, I would never be able to figure out the combination.
>
> This is a classic imaging dream of having the information and knowledge that you need in your head and an inability to get it in and out, and that's exactly what LD is about. People do have the information in their head that they need to be functional, but there is no way within the traditional means of education that they can get it in and out.

In addition to sleep disturbances, stress can result in a variety of physical symptoms and illnesses. Eating issues may result, as Terry laments:

> I have a weight problem. I've had it for a lot of years, and I often wonder. You see me in nursery school as this little, petite kind of

kid, and then you see me in second grade and I am huge. I'm sure that I was very stressed over the learning stuff. And I think that over the years I used food as a pacifier for those kinds of things.

Stomach distress, headaches, chest pains, dizziness, fainting, and stiff neck are further symptoms that have been tied to anxiety. Nonnie is convinced that disability-related stress caused her to become sick early in her marriage:

> I was in bed for 3 years without touching the ground except to take a bath and go to the refrigerator. I gave up 3 years of my life needlessly—if I had known I had a learning disability, I could have learned how to deal with the stress part better. I realize now that it was an autoimmune disease, Epstein-Barr, but I have been back and forth with physical illnesses because of the stress, the enormity of it.

### SUBSTANCE ABUSE

Several of the adults with LD/ADHD whom I interviewed spoke of past struggles with substance abuse. Jule observes that she and other individuals with ADHD are prone to excess in all areas, including the use of cigarettes, alcohol, and other drugs. Indeed, research tells us that, as early as adolescence, certain individuals with ADHD are more at risk of substance abuse than others. Those "who are hyperactive, impulsive, and show some degree of conduct disorder are statistically much more likely to develop patterns of substance abuse than are adolescents with the primarily inattentive subtype of ADHD" (Nadeau, 1996, p. 29).

Some individuals with LD/ADHD use alcohol or other drugs to ease the pressure and to mask the discomfort associated with their symptoms. Andre describes how he drank to escape his emotional distress:

> I self-medicated with drinking in college. I experienced different mood swings up and down. With the alcohol, I killed some of the pain at the time, but it didn't work for me in the long haul, because what happens is that you find out you're more depressed than you were initially.

Allyssa, too, used drugs to self-anesthetize. She experimented with a variety of substances to cover feelings of self-loathing associated with a lifetime of being demeaned by others: "I think that I felt so crappy about myself that I had to fill that crappy feeling with something, and I turned to different things. I did a lot of things, like buying drugs and drinking to numb the bad feelings I had about myself."

Although many adolescents turn to drugs to experiment with the feeling of being out of control, individuals with ADHD often experience a calming effect with stimulant drugs that paradoxically help them gain control. Jule welcomes the quietness that stimulants create in her hyperactive mind. As she explains, "You're always thinking. I go to bed thinking, and I think when I sleep. With drugs, it was just a little bit slower." Nina, too, describes this phenomenon of being calmed rather than stimulated by the same drugs that for most people produce a rush of energy. She remembers taking speed at parties in her youth, and while others were high, she would be off in a corner reading quietly. She and others in her family turned to alcohol as well for its calming effect: "I've had issues with alcoholism and drug abuse, which I really believe were very related to attention-deficit disorder. I believe I was self-medicating. [Others in my family did the same.] Alcohol calmed us down."

Some of the individuals interviewed were convinced that drugs allowed them to tap into their creativity. Jule recalls that drugs became a significant factor in her life during a time when she was bedridden and credits them with not only serving to ease both physical and psychological pain, but also with putting an extra creative spin on the book she was writing:

> We discovered marijuana, which we called dope. My ex-husband would kind of drift off into a coma, and I would just be able to get into my art and my music. Then I ran into a lot of physical problems and had about eight major surgeries. I got into pain killers. That was good. And then I got into coke, and that was really good. I didn't do anything straight. With coke, I was very creative. In fact, I jokingly named the chapters of the book I wrote during that time after the drugs I took—one was "Demerol," one was "Morphine," one was "Coke." While I was in bed, the Morphine and the Demerol were prescribed, but I smoked [marijuana] the whole time. The drugs made it easier to get through. It softened the thinking.

Although, like Jule, several of the "baby boomer" adults interviewed did resort to self-medication at some point in their youths, they have since recognized the dangers of this alternative to treatment. More than one expressed appreciation for the controlled effects of the legitimate medications now available.

## SEEKING TREATMENT

There are a variety of routes to good mental health. Although many people with LD/ADHD pursue traditional treatment with psychiatrists, psychologists, or social workers, many benefit from alternatives, such as psychodrama, self-help, spirituality, or exercise.

### TRADITIONAL THERAPY

Mental health providers come from a variety of professional disciplines, such as psychiatry, psychology, social work, and expressive therapy. In most cases, the professional field of the provider is less important than his or her background and understanding of LD. Adults with LD/ADHD seeking a traditional counseling relationship are urged to make a careful check of the therapist's background and style, approach to therapy, and ability to offer other types of treatment or make referrals, if necessary.

#### Check Background and Style

There are several steps one can follow to check the background and style of a potential mental health provider.

*Check the Therapist's Training and Experience* Unfortunately, many mental health professionals lack appropriate training to serve adults with LD/ADHD adequately. Betty, a social worker, reports that, according to her observations:

> Mental health professionals are not trained in LD and ADHD issues. They treat them for depression. They treat them for all sorts of things. I've seen major psychiatric institutions' psych evaluations done on my [social work] clients that have totally overlooked blatant LD issues and ADHD issues. The hard thing about being LD is that we sound great and we look perfectly normal. The only person to be executed in Maryland in umpteen years happened to have ADHD. I

wonder how that life would have been different if he had been effectively treated for the ADHD.

It is important to check the therapist's experience with LD/ADHD and his or her understanding of the underlying issues affecting those with LD/ADHD. Has the therapist had any formal training in this area? Has he or she treated others with LD/ADHD? Has he or she attended conferences related to these disabilities? Regarding the challenge of finding an informed mental health provider with an adequate background, Glenn advises:

> The first point is to become an informed consumer and don't just go in to a therapist because they have a shingle. You have to know what type of therapy they do, if they understand LD and how it manifests itself in perception, in self-concept, in all areas that most therapists do not know about. I was a fortunate person. I actually found two different therapists who said to me, "This is interesting, and let us learn about this together," who were willing to commit to developing an understanding of LD and going from there. We helped each other learn about LD.

Some of the specific symptoms of LD confuse uninformed therapists, compromising their ability to make an accurate diagnosis. For instance, a client who misses appointments or arrives late at therapy sessions could be accused of being "resistant" when his real problem is that he struggles to understand time concepts and cannot estimate the period needed for travel. A family history of a significant psychiatric disorder can lead the therapist to associate troublesome symptoms with that disorder rather than with the LD/ADHD that is the accurate diagnosis. Nina describes how this has happened in her case:

> The whole part about diagnosis is really so key—therapists should just not be afraid to look at all possibilities before they diagnose. All of my stuff is always attributed to having a schizophrenic mother and a Russian Orthodox alcoholic father. But the ADHD stuff puts that all in a context that makes me able to look at it.

Further, a therapist who lacks a full understanding of the inconsistencies inherent in LD/ADHD may be fooled by a client who seems too "together" to meet the criteria for diagnosis with either disability. Sari Solden explained how the emotional toll of such a presentation must be taken into consideration:

A person who is coping may . . . be doing very well . . . but it is the inner process, not the final product that needs to be examined. The level of difficulty needed to sustain the achievement and the impact—emotionally and physically—needs to be considered. (1995, p. 138)

Jule is one of those people with LD/ADHD whose strong coping skills can fool a therapist. She manages best, though at considerable emotional cost, when she is overcontrolling her life. Thus, on a day when her rather elaborate array of systems is working, she might appear to have no significant issues to address in therapy; on a day when her systems teeter, however, she is highly vulnerable and would benefit from treatment by a knowledgeable therapist. She recounts an experience that illustrates the challenge of working with clients like herself:

I don't know if this goes along with the ADHD, but I think it might, that when things are good, they're really good, but when they're shitty, they're *really* shitty. The first contact I had with the therapist was a good day when things were good, so by the time I finished explaining to him why I was the way I was, he told me I was fine. I went home thinking to myself, "Well, that was one really stupid therapist."

Nina had an unfortunate experience with an uninformed psychiatrist who made a number of errors in diagnosis and treatment:

In my twenties I went to see a psychiatrist. She told me I was manic-depressive and put me on Lithium. I was so depressed. I knew it was wrong—it felt wrong for my system, and I would go to her saying, "Isn't there something else I could take with less side effects?" and she basically said, "This is the treatment." I just took myself off it and stopped seeing her.

Although Nina clearly disagreed with the treatment approach, withdrawing from prescribed medication without medical supervision can be physically dangerous. Later Nina tried therapy again, this time being prescribed the most glib and superficial of treatment plans, the suggestion that if she could just find some engaging hobbies, she would be fine. Eventually she did find a knowledgeable mental health provider who was able to provide effective therapy that incorporated appropriate medication along with counseling and coaching.

It is critical that the mental health provider be aware of all of the characteristics of LD and ADHD and how they may surface in an individual's life. He or she must be able to listen with an ear attuned to the fact that the symptoms may or may not suggest additional psychological concerns.

*Check the Mental Health Provider's Therapeutic Style*    Mental health providers approach treatment from a wide variety of orientations, labeled with such terms as "psychodynamic," "cognitive behavioral," and "eclectic." In addition to checking what the goals of therapy would be and how they would be determined, it is wise to ask the provider to describe his or her orientation and how that would translate into sessions of treatment.

*Check the Provider's Personal Style*    Personal style is another factor that varies from therapist to therapist. Several of the adults interviewed for this book describe the personal qualities in a therapist that they value:

- *Warmth and acceptance*: Nonnie appreciates how unconditionally accepted she felt in treatment, recalling, "Her voice was kind and always accepting of all the mistakes I'd always made."
- *Empathy*: Several individuals report that they feel it is important to have a therapist who shows authentic concern, who recognizes and validates their difficulties and feelings and is ready to address such emotions as sadness, defensiveness, embarrassment, guilt, and rage. Glenn describes how emotionally vulnerable he felt when he entered counseling and how important it was for his therapist to recognize the roots of his reactions: "I was extremely defensive about my inabilities, and I would do everything I could to hide my inabilities from people, including walking away. If anyone got too close, and they started to understand, I was gone."
- *Affirmation*: Another form of validation, affirmation is particularly important to individuals who may be wracked by self-doubt, shame, and/or low self-esteem. Betty notes how important it is

to have "people who believe in you when you are having a hard time believing in yourself."

- *Orientation toward the positive*: Allyssa expresses appreciation for therapists who not only affirm but also celebrate and build upon strengths and achievements in the process of working on problem areas: "I think that anybody with any disability needs to be praised, really. We all need that. They need to be praised for what they're doing—not, 'Oh, let's talk about what you're *not* doing.' "
- *Humor*: Humor provides an extremely helpful element in relieving tension. However, therapists must be sensitive to language-processing problems in clients with LD, who may not always understand idioms or other figurative language or who may misinterpret and be offended by humorous comments.

*Check the Therapist's Ability to Write Prescriptions*   For some people, particularly those with ADHD who may benefit from the medication, it is important to know whether the therapist has prescription-providing ability. Those mental health providers who do not write prescriptions themselves generally collaborate with psychopharmacologists or psychiatrists to ensure that their clients receive and are monitored for any medications they may need.

*Check the Mental Health Provider's Fees*   In the fact-finding process, it is crucial to discuss the fee schedule and whether he or she accepts third-party payments through insurance. In these days of managed care, not all therapists are affiliated with every health maintenance organization (HMO) plan. Insurance coverage must be considered in the decision-making process.

### Check the Therapist's Approach to Treatment

It is important to develop a sense of how the counseling will proceed. The experiences of those people whom I interviewed and the clients whom I've served suggest that there are several qualities that adults with LD/ADHD should look for in therapy.

*Therapy that Is Directive and Problem-Driven*   Therapy should be practical and directive, problem-driven and focused on day-to-day issues. Therapy should not only help individuals develop insights into patterns that may exist in their behavior and thinking, but should also focus on strategizing possible action steps to contend with these patterns. As Jule notes, the therapist should understand that dwelling on the problem may be what the client needs to do "to get empathy and sympathy and all that, but there's got to be some resolution of how to move forward." Questions such as, "Given where you are right now, how can we get you beyond that?" can be extremely helpful. The opportunity to engage in active dialogue with a therapist who is willing to express opinions and to be directive is valued by clients like Jule: "Therapists need to be explicit. There would be times when the good therapist I went to would just listen. I'd talk about something, but then I would turn to him and I'd say, 'Okay, I need some feedback.' " Providing concrete suggestions, such as coping mechanisms, can be highly valued. Nonnie describes one very practical survival strategy suggested by her therapist; she puts on a Walkman to give herself time out from the world when she finds herself " on overload." Concrete suggestions may help clients with LD/ADHD structure their lives in such areas as organizing their surroundings, prioritizing tasks, keeping schedules, being on time, and making plans. It is important that therapists guide clients in all of this rather than do it for them, as guiding them fosters self-determination and serves to reduce the learned helplessness exhibited by so many individuals with LD/ADHD.

*Therapy that Is Goal-Directed*   The therapist should help the client identify goals and plan steps to reach those goals. Through goal-directed work with her therapist, Nina describes how she was able to overcome psychological barriers step by step to return to a singing career that had eluded her for many years:

I did my first singing performance in 15 years, largely through the help of the therapist I have now. The second time I went to see her, I brought in my résumé, which starts out saying that I'm a performance artist, and she said, "This is interesting." I said, "You know what, I don't have a lot of time to go through this whole thing in five sessions. I want you to read this and then talk to me about it. But the reason I want you to see this is I haven't done this in over 10 years on a regular basis." And she really heard it in the next couple of sessions. By the fifth session, she said, "What we want to get at is your brilliance—you're incredible!" It was so helpful having a therapist who said, "Let's get to the stuff that you're really interested in. Let's go for that," and redirecting me just to do it. I just received a grant to do the show again, which was a wonderful thing, so for the last couple of weeks she's asked, "What's happening with the show?" I said, "I haven't been working on it," and she said, "Next week I want you to bring me an outline of the show." So she's actively pushing me to identify what I really want to do.

Jule similarly benefitted from a goal-oriented approach, which helped her avoid intellectual stagnation and depression during a prolonged illness:

When I was bedridden, my therapist said to me, "You must do something. You're getting too depressed, so I will call you at 10:00 A.M. and you will start to read [or write]." So, my therapist would call to check in. I got up every morning and worked on my book for the entire 2 years I was recuperating, all the way through.

Such structure can be invaluable, particularly for those with both LD and ADHD, who "need external structure so much because they so lack internal structure" (Hallowell & Ratey, 1994, p. 91). Specific strategies for structuring the therapy sessions themselves, including taking notes of key points or tape recording the whole session for later review, can be very helpful. Nonnie explains how this worked for her:

I taped every single therapy session I ever had. I had a memory problem, and a lot of things were hard for me to accept because she was telling me the truth as she saw it, and she was also telling me what I should do. I would tape our session, and then I would listen to it in the car. Many things that are painful people forget or perceive wrong. Also, I'd listen and think, "This is what I said, but I really didn't mean that."

Providing a formal summary of major points covered at the end of the session is another form of structure that can be beneficial to those with LD/ADHD. A further element of structure is provided when therapists institute regular check-ins, evaluating and reevaluating in order to keep their finger on the psychological pulse of their clients

*Therapy that Addresses Distressing Past Experiences*   The therapist should help clients with LD/ADHD process past experiences and manage any related psychological repercussions. Psychological trauma related to experiencing multiple and repeated failures in school, as experienced by Glenn, should be processed:

> As a person with LD, I grew up in an environment of educational abuse. In many ways my response to being near an educational setting was the classic response of, say, a woman who had been sexually abused by her father going near her father—posttraumatic stress. There would be withdrawal, there would anger, hate, rage.

Therapy provided a forum for Rich to express the deep frustration he felt in dealing with his severe writing problems. He explains, "Even though you had it in your head, it didn't come out your fingertips on a piece of paper. You didn't know how to deal with feelings. You didn't know how to deal with the failures."

Therapists may find that they need to pose a series of focused questions to clients to help them access feelings that may have been buried over time. Questions such as, "How did you feel when your grade-school teachers asked you to pull out your reading books?" or "Were you ever teased due to your learning problems?" may prove helpful in triggering memories. Active listening to the client's answers will help him or her process the feelings that surface.

*Therapy that Addresses Self-Esteem*    The therapist should be able to really "hear" the feelings common to many with LD/ADHD and see through the masks that so often cover the person's self-doubt, fear, and self-loathing. Therapists must listen for and address self-image problems. For example, individuals like Harry, who felt stupid to his core, often suffer shame due to their own underachievement. Harry admits that he was very reluctant to let anybody know how he felt:

> I was so ashamed of my literacy troubles. That was a big secret, and I spent a great deal of my time keeping that secret so that nobody found it out. Now, as I look back at all of that, I think that keeping that disability a secret was probably more disabling than the disability.

Particular attention must be paid to detecting and addressing the underlying shame of women with LD/ADHD. Many feel burdened by cultural expectations that they will manage not only the organizational demands of their own individual lives, but those of their husbands and children as well. Specific therapeutic approaches may be particularly beneficial in this area. For example, cognitive therapy helps individuals learn positive self-statement training to break the negative cycle of self-contempt and worry. One of my female clients was able to turn around self-recriminating thoughts about her supposed failure in family management with the positive self-statement, "I may forget things now and then, but my system of writing everything down does work most of the time. No one is perfect. I'll just keep trying."

*Therapy that Provides Explanation*   The health care provider should explain the client's test results and diagnosis and help the client learn to do the same. It is extremely important that the therapist help clients understand and come to terms with their LD/ADHD. Once that is accomplished, those who are hiding behind masks will gradually be able to expose their true selves:

> Once adults with LD realize that they are not stupid or lazy or bad or incompetent, but are intelligent people with a mass of potential, their masks can gradually drop. Shame can melt away. Slowly they can begin to prize their differences and develop their unique talents into something productive. (Smith, 1991, p. 55)

Once the clients understand and accept themselves, they are in the position to begin to self-advocate. Rich describes the benefits:

> If you understand your own processing, then you can be in control of it. And once you're in control of it, then it's not a disadvantage— it can be an advantage. It becomes a disadvantage if you're not empowered to be in control of it. So if you're ever at the mercy of, say, somebody's lousy teaching style and you don't know your own style of learning, then you're forever at their mercy. But if you understand your own style of learning, you can do your own adaptations and accommodations and utilizations of strategies.

*Therapy that Helps Reframe the Diagnosis*   It is very important that the client with LD/ADHD be helped to reframe the diagnosis so it is no longer viewed unilaterally as a liability. The research of Gerber, Ginsberg, and Reiff (1992) on successful adults has shown the importance of recognizing and appreciating the plus side of LD. Jule describes how she was able to cast a positive spin on her hyperactive mind:

> I learned that my mind was going continue to race, that I was going to be hyper and intense, that that was just going to be part of the way I was. But what I also learned was that I needed to figure out as best I could the ways of using it more to my advantage.

Andre sees the difference he can make in the world by making the most of what could be viewed solely as negative symptoms. He explains:

> I think once I realized [about my disability], I started linking a purpose to everything. I was doing a lot of things, but I was still unhappy. The moment that I was diagnosed, I began to understand why I was like I was. On the flip side of the coin, I realized what I could do with that extra energy to help me. It was not negative. Now, I can see where I may be able to help others.

Nancie reports that she benefited during her high school years from extraordinary teaching that helped her frame a positive view of her abilities. Although this shift in self-assessment was accomplished through the guidance of a teacher rather than a therapist, it is notable for having shored her self-concept during difficult times in her life. Therapists should aim for the same result, actively facilitating a positive self-perception:

> One high school teacher I had didn't teach U.S. history but taught us how to believe in ourselves. That's all he taught all year. I thought, "No matter what anybody says, I know I can do something right, and I know I can be somebody or do the right thing some way." I don't know that we give that message to folks very well. The most important strategy one can believe in is that there are no failures. I would never say this to somebody directly, because they would think I was being facetious, but I really don't believe I've ever failed in anything. You're always trying to evaluate and improve, and if I was going to share anything with anybody, I would say, "You really have to see yourself a success or know that you can be successful."

In an interesting twist, Allyssa was able to take a similarly therapeutic role in her work with children with disabilities, where she facilitated reframing by accentuating the positive in her own clients. She recounts a delightful scene with a young girl:

> I worked with a handicapped girl who got into a fight when she was in kindergarten. Half her body is numb. She can't walk good, she can't stand up too long or she'll fall. When I worked with her on her birthday, I danced with her. This was like the first time she probably ever danced in her whole life. Even though she can't talk fast or she's not like me, I pointed out all the great things about her to herself, like, "Wow, Diane, look at you dancing!" and she was hysterical laughing. You have to point out the positive. Don't pay attention to the negative. There's no reason to, because the more I focus on what's bad, the more I feel negative; the more I focus on what's positive, the more positive I'll feel.

*Therapy that Accomodates LD/ADHD Limitations* The provider should build in accommodations for the LD/ADHD as needed. One such accommodation is ensuring that communication skills are explicitly taught, when necessary, to help the client fully benefit from therapy sessions. Rich explains why this is so important:

> Oftentimes people with disabilities go to counseling, and all they're reacting to are the anxieties associated with the disabilities. They don't necessarily have the mechanisms whereby they can communicate what's going on or cognitively have it structured to deal with what their issues are. You have to empower them to communicate in an effective way and be analytical about what's going on. Then you can be problem-oriented or solution-oriented. Unless you can provide them a means to process the information, it's not going to work—it just becomes repetitive. They relive it, relive it, relive it, and they'll never move on.

Another important accommodation is helping the client understand abstract concepts. Nonnie offers a fine example of this need and how it was met in her case:

> [My therapist] taught me cause and effect, that when I had a car accident, it was due to my impulsivity because I didn't stop to look

where I was turning. I know now about cause and effect—I think, "If this is what I do, how will it affect other people?"

Therapists should use methods geared to the specific special needs of their clients. They may let their hyperactive clients pace or periodically get up and walk around during sessions. They may incorporate graphic organizers to facilitate decision-making or artistic illustrations to explain concepts more concretely. Nonnie describes how her therapist was able to reach her through drawing:

> I have to picture things in my mind. If I don't, I lose them. So my therapist told me, "Stop, and somehow your unconscious will put a picture in your mind." She would draw a triangle and say, "You can't have three people in your family fighting. You have to knock off a person, because you can only have a dyad fighting at any one time."

Many clients with LD/ADHD need help from their therapists to prevent them from talking in tangents. Nonnie's therapist worked hard to keep her on target.

> She figured out how to stop me from rambling. I would have to focus. She didn't sit back. She was heavy duty into helping me by always checking me out—"Is this what you mean to say?" She would draw me back into what we were focusing on by saying, "Don't tell me a whole story. Get to the point."

A further accommodation is that therapists may employ a more physical, hands-on approach than they would normally use. Nonnie's therapist instinctively reached out to her:

> If I needed help, she would put her hand on my hand. Because I'm a tactile person, one touch on a shoulder or a hand would be a thousand words eliminated. That's important. I think actually she directly saved my life.

*Therapy that Incorporates Relaxation Training*    It is important to help adults with LD/ADHD identify and possibly eliminate the significant sources of stress in their lives. When they cannot be removed, clients must learn to tolerate them. Relaxation training is one tool that may be employed to help them better cope with the persistent tensions in their lives. The therapist may teach the client to recognize signs of stress in his or her body and encourage such activities as vigorously exercising or taking hot baths to relieve tension before it builds. Further, such relaxation training techniques as deep breathing and use of imagery may be embedded in treatment. Hallowell and Ratey described how imagery worked with one client who hoped to let go of her excessive worry. After beginning medication, she envisioned the weight of her worry sinking to the bottom of the sea:

> We ... worked on letting go of the weight, leaning over the rowboat in fantasy, in psychotherapy, letting the weight go, watching it fall. Laura would watch and describe it to me as it grew smaller to her eyes before disappearing into the depth of the water ... Gradually the stress did subside and take on proportions that most people carry every day. (1994, p. 85)

### Check the Provider's Ability to Offer Other Treatments

There are a variety of circumstances under which individual treatment is insufficient to meet a person's therapy goals. Couples counseling, family therapy, and group work can be highly effective when interpersonal concerns are the focus of treatment. Thus, adults with LD/ADHD should also check the therapist's ability to offer other types of treatment or to make referrals for them.

*Marital Therapy*  Much can be accomplished in couples counseling, particularly in marriages where communication has broken down. Through marital therapy, it is possible for couples to learn effective ways to communicate even when they disagree. Rich reports that couples work helped his marriage by teaching his wife and him "how to fight in the right way."

A spouse brings his or her observations about the partner with LD/ADHD to the sessions, providing an additional viewpoint that can reduce problems related to potentially skewed self-reporting by the client with LD/ADHD and that can help the therapist develop a more complete picture of the individual's family dynamics. The therapist can more effectively facilitate discussion when the partner has an opportunity to air grievances that may have built up.

In some cases, marital therapy will reveal unhealthy co-dependency patterns that may have developed. Such was the case with Janet and her husband:

I know that I was attracted to Harry for a lot of the wrong reasons. They were very dysfunctional and sick. I could take care of him and probably be his mother. He was very needy, so I could save him—but you must realize, he allowed me to do this. In that regard we had a very sick, dysfunctional relationship. It is very much like an alcoholic relationship—you have the enabling and the denial. For us, finding help was a lot like recovery from alcoholism, though there was no alcoholism in the family. A 12-step program worked for us. It has taken years and years of work. It didn't happen overnight. We both had to accept the responsibility for changing ourselves, not each other. We had to give each other a chance to grow. I've had to work hard to stop enabling.

*Family Therapy*   Families often find that it helps to have therapy sessions together. In family work, the therapist can help the client's spouse and children understand LD-related issues and learn skills to deal with those that have a negative impact upon their nuclear family. Understanding can help reduce resentment that may have risen out of ruined family outings, forgotten birthdays, missed appointments, and other disappointing events. This structured time provides a forum for talking, an occasion to look at the family's patterns of interactions, a chance to develop an understanding of those patterns, and the opportunity to overcome any existing resistance to changing family dynamics. Goals may be set, and members of the family can brainstorm how to work toward their objectives (Hallowell & Ratey, 1994).

*Group Therapy*   Group therapy can be very effective in helping individuals with LD/ADHD realize that they are not alone in their struggles. It provides an opportunity for vicarious learning from other members of the group, as they share techniques and strategies that they have tried and found to be beneficial. Finally, in group therapy there is ample support for learning self-acceptance, a critical goal of any form of mental health treatment.

## MEDICATIONS

Few who are diagnosed with LD alone are prescribed medication, but those found to have both LD and ADHD may well have the opportunity to test the effectiveness of medication in controlling their ADHD symptoms. Although 75%–80% of children benefit from medications, the percentages are less promising for adults (e.g., Silver, 1999). However, many of the adults who do benefit from medications report a welcome increase in attention span along with decreases in impulsivity, distractibility, and off-task behavior. In addition, motor control often increases, resulting in improvement of such motor activities as handwriting. Silver provided a clear explanation of the potential benefits of medication:

> ADHD is caused by a deficiency of a specific neurotransmitter, norepinephrine. The goal of medication is to increase the level of this neurotransmitter at the nerve interfaces in the areas of the brain involved. Currently two different mechanisms accomplish this increase. I like to use the analogy of a lake without enough water in it. One could increase the level of water in the lake in one of two ways. First, one could pour more water into the lake. Alternatively, one could build a dam. No more water is flowing into the lake than before, but the water flows out more slowly; thus, the water level goes up. (1999, p. 184)

### Stimulants

Stimulants represent the first mechanism. By increasing the level of the norepinephrine, drugs such as Ritalin (methylphenidate), Dexedrine (dextroamphetamine), Cylert (pemoline), and Adderol (a dextroamphetamine and levoamphetamine mixture) allow the brain to exert better control, to monitor actions and reactions more effectively, to reduce impulsivity, and to increase focus.

Ritalin is the most frequently prescribed of the stimulants in the treatment of ADHD. Unlike many other drugs, the amount prescribed does not seem to relate to body weight but instead is based upon how fast the individual metabolizes the medication. Clinical observations are used to establish Ritalin dosages (Silver, 1999). Because ADHD symptoms, including hyperactivity, distractibility, and impulsivity, may be present throughout each day, it is recommended that doses be taken "whenever these behaviors interfere with the individual's success in life" (Silver, 1999, p. 196). Ritalin is available in short-acting (4 hours) and long-acting (6–12 hour) forms, a feature that provides a flexibility appreciated by individuals like Nina, who reports:

> I do take Ritalin every day. I vary the dosage. The thing that I like about Ritalin is I could pretty much play with the dosage. I take

5 milligrams in small increments, every hour and a half or so. I take between 5 and 40 milligrams a day, depending on what my day looks like. If I have meetings into the night, I take it later. The thing that I liked about it is that I could *not* take it, and I wouldn't have to do withdrawals.

Andre explains his conceptualization of how Ritalin works:

Being ADHD affects me enormously. I manage my ADHD with medication. I currently take Ritalin. I understand attention deficit to be a system. If you would compare it to a mechanical system, it would be like the brake didn't work properly; with medication, the brakes work fine. It's like wearing eyeglasses; with medication, I can see a whole lot of things, whereas without it, I can't tell the difference.

### Antidepressants

Antidepressants represent the second mechanism described above. They decrease the breakdown or absorption of norepinephrine at the nerve ending, which increases the overall level of norepinephrine in the body (Silver, 1999). Antidepressants metabolize more slowly than stimulants, providing a more steady flow of medication, thereby avoiding some of the uneven ups and downs sometimes experienced with stimulants.

Antidepressants are often prescribed in tandem with stimulants to establish more even medication coverage. Tofranil (imipramine), Norpramin (desiprimine), and Pamelor (nortriptyline) are antide-pressant drugs in a pharmaceutical category referred to as tricyclic antidepressants. Drugs in a second pharmaceutical category, selective serotonin reuptake inhibitors (SSRIs), are also prescribed. Among the more commonly prescribed SSRIs are Prozac (fluoxetine), Zoloft (sertraline), and Paxil (paroxetine). The drugs in this category are long-acting. Because they are always in the bloodstream, liver functioning must be monitored through blood tests every 6 months.

Those who are prescribed medications must be closely monitored by a qualified professional, often a medical doctor. This may mean that a client who is in therapy with a psychologist or social worker must make separate visits for medical monitoring. In some cases, the client may also be working closely with a coach on practical matters. The disadvantage of this scenario is the potential for fragmentation of services. Nina describes her dissatisfaction with this arrangement:

> I see one person as my coach and therapist, and I see another doctor to have my medication prescribed. The doctor who prescribes Ritalin, a psychopharmacologist, sees me only for a few minutes once a month. He asks how I'm doing and how things are going, and I'm out of there. That feels not quite right to me—it just feels too disjointed. It feels disconnected from who I am and what I'm doing. I feel like I want to tell him stuff. He's pretty business-like—"I'm here for the meds, and your 20 minutes is up."

## INFORMAL AND ALTERNATIVE MENTAL HEALTH SUPPORT SYSTEMS

Not all adults with LD/ADHD find traditional mental health services either appropriate or desirable. Individuals may seek a variety of alternative channels for developing a greater understanding of themselves and their disability and for learning effective coping strategies.

### Coaching

Many adults with LD/ADHD choose to establish an ongoing alliance with a coach. After a full review of the individual's needs and goals, the coach provides structure and support toward the realization of identified objectives through regular, if not daily, contact via personal meetings, telephone calls, e-mail, or FAX. The focus is on pragmatic rather than psychological concerns, as the coach helps the individual develop new habits, skills, and thinking about such matters as time management and organizational skills. Although some choose to use coaching either alone or as a supplement to psychotherapy, Nina sought and found a therapist who is able to play both roles:

> Coaching goes hand-in-hand with my therapy. I needed to see somebody who was not only a skilled coach but a skilled therapist since I had a lot of issues—the shame and the whole sense of loss and the mourning. Somebody needs to be able to handle that. The tears come up easily; it's fairly intense for me. Somebody also needs to be able to be clear about what's happening with the

coaching stuff, because sometimes we'll talk about something that on the surface might seem pretty benign, such as my bank account, and I'll shut down completely. I see my therapist in person once a week. I don't always call her for coaching.

## Psychodrama

An alternative to traditional group therapy is psychodrama, which engages participants in improvisational role playing of emotionally charged situations. This option provided Glenn with the most effective route to learning about his impact on others. It helped him develop interpersonal insights and provided a forum where he could practice new social behaviors:

I found a great approach, a wonderful approach, one that is very well-suited for LD and ADHD—a psychodrama work group. I was in the same basic psychodrama work group for about 7 years. You could be auditory, visual, kinesthetic all [at] the same time in your therapy, which is exactly how you are supposed to try to learn how to read. Psychodrama therapy helped me greatly to understand and empathize and be aware of how other people are perceiving me and how I was perceiving other people. So, it met my needs as a person who was LD and ADHD, and it also met my therapeutic needs. The psychodrama people and a couple of other people worked with me and supported me in coming to terms with the pain, coming to terms with the anger, coming to terms with the incredible images that I had of myself as a dysfunctional person and as a failure.

## Training and Education

Some people find that different kinds of training and education have a positive effect on their mental health.

*Academic Tutoring*    Academic tutoring can have benefits that extend well beyond improvement of reading and writing skills. Glenn explains:

My LD tutor was just beyond belief. I mean there was someone who not only could help me learn what I needed to learn, but who actually understood the angst involved in having these problems. Our literacy training oftentimes had about 5 minutes of "a" equals "ah" and an hour and 45 minutes of talking about pain. Her understanding of the pain involved in being who I was was absolutely, inescapably, a major component [of our work together].

*Organizational Tutoring*    Organizational tutoring can be effective as well, offering the client techniques for organization along with the peace-of-mind that his or her world has order.

*Assertiveness Training*    Assertiveness training can be highly effective in providing the tools to express feelings and wishes to others. Through assertiveness, an adult with LD/ADHD can learn to refuse requests effectively and thus avoid many of the emotional repercussions of being overwhelmed by having too much to do. Andre explains how it worked for him:

Eventually, even on medication, if you don't slow down and organize, you can still hit some walls. So I just have to remind myself, like most people do, not to take on too much. Most of us will say yes to anything. I had to learn those skills, not to say yes to everything, because I don't want to hurt people's feelings. I had to purchase some material on assertiveness because I was too passive in a lot of situations. There were also a lot of situations where I was just too overconfident, and so I had to learn the difference between being aggressive and being assertive.

*Self-Education*    Self-education is also an option. Many people find that it is informative and comforting to learn more about themselves and their LD/ADHD. Some attend conferences on the topic of LD/ADHD. Andre has been attending the Learning Disabilities Association of America (LDA) conference for the past several years. He describes the benefits:

I've been to two or three LDA conferences now. I'm still learning. It's great. The more I learn, the more excited I am, and it makes the transition a whole lot easier for me to deal with. It helps me to talk more confidently to other people who otherwise I wouldn't even talk to about it, especially if they're not LD.

*Self-Help*    Other adults with LD choose to do their psychological work alone in the form of self-help. Some people find that homilies and clichés can help them cope with the difficult moments in life. Jo Ann offers an example:

> I don't have enough money to have a therapist. I don't like to dwell on a problem. What I usually do is think it through and say, "Okay, it's like the day when the sun's out and the clouds go over a band of the sun and after a while, the sun's back out." One phrase that I always appreciated was, "Take 10 minutes to feel sorry for yourself, and spend 45 minutes as constructive, doing what you can do about it." So that's what I do, basically.

Rich turns to self-help manuals and audiotapes. He reports that when he is on road trips, he listens to and learns much from tapes on stress management, organization, and time management.

Many have sought support through the self-help movement, which offers individuals with LD/ADHD an opportunity not only to share their experiences, but also to support one another in problem solving. For a very long time, there was little opportunity for self-help among individuals with LD. Jule comments:

> They didn't have anything like a self-help movement when I was growing up. I mean you were called spacy, dizzy, and you didn't have people that thought that you really had a lot going for you intellectually. There was not a recognition, there was not a banding together.

As a result, many adults with LD/ADHD like Glenn turn to some of the 12-step programs for support:

> When I was 30 in 1980, there were not a lot of people who understood what was going on. This was the time when Dale Brown was trying to set up self-help groups around the country, but it didn't take off in Seattle where I lived at the time. I ended up being in unrelated self-help groups, such as Adult Children of Alcoholics. My parents were not alcoholics, but they were very dysfunctional, I was very dysfunctional, and there was a great deal of overlap.

While dating an alcoholic, Jule found Al-Anon to be a superb support, even for those with no alcoholism in their lives. She explains:

The best support program I ever went to was Al-Anon. Unlike AA, where you get up to complain about everybody screwing up your life, with Al-Anon you have to take responsibility for your life but you also allow other people to do their own thing. I always had to be one step ahead to set things up to avoid disorder and being thrown. Al-Anon released me from that behavior. That's what people should do. That was the best therapy I ever had.

*Peer Support*    Adults with LD/ADHD may also become involved in more LD-focused peer support, which can entail one-to-one or small-group support and opportunities to share experiences and strategies with others who have similar issues and a shared diagnosis. Dale Brown (1992) considered peer counseling and relationship building key to both personal and political empowerment. Opportunities to participate in peer support may be available through organizations, such as LDA. Andre describes added benefits of such involvement:

I got connected in the self-help group. I was determined and showed leadership qualities. I was nominated to represent the group on a national level at the LDA conference. I'm still learning. It's great. The more I learn, the more excited I am.

Jo Ann, too, became intensely involved in the self-help movement through LDA; ultimately, it shaped her professional activities for more than 20 years:

Along with the Puzzle People movement, I also got very involved with LDA. I can still remember my first conference, Kansas City in 1978. How I even got there was a miracle, because my folks didn't have the money to send me. What drew me was that was the first year they had the LD adult breakfast. I saw it in the ACLD Newsbrief and thought, "I'd love to go to that, but there's no way." John Arena suggested I write a letter. I didn't ask about coming—I just said, "Could you give this message to LD adults? Tell the adults how I'd like to meet them." I guess the letter was so powerful that the person in charge turned around and sent an airline ticket! Then a week or two later, the local volunteer bureau gave me money, and things just started to fall into place, and I got to go. It was my first time in a hotel alone. I had flown alone maybe once or twice before, but this was a whole different aspect, going to my first conference. I had no expectations. I got so much out of that. From that I was on the first committee for the youth and adults of LDA and then, down the road, I became the chairman twice. And so, I just got really involved.

### Spiritual Pursuits

Some adults with LD/ADHD look beyond themselves and others for help. Religious support and spirituality are very personal, but many people find they provide an invaluable channel to self-understanding and self-acceptance. Betty details her unusual path to good mental health:

> I always chose healthy spirituality over mental health. I never went to a therapist. I saw a priest because I felt that I could educate a priest about LD and ADHD issues more than I could a therapist. I go on 8-day silent retreats once a year. For someone with ADHD to keep my mouth shut for 8 days usually takes somebody threatening to throw me out if I talk. I find that, with the ADHD, to go on silent retreats eliminates a lot of the stimuli. It does two things: first of all, it shuts me up, which takes a major movement in itself; second, it frees me from other people's problems.
>
> I find that the contemplative, the meditative, the taking a day off and going into complete silence is helpful. It gets you in touch with yourself. I think any kind of counselor who is therapeutic, who accepts, who nurtures, who understands, and who gives us a chance for who we are and the freedom of exploring that without judgment and with compassionate understanding is therapeutic, whether they be religious or [in] mental health.

Allyssa describes the enormous shift that happened in her self-concept, with repercussions throughout her life, when she turned to religion:

> I still have to work through things that I felt about myself for a long time. Today I go to God with them, and I really feel that I don't need to go to therapy. When I found God, I realized that I'm a human being just like everybody else. That's when I started to feel like I'm worth something. God loves me as much as he loves a billionaire

on Park Avenue, and we're equal. It doesn't matter that I see numbers backwards—that absolutely means nothing.

Lilia, too, found that it was the spiritual support that made the biggest difference in her life:

> I've been depressed many times, wanted to commit suicide many times. But the only help that I had was God. That's the only help that I had because financially I couldn't afford to [do otherwise]. Sometimes I was told by people at Dorca's Place [the adult literacy center I attend], "You need to go see a psychiatrist. You need someone to talk to." Before I started school, my sisters would tell me that and my friends. My mom, who is a very strong woman, who has a lot of faith, says, "Lilia, God doesn't close one door that he doesn't open another one," and I strongly believe in that. When I thought there was no reason for living, I would say, "God, please give me the strength," and for some reason or another, God did open doors.

### Meditation

Meditation provides a deeply personal psychic space where individuals can discover calm and develop greater self-understanding. Prior to his diagnosis and to beginning on medication, Andre found meditation to have a calming effect and instinctively turned to it to find peace in his hyperactive world. Rich, too, finds meditation deeply fortifying. He explains that meditation is more meaningful to him than attending traditional church services:

> I meditate. I don't go too frequently to formalized religious services, although I think I'm a spiritual person. My concept of going to church is much more laid back. My walks and my meditations and my runs can be very meditative for me in that it helps me to work out situations within my own head. They can be calming at times when I begin to get depressed. I do breathing exercises for relaxation. I was into the martial arts at one point, which was a real good combination of mental and physical self-analysis.

### Friendship

Friends provide another source of emotional support. Friendship cannot be overestimated in its value to good mental health. Glenn reports how his former wife was a true friend in providing firm and insistent support as he edged quite resistently into the world of literacy:

> My partner for 10 years helped me start to understand what it was to be an adult. She pulled me kicking and screaming out of a dysfunctional adolescence into adulthood. She also pulled me kicking and screaming into getting diagnosed. She took me kicking and screaming into the literacy provider. She took me kicking and screaming everywhere. She was that solid support thing. I am now other people's counselor. I do a lot of work with people in a kind of informal thing. I am the one helping them understand that there are options, that you can always find good options.

Nina very touchingly paints a picture of physical support offered by her friends who psychologically stand by to help her through the many challenges in her day-to-day life:

> I'm in a circle of people at this point in my life who say, "I'll hold your hand." It's taken me a long time to figure out how to do that.

### Healthy Living

Eating right, getting adequate rest, and being attuned to one's body are important aspects of healthy living. Betty describes a routine that she considers important to maintaining overall good physical and mental health:

> Outside of being 50 and overweight—but not obese—I'm in good health. I watch what I eat—salt, sugar and that type of thing—all things in moderation. I know to get enough rest. I know to keep on a structured schedule. I know when I'm having a good day and a bad day, and I know to do tasks that I can on good days and on bad days to just back it down to other things.

Exercise can help reduce stress and relieve energy surges. Rich found boxing to be an effective, if nontraditional, means of dealing with his anger:

> The first year I was in the seminary, because of my attitude and my overt anger and hostility, when people gave me lip, my response

was to immediately give it back or to immediately get into it with people. One priest took me under his wing and told me he had to help me with anger management, and he did that through boxing, which is a hell of a way to get control of your anger.

Several people interviewed described daily exercise routines that help them "zone out," "feel high," "self-medicate," and "feel alive." Rich reports:

I have to expend a lot of energy other than sitting at my desk in order for me just to maintain and have a certain level of equilibrium. If I exercise, if I expend that energy, get that adrenaline going in that area, then it doesn't build up in other areas. It just keeps me on a more even keel. The more I'm in a consistent exercise routine, the better off I am in my head.

Nina describes the benefits of her exercise routine:

I walk probably six times a week, for almost an hour every day. I do lifting weights or sit-ups or stuff like that. I've always been driven to physical activity. I think a lot of it is because it's one of those instinctual survival mechanisms that I had to develop to not jump out of my skin, to get through a day at work or get through a meeting. I recognize that as a stress reducer.

Betty, too, sees exercise as essential to her maintaining mental health and reports, "People who are around me know that when I get restless and wired, they should just let me run, literally."

A number of clients with LD/ADHD have extolled the virtues of yoga as a wonderful physical way to not only increase concentration and focus, but also to achieve much-desired inner peace.

## SUMMARY

LD/ADHD often has a significant impact on mental health. Living long term with the symptoms often results in emotional overlay, secondary symptoms such as irritability and mood swings, problems of self-esteem, depression, stress, anxiety, and substance abuse. Treatment by a qualified mental health provider can be very effective.

Adults with LD/ADHD who seek traditional mental health support are urged to carefully check the therapist's background and style; his or her approach to therapy; and his or her ability to offer allied treatments, such as marital therapy or prescribed medications. Beyond traditional counseling relationships, there are a variety of informal and alternative mental health support systems, such as coaching, psychodrama, assertiveness training, self-help, religious support, meditation, friendships, and exercise.

# 3

## Family of Origin

Reaction by the family of origin to LD/ADHD in a member of its ranks can vary widely. Family members who learn about the diagnosis when the child or sibling is quite young may respond differently from those who learn about his or her disability after decades of living with a mishmash of distressing and misunderstood symptoms.

### POSITIVE FAMILY RELATIONSHIPS

Many parents are unconditionally accepting and devote their lives to reassuring their children with LD/ADHD that they can shine in one area, if not in all. Jo Ann gratefully acknowledges that this was the case in her family. Her mother helped her see what she could do rather than focusing solely on areas in which she did not seem to be able to succeed. Nancie's parents, too, continually believed in her. She credits their high expectations with keeping her in school despite a turbulent adolescence that she believes was caused by disability-related self-esteem issues:

> I graduated from high school pregnant. They wouldn't let me participate in graduation; they just sent me my diploma in the mail. I don't know how I finished school or why. I think it was because I came from well-educated parents, and it was just part of what I was supposed to do. I don't know that I ever thought that there was an option of not finishing high school.

Andre appreciates the confidence–building fostered by his mom, who never once stopped believing that her son could achieve great things. He credits her with positively molding his character and with having a protective influence on his life, veering him from social pressures that could well have led to criminal pursuits:

> My mother realized that I could do almost anything once I slowed down to think. I was really isolated as a teenager and had low self-esteem. But once my mother started supporting me [that changed]. To make a long story short, in high school I was captain of the football team, soccer team, track team, chairman of student council. Had it not been for that support of my mother pointing out that I could do these things, I would probably be in jail. A lot of people I know are in jail because they don't know how to cope. In a lot of cases, they simply didn't have anybody to support them or give them the extra boost that they needed to get through those stages of life.

Like Andre's mother, many parents are determined that their children not compromise their ambitions in life due to LD. Indeed, they often try to downplay their child's differences altogether. Jule reports that her mother's attitude and advice helped diminish her limitations in her own mind, gave her a positive, empowering outlook, and fostered a spunky "I can do it!" approach to life. She recalls:

> There was always my mother saying to me, "What do you mean, you can't do it? If you want it, do it!" She was a normal mother, but there was always a sense that you figured out what you needed to do. She said to me once, "If you place the limitations on yourself that others are placing on you, you will do nothing." My mother was a real advocate and not because she was ambitious and wanted me to be this or be that. It was that she was not about to watch me compromise unless I chose to negotiate.

Jule chuckles as she reports an example of her mother's cheer-leading, when she was encouraged to "stand up and fight" for entry into a prestigious college, despite weak scores on the graduate record exam (GRE):

When I took my GREs and went down and was going to pull my application from Emory College, my mother said, "You will not! You just walk in and you tell them you listen with a third ear!" and I said, "Mother, are you nuts?" She said, "No, you just go in there and do that." I said that my legs were going to be shaky, and she said, "Well, just stand behind the desk so they don't see!"

Some parents are able to maintain this level of encouragement. These are the mothers and fathers who successfully avoid the excessive criticism that unfortunately tends to characterize some families of individuals with LD/ADHD, criticism that deflates self-esteem and that inevitably compromises relationships. Betty voices deep appreciation for her father's uncritical outlook on her many problems, which in her youth were still years from being diagnosed as LD:

Various members of the family relate to me in different ways. My father was very positive. He had the guilt that I inherited it from his side of the family and the understanding, which was extremely helpful. My grandfather used to scream at my learning disabled uncle because Grandpa admired education, and my uncle couldn't read. Dad realized that yelling and screaming didn't work.

His encouragement and pride in her hard-won accomplishments strengthened her confidence to continue on, even in the face of potential failure:

I credit my father for my success because Daddy never really criticized. He understood what I was going through. He appreciated the effort that it took to go through school, and he was always there for me. When I went on academic probation in college, he said, "Every minute you spend in college is worth a million dollars to me. Hang in there. We're behind you. We'll be there for you."

Indeed, parental attitude can make a big difference in shaping whether individuals perceive LD/ADHD as a handicap and whether they revert to using it as an excuse. Betty continues reminiscing and also fondly remembers the power of her father's role modeling of tackling problems head-on:

I was raised with the idea that if you have a problem, you don't complain about it; you go fix it. [For example], when Dad was young, he decided he wanted to go play tennis. Well, tennis courts were 60 miles away, so somehow he got a book on how to build a tennis court, built one, and learned how to play tennis on his own court.

Parental attitude positively affected Jule, too. She recalls how her stepfather encouraged her to rise to her potential. He patiently let her take her time to discover the value of his advice:

My stepfather, who is a tremendous support, has helped me with my business, so that I have a sounding board. He doesn't tell me what to do; he gives me advice. He used to say, "Why is it that when I tell you there's a rock in the road, you still trip over it?" Now if I know there's a rock in the road, I walk around it, but in the beginning, when I didn't follow [his warnings], he'd just say, "That's okay. No problem. It's totally your choice." If I chose not to do it, then that was not a problem, except that when I got older, the consequence was that he was not going to be there to give me his input.

He helped her understand that she must not use her problems as an excuse:

I began to realize that in order to get more from people who were willing to help me, there were no excuses. When you get to the airport, you don't say, "Gee, I got stuck in traffic" and expect the plane to be there. If you're late, it's gone. And that's what he taught me—you don't make excuses.

Some parents are very matter-of-fact about dealing with the challenges faced by their child—without fanfare or drama, they simply secure any help that is needed. Rich explains how his working-class parents valued education and doggedly sought the support he would need to succeed in school:

My parents recognized my problems when I was young. They always valued education. They're immigrants, and their whole thing for all my brothers and me was, "Get an education, get an education, get an education." They recognized pretty early that I wasn't getting an education. My mother was a cleaning lady, and my father was a truck driver. They wanted us to have every advantage, and they made sure that we did, which is why back in the 1950s they sent me to the Mass General Hospital Clinic. I don't think they looked at it as getting remediated, so nobody ever really looked at me as being dyslexic or having an attention deficit. They just looked at it as, "Well, you need to get this done. Take care of this." And that was it.

Terry's parents were similarly matter-of-fact and ready to provide support when she declared her interest in pursuing higher education. Until that moment, she had been unaware of their long-held silent hopes:

> I had this sense in growing up that my brother should be a doctor and I should marry one, and that's what happened. So it wasn't like they were worried that I wouldn't succeed. But I don't think that they had high expectations for me. On the other hand, when I decided to get a master's, my mother said to me, "You know, I'm going to pay for it," and I said, "You are?" And she said, "Yeah, we paid for your brother to go to medical school, and I remember thinking to myself that if Terry decides to go back to school, then I'm going to pay for it because I should." I said great. So I guess she did think I'd go on eventually.

Some parents seem to know instinctively how to help their children approach and overcome the hurdles in their path. Although Jo Ann's mother was not a teacher by training, she had a knack for helping her daughter succeed in learning:

> My mom didn't have a degree to teach or even a college degree, but she was doing things at home with me instinctively. I wasn't diagnosed, so she didn't have any idea that I had a learning disability but I can remember at 4 years old learning how to spell "post office"—she told me to think of "off" and "ice." I mean that was her way of teaching me, and that was the best way for me to learn.

Nancie's mother capitalized on her daughter's interests and abilities and directed her toward her natural strengths:

My mother was always there if I wanted to do something. If I wanted to play the piano and bugged her to play the piano, lo, the piano was provided, and I got music lessons. I think she always looked for the talent and just kind of pursued the talent and moved forward and allowed those things to blossom. So I probably got a good foundation. I don't know that as a kid I could have said, "These are my strengths," but I knew them and I kind of went toward them.

Like many other adults with LD, Jule is so appreciative of her parents' lifelong support that the bond has remained extremely tight. She expresses her gnawing concern about the future without them:

I'm very, very close to my parents. I just turned 50. I worry, now that I've gotten older and am so close to my parents, about losing them. I can't come to terms with losing them—I'll lose something very much a part of my life. My life is so much fuller than it would be if they were not there.

## TENSION WITHIN THE FAMILY

Unfortunately, the relationship between the adult with LD/ADHD and his or her family of origin is sometimes strained. Many families are dysfunctional to begin with, and LD simply complicates what is an already difficult life. Glenn describes the too-frequent basis of discussions of families in which a child has an LD:

There is an assumption of functionality in the family, and I think that is an extremely false premise. Kids with LD do not necessarily come from fully intact, fully functioning, well-heeled families. That is definitely not what my family was. In my family there was divorce, separation, early death of parents. There was a lot of poverty; there were not a lot of resources; there was not a lot of focus on me as a child nor on me as a student or on me as whatever. My family was in severe, dire survival mode.

A pattern of unhealthy dynamics may be established during the childhood of individuals with LD/ADHD, when, because of persistent difficulties, they are cast in the role of "problem child" within the family. In that role, he or she is thereafter the scapegoat for a broad range of issues, many of which have nothing to do with the disability (Hallowell & Ratey, 1994). This cycle can and often does persist well into adulthood. Betty describes the pattern of conflict that developed when she emerged as the black sheep in what she refers to as her "toxic" family:

> I had a tough relationship with my family. My mother was hypercritical of me, as were my sister and brothers. Everything I did was wrong or screwed up or whatever. They were very negative because they didn't understand. They were always saying, "Why can't you XYZ? Why are you acting that way? Why are you acting so stupid when you're not stupid? You're a chronic underachiever." I was always being balled out, looked on as the black sheep of the family. I think part of the reason I've been a success is that I've largely separated myself from family.

Other reasons for discord with the family relate to characteristics of the LD itself. The child who was tactilely defensive may have provoked negative parental reactions by responding stiffly to his or her parents' hugs and by being unable to relax and cuddle and reinforce their warmth. The child who was hyperactive may have exhausted his or her parents by constantly being on the move. The child with significant organizational problems may have regularly missed the mark in terms of maintaining family norms; his or her forgetfulness, chronic lateness, untidy nature, and pattern of continually losing belongings may well have resulted in a destructive dynamic cycle. Within this cycle, it is likely that the child's parents devoted a great deal of time to monitoring and punishing him or her, leading him or her to become defiant or to devalue himself or herself, which further intensified the parents' exasperation and their sense of failure.

Many families have been unable to accept the reality of the LD and devalue the coping mechanisms or achievements of their family member with LD/ADHD. Nina notes:

> I've often told my family that I haven't done anything in my life that somebody hasn't basically held my hand and helped me do. My family has reacted with, "Well if you can't do it by yourself, then you're really not going to do it."

Indeed, her family reacted with suspicion to the explanations she offered for her LD/ADHD symptoms:

> I did talk to my older sister about being in treatment for my LD and ADHD. We're an estranged family, so her reaction was pretty much, "So this is the new thing that you're saying it is." I have other relatives who, over the years—because I've started things and not finished them—have kind of had this mocking sense of, "Is this another one of your little projects that you want to try, or is this another one of your schemes?" I understand it at this point. They did see this cycle of, "Well, first I'm gonna do this and then I'm gonna do that" and not ever being able to stay with it. There is the recurring sense that I'm doing this as some kind of way to get out of whatever I should do. If I didn't finish a project in high school, they'd tell me I was lazy, and they'd say, "You're so smart, I can't believe you can't finish this project." I remember thinking, "Me?" And then the sense of shame would come over me that I couldn't finish it. So, then I wouldn't finish it just because I was smart and ashamed. Part of our estrangement is my saying, "I'm not going to take your negative treatment."

Family members may make subtle, less direct remarks that can be equally hurtful to the adult with LD. Terry offers an example:

> My mother said something to me once that hurt my feelings. It was before I got married. She said, "You know, you've got to be careful because the thing that you really dislike about your mate is probably going to come up in your kids," and I knew she was talking about my father's LD stuff.

## PARENTAL RELATIONSHIPS

Tension between parents is inevitable under these conditions. Many parents bear the weight of a complex set of emotions in relation to their child with LD. Betty Osman wrote:

> Following the initial feelings of guilt and anger, disappointment and anxiety are perhaps the most universal feelings that parents

have about their children's learning differences. Parents have wishes and fantasies about their children, and it is hard for them to accept their unrealized dreams. (1997, pp. 37–38)

In circumstances in which an individual was diagnosed late, the parents may feel guilty that they failed to seek answers sooner in their child's life and may feel a deep resentment that is quite apparent to others. As Siegel noted:

Retrospective thinking may [have led these parents] to feel that they should have given more attention to siblings or perhaps planned a larger family or nurtured the husband–wife relationship. They may regret that they missed so much and did not enjoy life as they might have. (1974, p. 66)

Resentment particularly arises for those parents who have had to bear the burden of blame for causing "the problem" in their child. Betty sighs as she describes her relationship with her own mother:

My mother cannot be around me for more than 5 minutes without being very critical of me. The schools were always blaming her for my problems, which made her feel like a failure. And her feeling like a failure was put right back on me.

Some parents fail to recognize the larger picture of the disability; they perceive only isolated symptoms and reject the terms *LD* or *ADHD*. Terry recounts an experience that demonstrates this:

I talked to [family members] about the idea that it's a learning disability. I was asking my mother some things, and she said, "You don't have a learning disability. You just can't spell." It's not 'just can't spell'—it's bigger than that. It's like I have this block of an ability to communicate. I think that it just feels to her that I'm very competent. I mean, here I am, a person who basically, since the day I graduated high school, has run my life—I found my own job, I found my own husband—in every way I feel very successful.

She regrets that her mother views her LD rather simplistically and has often discounted the emotions that arise along with each of the symptoms:

> My mother just doesn't get it. I have this vivid memory of me standing up on the landing of our split-level house—I was in high school writing a paper or something, and I came out on the landing and said to my mother, "How do you spell such-and-such?" And she's looking up from the kitchen, saying, "Well, sound it out. What do you think the first letter is? Well, you know the first letter. What's the next letter. Sound it out." And me just having a screaming fit, saying, "Just tell me! I can't think. I can't stop to think about this. I'm thinking about what I want to say!" So I think there are a lot of ways she felt, "Well, you can just do this, and then it'll be better." But, you know, it really wasn't true.

Jo Ann has a remarkably similar story to tell. She reports that when she was having difficulty reading an article one day and her mother was urging her to sound out the words, she became so frustrated and angry that she put her foot through the nearest wall.

## SIBLING RELATIONSHIPS

Learning disabilities have a direct effect on relationships among siblings as well. Many are very loving and supportive, able to look beyond the weaknesses of their brother or sister with LD/ADHD, ready to cheer for his or her hard-won achievements. Indeed, in many cases, the entire family is accepting and encouraging, downplaying challenges and celebrating strengths. Allyssa credits her siblings with doing the best they could in responding to her LD. Having come through a particularly turbulent and troubled youth, she expresses pride in the role she is now able to play with her younger sisters:

> My family was there for me to the best of their ability. They did a lot of different things. I have a big brother who's kind of always tried to make me feel good about myself. I have two baby sisters, seven and four. They don't know I have a learning disability. All they know

is that I live a life today that they want to live. They look up to me today, and it's awesome. They say, "Wow, look at our big sister. She's young, she's cool. She doesn't drink, she doesn't do drugs, she doesn't do things that aren't right." My whole life I wanted a role model that was positive, that I could look up to and say, "Wow, I want to someday be like that." I'm not talking about a pedestal. When I was younger, I wanted to look up to a woman that was living the right way and say, "I want to live a life like she's living." I had nobody to really look up to like that. I'm that person for my sisters.

In some families, however, LD is not so readily accepted by the other children. Such was the case in Betty's family:

My sister, who was 4 years older than I, was a Phi Beta Kappa and extremely bright. She was very judgmental and critical and a perfectionist. I'm not a perfectionist; I'm the exact opposite, and there were a lot of difficulties relating to my sister in terms of seeking acceptance, seeking understanding. Everything I did was wrong. She died of Lupus at the age of 28 before we really understood each other as adults.

Some siblings feel the child with LD/ADHD was overindulged, that their parents were overprotective and expected too little of him or her. Some resent the attention parents have always had to devote to their sister or brother with LD/ADHD. Siblings in some families grew up feeling guilty about their own success in academics and feeling burdened by too-high expectations from their parents, who seemed to need their other children's successes to offset their own guilt and disappointment about the learning problems of the child with LD. These siblings may still feel hurt if their parents downplayed their own high grades to protect the brother or sister with LD/ADHD from the pain of comparison (Osman, 1997). Allyssa laments her brother's jealousy:

I have a brother who's 3½ years older than me. He's always felt, "I wish I had a learning disability, for the attention [I'd get]." That was not a healthy thing. I really feel that it's so wrong to classify people. It does them such an injustice. They gave me all this attention, and my brother was like, "Hey, what about me? I'm a person, too, you know!"

Some siblings resent the accomplishments of their brother or sister with LD/ADHD and are jealous of parents' positive regard for those achievements. Some harbor resentment for the embarrassment they felt throughout their childhood due to the LD-related social skills problems or academic difficulties of their sister or brother. They may feel resentful that throughout their childhood, they were expected to "drag along" a sibling with LD/ADHD to social events. Lacking an understanding of the inconsistencies of LD, they may resent the term, seeing it as a "cop-out" diagnosis. Lilia describes how a sister to whom she is very attached simply refuses to accept the diagnosis as valid:

> I have a sister who I'm very, very close to and when I talk to her about my LD, she says, "I don't think that's it. I think you just didn't like school." I said, "You weren't in my shoes. You don't know how I felt when the teacher would tell me to stand up and all the other kids laughed. That was degrading! I wanted to crawl in my seat and just cry. So don't tell me that I didn't like school. I didn't like school for a lot of reasons—I didn't understand what was going on every day. People are still having a hard time with people with learning disabilities." "That's not true," she said. "It's just that you didn't try hard enough."

Some siblings grow up with a deep and unexpressed fear that LD/ADHD in the family means there is also something wrong with them or that they may pass the disability on to their own children. Andre describes how this fear has created an unfortunate distance between him and his family:

> My mother and father and sisters and brothers—they've been somewhat surprised with me. I think it scares them. I try to tell them and they say, "Oh, it's just this. Oh, it's just that." I think the underlying fear is that they have it and don't want to accept it. The more I say it, the more they deny it. I educate them, but they don't want to hear it. That hurts me, too because I feel somehow rejected. Actually, that hurts me deeply. Sometimes it results in my not calling them for a whole month.

Siblings may indeed have LD or ADHD too, and their resentment can be affected by their own disability-related symptoms. Jule describes her own sibling scenario:

> There really is this thing to [LD] running in families. My sister was very well behaved, made straight A's—the perfect child, who probably has a nonverbal social disability. She is incredibly spacy, so when she got into an unstructured situation, she went wild and promiscuous, the whole thing, without it bothering her. She's never had strong friendships or relationships except with the guy she married, [who is] her only friend, her only everything. Very self-centered. She's gotten nicer since she met this guy, but there's that spaciness there. There's also that lack of awareness of the feelings of others.
>
> My mother had my second brother run track because he had so much energy. She got him a trampoline. He was a behavior problem, and he wasn't a nice behavior problem. There are big differences between us, even though we both have the ADHD with the hyperactivity. He is overtly jealous of me, and it's so stupid because he has so much.

Some siblings respond to the diagnosis with pity. Lilia bristles as she recalls her sister's response to her disclosure that test results indicated she had a LD:

> I said to my sister, "I got my results. I have a learning disability." I can still see her facial expression. She went, "Oh, Lilia. Oh, honey." It was like, "Oh, you poor thing. When are you gonna die? How much longer do you have to live?" I don't know. Maybe it was the way I said it. Maybe because I didn't understand it. I was like, "Hellooooo, I can do circles around you!"

## EXTENDED FAMILY

Even grandparents are affected by LD in the family. Many adults gratefully report that their grandparents were champions who believed in them despite their significant learning problems. Jule deeply appreciates the unconditional positive regard of her grandmother, who was always totally accepting.

However, grandparents may also react negatively. They may be critical of their son or daughter for the way he or she handled the LD/ADHD, concerned that the grandchild with the LD/ADHD was spoiled or, conversely, not taken care of enough. Some grandparents feel resentful of the grandchild's negative effects on the adult life of their own son or daughter.

## STRATEGIES FOR STRONGER FAMILY TIES

There are several steps that can be taken to bolster family ties.

### EDUCATING THE FAMILY

LD/ADHD affects not only the individual but also the family as a whole. One woman, providing an example of this broad effect, sadly notes tension whenever she returns home for Thanksgiving, as everyone struggles to readjust to her symptoms. It is very important that members of both the immediate and extended family be educated about LD and ADHD because education helps relieve such tension. As they learn, family members come to understand that LD/ADHD is neither purposeful nor an excuse for laziness or irresponsibility. Education can be achieved through books, on the Internet, at many doctors' offices, and through organizations such as the National Center for Learning Disabilities or the Learning Disabilities Association of America (see Resources).

### CAPITALIZING ON TALENTS

Armed with understanding, family members stop blaming their relative for having LD/ADHD and are able to look beyond weaknesses to identify and appreciate his or her unique talents and, to the extent possible, how to circumvent weaknesses. Accentuating the positive changes the individual's family reputation (Hallowell & Ratey, 1994) and sets the stage for healthier dynamics.

### DISCUSSING NEGATIVE EMOTIONS

Family members should have an opportunity to discuss any fears or resentments they may have related to LD/ADHD. It is important that they speak frankly and freely. One woman reported, "It was so helpful to my relationship with my sister when she finally aired her fears that she would give birth to kids with LD. She cried and I cried and the tension between us was dissolved." Such candor is not always achievable without assistance; thus, many families seek the services of a mental health provider to create a safe environment in which to communicate effectively.

## LEARNING TO NEGOTIATE

It is important for the family to learn how to work out their differences and relate to one another in harmony. Family members need to learn negotiation skills, possibly in family therapy, targeting specific problems of the individual with LD/ADHD, such as chronic lateness, and then developing a plan of action to correct those problems. One man reported that his family targeted his tendency to lose track of time at work and to miss dinner night after night:

> They worked out a plan to call me at the office 45 minutes before dinnertime to remind me to knock it off and come home. Because it was my kids doing the reminding, it really helped. I heard their voices and remembered how much I wanted to be with them.

Facing the same type of problem with a mother who missed her children's soccer games due to distractions as she completed pre-game chores, another family opted to give her a watch with an alarm, which she could set to ring when it was time to prepare to go to the soccer field.

## MAINTAINING A SENSE OF HUMOR

Families need to maintain perspective and a sense of humor. One woman reported that her family has dealt with her symptoms with humor since learning about her LD. Indeed supportive humor is advocated by Hallowell and Ratey, who noted, "Sometimes the key to success in treatment is just to persist and to keep a sense of humor. Get a second consultation, get additional help, but don't give up" (1994, p. 146).

## SUMMARY

Reactions tend to vary when one member of a family has LD/ADHD. Although many parents are very supportive, some struggle with feelings of guilt or resentment, and some deny the problem altogether. Similarly varying reactions are apparent in siblings. While many are loving and supportive, some feel unresolved jealousy and embarrassment and may bear continuing resentment over attention lost to the brother or sister with LD/ADHD. Grandparents also exhibit mixed reactions. Family ties may be strengthened by educating all concerned about LD/ADHD, by letting family members air their feelings, by providing training in negotiation to resolve ongoing problems, and by maintaining perspective and a sense of humor.

## Friendships and Dating

LD/ADHD can have a significant impact on friendships and dating. Although some adults with LD/ADHD enjoy very rich and satisfying social lives, many, unfortunately, do not. Even those who do enjoy numerous friendships may find that LD/ADHD-related challenges periodically complicate their relationships. Nina describes how this affects her interpersonal dealings with others:

> I'm smart, I'm funny. I entertain people enough on a regular basis, day-to-day stuff. But many of my friends get upset with me because I can't pay attention to them, sometimes for long periods of time, and I tend to interrupt a lot [because] I think so fast, I just think all over the place.

As a defense, many adults with LD/ADHD choose to isolate themselves rather than expose weaknesses associated with LD to the scrutiny and judgment of others. For example, despite her charisma and love of people, Nina often chooses solitude. She explains, "I've been a loner in a lot of ways and that's a survival thing because I didn't want anyone to see how bad I was." Jule, too, admits to feeling vulnerable and in need of self-protection:

> I'm very fun-loving and all, but I keep my distance from people in lots of ways. If I have bad vibes about someone, I steer clear. I get hurt real easily. I believe people say what they mean—if a friend makes an unkind comment, somebody else might not be affected by it, but I will be.

Some adults with LD/ADHD were open and friendly as children, but, after a lifetime of being hurt by others, now find it difficult to believe that people will react to them positively. They become rather guarded and often keep a distance in their interactions with others. Allyssa reflects:

> I was a very trusting little kid, and I've been hurt. I think the idea of being hurt by people in my life—being told you're not worth it and having people always break trust—has affected my relationships.

Caution in social situations is not unreasonable when one considers that even among friends adults with LD/ADHD can experience subtle disapproval. Glenn's assessment that he was losing social acceptance from his long-time circle of friends was deeply painful and ultimately led him to relocate to a new city. There he was able to try to reestablish his identity with new peers. He recalls:

> For 18 years my job was running up and down the steps selling beer at sporting events. That was the job I could handle as a basically illiterate person. My friends and peers were in college—some were becoming lawyers and some were becoming doctors, social workers, white-collar successful people. They knew me, and they loved me, and they supported me, but I knew I was falling further and further behind them. They were becoming judges; they were becoming elected officials. We are still friends, but their lives and my life were changing dramatically. We went from becoming hippie-radical organizers to [people with] very different roles. I was still socially accepted, but the "socially accepted curve" was dropping dramatically.
>
> A lot of people faded out of my life when they became more successful. I was stuck in this nonliterate, nonfunctional world. I was psychologically slipping away from my peers a great deal, and who do I relate to among the other people who are there? I can't really relate to them, and because of that, I become more and more isolated. Try dating a quality woman in her thirties and you get, "What do you do? You sell beer? God!" So, the ability to relate to people I would want to relate to on a social level, an emotional level, and a sexual level—they were not very accepting of me because I was illiterate and dysfunctional. I was very cognizant of this, and I was very aware that I was slipping further and further away. Part of the mad rush when I got identified [as having LD] was

that I tried to get back up to my peers. I haven't quite done that. In some ways, I am actually surpassing some of my peers, but the stigma is still there because some of them still think of me as what I was, not what I've become. They know my history. One of the reasons I wanted to move to [a new city] is that in some ways, I am socially just starting out here. People don't all know my past, and I can be who I am now, as opposed to who I was.

## SOCIAL CHALLENGES RELATED PRIMARILY TO SYMPTOMS OF LD/ADHD

The characteristics of LD/ADHD have varying effects on friendships and dating relationships.

### SOFT NEUROLOGICAL SIGNS

Individuals with LD/ADHD who have soft neurological signs that make them appear different from others sometimes experience disapproval and social exclusion. Soft neurological signs include overreacting with a startle response to stimuli; moving in a disorganized fashion; holding the head somewhat askew; talking too fast, too slowly, or too loudly; and either staring or not being able to maintain eye contact. Dale Brown described her acute and painful awareness of the effect that her appearance had on others during her college years:

> I learned that certain aspects of my appearance made it difficult for others to relate to me. I tilted my head slightly. In order to look at something, I often moved my head and entire body instead of my eyes. To repress my hyperactivity, I held my muscles rigid. I was often startled and would make sudden movements. These were the visible signs of the dysfunction of my central nervous system. (1982, p. 21)

### PERCEPTUAL PROBLEMS

Perceptual problems can interfere with social relationships in a number of ways. Those with **weak visual discrimination** have difficulty differentiating and interpreting facial expressions and gestures. One person explained how this resulted in frequent misinterpretations of friends' reactions to her. She complained to me that she could not judge whether she was being joked with or mocked by her friends. As a defense against the tension and sadness of feeling rejected, she reported that she tends to withdraw; she would rather be alone than subject herself to the humiliation of not knowing where she stands with people. For many adults with LD/ADHD, a parallel **auditory discrimination problem** exists; they cannot readily distinguish between voice tones, so it is difficult to differentiate between genuine and sarcastic comments.

Adults with **visual figure–ground difficulties,** who cannot easily pick one figure out from a visual field, may decide that it is more comfortable to limit their social life than to cope with the visual overload that occurs in certain settings. Glenn describes how this tension arises:

> If I go to a movie and sit in the back, everyone's heads make all this movement, and I lose concentration. I need to sit very close up front so I can just have the movie in front of me.

Similarly, individuals with **auditory figure–ground difficulties** often become overwhelmed at parties due to the mix of conversations and music. Glenn describes some of the limitations that this lack of filtering ability places on his social life: "There are several environments that are very disturbing to me. It is very difficult for me to go into loud environments, because I can't filter out the noise. I don't go [out] to [listen to] bands or to bars."

**Tactile differential problems** also affect the social interactions of adults with LD/ADHD. A simple hug or handshake can be a challenge. Some squeeze too hard in a handshake and make the other person wince; others hold the person's hand with too little pressure, giving an impression of weakness. Glenn chuckles but is serious as he comments, "Just patting someone on the shoulder, you can send him flying across the room."

## MEMORY IMPAIRMENTS

Poor memory can cause tension within friendships and dating relationships. People who have **difficulty with visual memory** tend to forget faces and experience awkward moments when they fail to recognize someone whom they have met before. They often cannot remember landmarks, which means they tend to get lost. This leads to being late, a behavior that rarely endears them to friends or lovers. Those with **poor auditory memory** may offend others when they forget that they have orally made plans. They may appear lazy or defiant to others when given multiple directions, as they just cannot remember the second step of what they have been asked to do. They frequently forget names and often have trouble remembering telephone numbers. As Pat describes:

> Having a problem with short-term memory does terrible things for relationships. I can remember faces and that sort of stuff, but I don't remember names. I have extreme difficulty putting things in time and space, which means I lose where I knew you. I know you are back there somewhere but I do not have any sense of time.

Many adults with LD/ADHD, like Terry, need both visual and auditory input in order to derive real meaning from an interaction. She explains:

> I spend a lot of time talking on the phone to people. I have a lot of trouble connecting who they are afterwards. I don't remember names really well if I haven't had a very real encounter with someone. It has to be that I've really interacted with them in person.

## LANGUAGE DISORDERS

People with language disorders run into difficult interpersonal moments when they either fail to understand what another person says or fumble in their efforts to express themselves to others. Many find themselves in awkward situations when others use figurative language, which they find difficult to understand. An example of this was provided several years ago, when one young woman with LD arrived in my office terribly distressed, explaining that she had been physically threatened by a male friend who was extremely angry with her. Her fear was nearly palpable as she breathlessly recounted the story and frantically worried aloud,

"This time he says he's going to let it ride!" She had no idea what "let it ride" meant and, thus, missed understanding that the danger of his hitting her had passed at least for the time being.

Jokes present a particular challenge for those with difficulties in language processing, as they so often end in a punchline expressed in idioms, puns, and other forms of figurative language. One woman reported that her parents astutely recognized her "humor deficit" when she was young and cleverly conducted "humor remediation" sessions each weekend as they read together and interpreted the jokes in the comics section of the Sunday paper.

Janet explains a positive social aspect of language concreteness. Noting that an individual who is so concrete is prone to neither manipulations nor game-playing, she reports that Harry "is absolutely incapable of sarcasm or manipulation—it's just part of the disability. He can't participate in that, and he doesn't understand that. He is incapable of being dishonest."

## SKILLS DEFICITS

Skills deficits can also have negative implications in friendships or dating relationships. Many adults with LD who have **difficulty with math,** for instance, struggle with money management. Those who resort to borrowing may experience much tension in friendships if they repeatedly ask for loans or forget to repay their debts.

People who have **difficulty reading** experience awkward moments in a variety of situations. For example, some try to avoid restaurants where they will be forced to read menus. One woman told me she compensates by going to the International House of Pancakes because there are pictures on the menu of all the meal choices, and it is not necessary to read at all.

Even a birthday party can be traumatic. Christopher Lee described a painful moment when his college buddies surprised him:

It was my perfect birthday—until I was asked to read my birthday cards aloud in front of a room full of people. I tried to get out of it by joking around, but when a person is surrounded by a bunch of friends, the peers usually have the advantage. They insisted, and I had to give in. I started reading, stumbling through verses that were supposed to rhyme and clichés that were supposed to make me blush. Instead of enjoying the moment, I became frustrated, and my face grew warm. I tensed up, and my mood switched from delight to apprehension. (Lee & Jackson, 1992, p. 110)

**Writing problems** may keep a person from jotting notes on greeting cards or from remaining in contact with friends. Glenn describes how for years he disappointed others who expected correspondence from him:

I don't sit down and write any long elegant letters. It's torturous. I don't correspond like normal people do. At one point of my life, before computers, I didn't write a letter to anyone for 5–10 years. I would communicate by phone. It was impossible for me to write a letter.

### DISTRACTIBILITY AND ATTENTION PROBLEMS

Problems of attention often contribute to strains in interpersonal relationships. Distracted adults may have lapses of attention and lose their train of thought or may be poor listeners in conversations. They regularly arrive late for dates because they become waylaid by a telephone call or a television show or by countless small matters. In contrast, adults who tend to hyperfocus may become overinvolved in projects, in their work on the computer, or in a good book they are reading, and lose track of time, the end result being that they, too, are chronically late.

### DISORGANIZATION

The reciprocal relationship that often exists between disorganization and anxiety has wide-ranging negative implications. One individual with LD/ADHD offered an example of this, reporting that she tends to be hopelessly disorganized, and her disorganization invariably makes her feel anxious because she knows she is "supposed to be able to handle things." Her anxiety further increases her disorganization, which makes her more likely to forget social plans or someone's birthday. The resulting interpersonal tension makes her even more anxious. It is a difficult cycle.

Many adults with LD/ADHD feel not only anxious but also deeply ashamed of their disorganization, so much so that they go into isolation rather than risk exposing themselves to the embarrassment of others seeing the chaos in which they live. One woman reported that her living room is nearly always in a messy state and she is too embarrassed to invite others over to visit.

## HYPERACTIVITY

Hyperactive adults often experience interpersonal tension. With a physical need to move more than other people typically do, they may repeatedly get up and walk around when talking with others, clicking their pens or engaging in other behaviors that can be considered annoying. As Nina has been advised, constant activity can be a social turn-off:

> A male friend of mine would always tell me, "Men are intimidated by you," and I'd ask, "But why?" He'd say, "You just don't stop." It was always a joke, and we would laugh about it, but, ultimately it's become painful just to recognize that and say, "Hmm, [this LD/ADHD thing] is not just about work and reading and all of that stuff."

Hyperactivity can have a negative impact on relationships even during a relatively sedentary activity such as television-watching, when the individual continually cruises the channels with the remote control. It may also surface in simple conversation, as it does for Betty:

> I tend to talk too much. People know I talk a lot, and when I start getting on their nerves they just say, "Hey, cool it," and I'm accepting of that. When I'm around a relaxed situation, the symptoms are not as bad. In new situations I can be—I hate to say the word—inappropriate. I always fear being inappropriate in these situations because I know under stress the mouth is gonna start running. And that's always scary. I think after people get to know me, they appreciate my finer qualities and I have no problems finding friends.

## IMPULSIVITY

Impulsivity causes many quick responses and knee-jerk reactions that are often socially inappropriate. For example, with the continual flood of ideas that flows through her mind, Nina finds she responds too quickly in conversation and tends to interrupt others. Ritalin helps her control this behavior:

> My impulse control is much better than it's ever been. That's some of the stuff that the Ritalin does. My brain is still going, but for some reason, I don't feel I have to comment on every single thing; I know I can file away things and come back to them, whereas before, I was thinking, "If I don't say it now, I'll lose it, and it'll never come back again to mention."

Impulsivity also leads some adults with LD/ADHD to blurt out whatever is on their minds without filtering offensive content. This can be destructive to relationships. Nancie regretfully notes, "Everything that I want to say, everything that's in my brain comes out of my mouth. Always."

People with LD/ADHD can be genuinely appalled by their own behavior when they find themselves unwittingly engaging in impulsive antisocial behaviors, such as telling secrets that they had sworn to keep or being harsh and rude. Betty recognizes that she offends others at times when she speaks crassly or swears.

## SOCIAL CHALLENGES RELATED TO SECONDARY SYMPTOMS OF LD/ADHD

In addition to the impact of the primary characteristics of LD/ADHD described above, several secondary symptoms—such as social immaturity, poor self-concept, disorganization, egocentricity, and a lack of social skills—also affect friendship and dating relationships. There are a variety of social skills problems associated with LD/ADHD that have a direct influence on friendships and dating. Some are attributable to the LD itself, such as staring behavior that can be a soft neurological symptom or shyness that may be rooted in difficulty with expressive language. Others are secondary effects, byproducts of living a life with LD, sometimes attributable to isolation during childhood.

### SOCIAL MATURATIONAL LAG

Many adults with LD/ADHD grew up consistently seeming younger than their years, socially responding as if they were 12 when they were 16, as if they were 16 when they were 20. This maturational lag launched them into a negative social cycle whereby they often were set apart from their peers, so they had fewer social opportunities. This limited their overall social growth, which meant that they continued to be set apart from their peers. Glenn describes the persistent delays:

> Most LD males tend to mature slower socially and emotionally than their peers. So when most boys are trying to get their first date, LD boys are still playing with Power Rangers; when people are starting to go steady, they are still trying to get laid for the first time or get their first date; and when people are starting to get married, they are still looking for whatever. They tend to be behind.

Social immaturity is not limited to males. Jo Ann also experienced a delay in social maturation. Throughout our interview, she described a lifetime of feeling discomfort that made her uneasy with her peers and contributed to long periods of isolation and loneliness in her life:

> [I had a couple of dates with] guys that did get a little too forward—not seriously or anything—but I fortunately was able to read enough clues to say, "I want out of here, I don't want any part of this." I always felt that it was a little soon on the first date to be doing any more than just sitting down and having coffee and maybe seeing if we had anything in common. That's my feeling. If you have something in common, then maybe things will develop. I mean I've never gotten that far [that anything developed].

The consequences of a maturational lag last far beyond childhood. Limited opportunities to practice social behaviors with peers during one's youth result in the development of a restricted repertoire of approaches for engaging with others in adulthood. As Glenn notes, "People with LD, including myself, very clearly often don't learn social skills. They don't understand etiquette, they don't know the social circles, so they become pretty isolated."

Adults with LD/ADHD may lack the social skills necessary to meet, launch, and maintain new friendships. Many feel uncomfortable even trying to do so. They may feel unsure of the "rules" of how to handle themselves in certain social situations, or they may lack the confidence necessary to put into play those rules that they know. Lack of social refinement is troublesome for many adults who have no LD at all; those who do have LD/ADHD often find their tendency to be out of step socially a painful issue that is at least as complicating in their lives as technical difficulties such as limited reading or writing skills.

## Low Self-Esteem

Low self-esteem can seriously undermine the social lives of adults with LD/ADHD. Individuals who are wracked by self-doubt feel insecure about the impression they make on others. If they are filled with self-loathing, they find it hard to project the confidence required for successful social interactions. The result may be further isolation, as they question whether they can possibly connect with others in the social world. Glenn, for example, doubts that he could be at all attractive to women. In recounting his history of illiteracy and dysfunction, he only half-jokingly asks, "What self-respecting woman, seeing the man that I was, would have been interested in this highly dysfunctional, crazy, weird, disheveled, angry, illiterate person? Why should she have been interested?"

Jo Ann offers a poignant description of the discomfort she experiences when faced with the complex social demands of attending an art exhibit or a cocktail party:

> I was glad I went and saw the art, but it was just such a challenge to get to the table to get a glass of wine and balance wine and cheese and look at pictures and look at your program. By doing all that, I didn't really have any energy left to really talk to somebody. Normally, if you go to something like that, you're supposed to go up and say, "Hello, my name is . . . and what do you think of this painting?" I couldn't. All I could do is basically go through and read the names of the artists.
>
> [It's] the same way at a cocktail party. I go because sometimes it's required—when you're in an executive position, you have to go to things like that. When they start picking my brains for the really important stuff, half of the time I know I won't hear or understand what they're saying. It sounds like I'm getting it, but I'm really not. Then I might call them back later and say, "Gee, you

know, I'd really like to talk to you more about this that you were mentioning the other night at the party."

Trying to move in and out of a room that's really crowded is a real challenge for me. I know the words to say, "Please excuse me" or something, but sometimes people are so intense talking, it's like when do you interrupt? I mean, am I going to annoy that person because they're right in a tense moment of conversation? Do you just stand there and wait? It's easiest for me just to go out of the room and come around to an exit where there's more room, but that's not always an option.

Jo Ann regularly feels the tension of her social uncertainties, even when involved in an activity as familiar and safe as attending her own church:

Sunday morning, when the minister gets really intense with somebody and I don't know whether it's a new person or something, do I stand in line and wait for my turn to shake hands, or do I just skip it because I see him every Sunday anyway, so why is it so important to see him now? That kind of thing just flips in and out my mind. I want to do things right, but I don't want to be intense because I know that in the past, as a young person, I was very intense. I think I still probably am.

## EGOCENTRICITY

Egocentricity is a particularly challenging aspect of LD in that has such a direct and detrimental effect on interpersonal relationships. As Glenn explains, self-absorption can be a byproduct of the self-preservation efforts of adults with a variety of disabilities:

How we tend to survive tends to make us much more insular and self-focused. It tends to be true with most people with disabilities, especially people with severe physical disabilities. The focal point becomes the discussion of how you are breathing or butt sores or bad personal care attendants. With people with LD, the conversation tends to be "how I can't read" or "how I'm dysfunctional." It becomes one of a negative, isolated view and your dysfunction. It's normal and it's okay and it's necessary to talk about surviving and how to survive, but to the population who is not LD and not involved

in it, they wonder what the hell is going on. You are very self-centered
and egocentric, so it's another level of isolation.

Egocentric adults have trouble effectively evaluating the impact
of such self-centered behaviors as breaking promises, forgetting
dates, or being chronically tardy. Janet keenly felt the sting of these
behaviors early in her relationship with Harry. She interpreted his
forgetfulness, his being late, and his poor eye contact as a lack of
caring and only later came to understand that these behaviors were
tied to his LD. Janet laughingly explains that she eventually grew
to recognize that there was actually an upside of his lack of
awareness of the goings-on around him, and that it had worked to
her advantage on at least one occasion: "I once planned a surprise
birthday party for my husband with over 60 people. It was at home.
Despite all the cooking and everything that was going on, he literally
never had a clue!"

Egocentrism plays out in a variety of ways. The self-
centeredness that keeps Harry from noticing the goings on in his
own home is also at the root of Jule's impatience, a trait that she
regretfully notes tends to destroy relationships:

> In my relationships with men—in the beginning, it's so wonderful.
> Everything is the same intensity. Everything is great. Relationships
> last about 2 years, then little things bother me. Impatience. First I
> am so understanding, so wonderful, so giving, so loving, and then
> I am short-tempered and impulsive, without monitoring what I say. I
> snap, short-fuse, let things drag on, get picky, intolerant, self-centered
> and then am real willing to quickly go, leave, end the relationship.

Impatience often stems from a lack of control, and the need
for control is often caused by egocentricity. For many adults with
LD/ADHD, control feels essential to their well-being. Nancie
recognizes her fragile hold on control and the negative effects when
it is lost. She admits that when something unexpected happens in
a relationship, it unnerves her. She admits, "If I'm not in control,
everything goes awry. If I'm in control, things will go okay, as long
as I can manage time."

Self-centeredness and a need for control generate an impatience
that can keep a person from considering the points of view of others,
particularly those of close friends and lovers. Jule notes:

If I had a bad day, I had a bad day—a lot of insensitivity, a lack of stopping and reflecting about where the other person was coming from. Especially once it was a very familiar kind of relationship, then I was bitchy.

Nina finds that she loses patience in relationships, too. At the time of our interview, she had recently broken up with a man who also had ADHD. She comments on how ironic it was that she should have so little patience:

I have an enormous amount of patience with my work and with my child and in terms of compassionate empathy, but when the guy in my life isn't ready to go, I'm all over the place with, "Come on let's go, let's do this, let's go places." I haven't been particularly good at just being in the moment and just enjoying someone's company. I'm always wondering what's coming next, what's going to happen.

Impatience, control, and egocentricity are, thus, closely linked. Nancie provides an example of how adults who rigidly maintain control in an effort to survive react with impatience and annoyance to interference with their habits:

I get really irritated when people call in the evening time—I don't want to talk in the evening! If you can get past that [attitude] for 30 seconds, then I can be engaged to talk. It's obviously not their problem. I really am an avid TV watcher, and I don't want anyone to interrupt me in the process [of watching a show]. It's the time when it's the only thing that's going on in my brain, and I can block everything else out. It's a down time, kind of a mechanism where I don't have to think about anything else. If you ask me what I watched last night, though, I often couldn't tell you.

## SOCIAL SKILLS DEFICITS

People with social skills deficits often have difficulty understanding body language, which puts them at a tremendous social disadvantage because up to 80% of communication tends to be nonverbal. They have trouble "reading" flirtatious body language; likewise, they have difficulty communicating their interest nonverbally to others. Lack of eye contact, misjudgments about how close to stand to someone else, and difficulty modulating voice volume can all impede social contacts. One woman attributed her lack of dating experience to an inability to read clues regarding what men want. She described painful shyness, lack of skill in making small talk, and the subsequent misery she felt in her few dating experiences with men.

Many adults with social skills problems are aware that they break social rules but are unsure of which specific behavior is offensive. One woman came to me after a series of single dates, wondering what she was doing to keep men from wanting to spend more time with her. She was not able to self-monitor and was, therefore, unable to self-evaluate. As we walked through her typical first-date behavior, it became apparent that she lacked a sense of the timing and disclosed too much about herself too soon. Nina describes how this happens to her as well:

> I just met this really cute guy, an artist. We met at this open studio situation, and we were having a nice conversation. I looked at him and thought, "Gee, he's awful cute," and when he said, "What brought you here?" I went with this thing about, "Well, you know, I'm a single parent and blah, blah, blah." I told him my life story in 2 seconds! If a friend were to tell me that she told this man all this stuff on her first date, I'd say, "What did you do that for?" But I do it all the time.

In fact, with time, Nina has come to understand that what works in platonic relationships may actually turn romantic partners away. She continues:

> With women you can get away with [divulging too much too soon]. A woman would laugh and say something like, "Oh my God, why is she telling me all this?" I have great women friends. And I have great male friends as long as it's not a sexual thing, but [my tendency to blurt out my whole life story] throws potential partners off.

## ISSUES IN FRIENDSHIPS

One of the primary social concerns faced by adults with LD/ADHD is the issue of disclosure. Whether to divulge the disability to others is a complex decision that must be made with each new acquaintance. One person with LD described the choice as being between "passing," in the hopes that symptoms will not interfere with the budding relationship, or "coming out" and potentially being judged in a negative light. Nina comments that it is not an easy decision to make and that she still fights to quiet the message in her mind that she heard repeatedly from her family over the years, "Oh, stop it. You're making excuses for yourself."

Adults with LD/ADHD face the risk that friends with whom they disclose will accuse them of overreacting to their symptoms. This tends to be particularly true for individuals who function well with their LD and who sometimes find themselves in the awkward position of having to defend their assertion that the diagnostic label indeed fits.

There is often a fear of rejection associated with disclosing, a fear that is especially powerful within dating relationships. When meeting someone new, the risks associated with self-disclosure must be weighed against the advantages associated with honesty. Nonnie describes her decision-making process when she met Mickey, her partner of the past several years:

> I was selective, because I thought, "So, how much can you tell him about yourself? How fast should you tell him?" I didn't want to lose him. I was doing a lot of soul searching, but then he called me. What did I want him to know? Would he leave me because of it? He was a very understanding person, but he'd never heard of the term *learning disability*.

Once the decision is made to disclose, there are still further decisions to be made about how and when to proceed toward this goal. Again, these are not simple decisions to make. Nina discusses this dilemma:

> About new people, I don't know how I would disclose. I almost feel like there's still a little bit of embarrassment about it. I wish I could call that guy [to whom I said way too much about myself too soon] and say, "You know, I didn't really mean to say that stuff, but I have attention deficit disorder, and I don't know how to shut up. My impulse control is bad." But then I would go and do a whole thing about that, and I'd sound just as stupid.

Timing is another element to be considered. The individual needs to decide whether to disclose right away or to wait, allowing the partner a period of time first to get to know who he or she is as a complete person. Nina explains the advantage of waiting a while:

> [Regarding disclosure] with new people, it's the way I felt when I was in fifth grade, when I had pointed glasses and bad teeth and badly permed hair—not a pretty creature. A lot of the girls had shunned me; all the cute girls and all the popular girls ignored me. I remember thinking, "As long as they can find out how smart, how funny, and how talented I am—after they find that out, then I'll worry about whether or not they're my friends. If I could just find a way to let them know this. . . . " So, what I would do was go sing in the next show or do really well in something in school, and they did come to like me. I needed that with new people. It's the same thing with guys now and with jobs. Once they get to know me, they'll date me or hire me or whatever. Once they get to see who I am, I'll be accepted.

Terry once was as wary of disclosure as Nina, but she has relaxed her guard in recent years: "If I have interactions with people and they know me for what my strengths are, I'm now able to sort of unmask what my disabilities or liabilities are—it doesn't feel like it's the sum total of what they think of me."

People vary in how they disclose. There is no single best disclosure approach that is least likely to result in unwanted reactions; however, one woman advocates the use of humor in the hopes of deflecting pity, a reaction she abhors. Many find it helpful to follow up on disclosure with a step-by-step education about LD. Nonnie describes how she took this approach when Mickey first came into her life:

> I gave him one article [that I'd written on LD] a night, because I didn't want to overwhelm him. I recommend that others be honest and open. This business about communicating is delicate because what you're doing is exposing yourself, exposing your inner core, your soul along with your low self-esteem. You have to have the intuition that this is going to work. My intuition was that this man was not going to run, although most people would be afraid

and worry, "What's the burden going to be? What do I have to do? What kind of pressure will there be for me? Do I want it?"

Nonnie's confidence in Mickey's reaction was well founded. She reports how deeply moving it was when he conveyed that he would be more than just a friend by responding, "Don't worry, I'll be your safety net." His reaction was profoundly comforting and foretold the strength of the bond that would develop in their long-term future together.

New partners often feel empowered by knowledge about LD/ADHD. Mickey, for example, felt better prepared to participate in an honest and genuine relationship with Nonnie when he learned about her LD. In particular, as he explains, he grew to understand that he should not take certain behaviors personally:

> I think that [people without the disability] need a depth of education with regard to behavior patterns and thought patterns in order to understand that some things are not personal but impersonal behavior and [in order] not to feel rejected or shut out or imposed upon. Sometimes Nonnie can do certain things, and in a way it seems somewhat personal to me, that she's reacting to me. She really isn't—she's just behaving in the way that she always would behave whether I was there or not. I may not have understood it initially, but once I did understand her thought processes and her behavior patterns, then I could understand and accept that and go along with it and just stand back and watch what was happening and not take any personal affront.

## FILTERING RELATIONSHIPS

Another friendship-related challenge faced by individuals with LD/ADHD is determining who will stand steadfastly behind them, who will fully accept them as friends despite symptoms that clearly affect relationships in a multitude of ways. As Nancie admits, she is not always the most reliable of friends:

> I tend to make friends and think I work at the relationship, but I get sidetracked and realize that I haven't called somebody or talked to somebody for a long time and wonder why they don't call me and don't want to talk to me. Sometimes they express irritation that I haven't phoned.

Adults with LD/ADHD need to identify and filter out those people who cannot be supportive friends. Nina describes how this works in her life:

> People that I know right now pretty much know I'm in treatment, and that's been good. It's been okay for me to say, "You know, when I've hurt your feelings in the past about not calling or not being consistent with you, it's really not about you and me and our relationship or how I feel about you. It's more about me and my stuff." There's almost a filtering in my friendships—a person can be my friend if he or she can deal with the fact that I don't call when I say that I will, that I get overloaded and I don't call. If people could put up with that without making me feel a sense of shame about it. . . . I guess that's where it starts to happen; if somebody says "Well, you never call me," my reaction is almost to get pissed off. It's a weird kind of thing—I don't want to have to go into why. It's hard for me.

Adults with LD/ADHD need to find relationships in which they can be themselves and in which they need not be defensive about the style of friendship they can offer. Nina spoke of how unpleasant and awkward it is when someone fails to take into account that LD/ADHD has a direct impact on her relationships and expects more than she can offer in a friendship. As she noted, "With one woman in particular, I remember I had this intuitive sense that she wouldn't get what [LD] was." Filtering should help Nina and others avoid relationships in which they need to be continually on the defensive.

It is possible to find people who will understand and provide meaningful and positive support. Allyssa appreciates that many good friends in her life have really helped her through a lot of "stuff" and have given her more confidence. This has been Nancie's experience as well. She takes pleasure in finding unconditional acceptance within her friendships:

> I have one friend that I would do anything for, and she would do anything for me. She really understands me. It doesn't matter if I'm in an irritable mood. I can even say to her, "Hi, I'm just in an irritable mood. " She goes, "It's okay. It's fine for you to be that way." So it's really an unconditional friendship, and it really means a lot. I have another friend that I don't see very often. I always feel

really guilty because I should have called her a lot more. When I say that, she says, "Oh, I know, we're all busy, and it doesn't matter because I care about you, no matter what."

Many adults with LD/ADHD find great satisfaction and comfort in meeting and getting to know others who share not only a diagnosis of LD/ADHD but also a deep understanding of its implications on day-to-day life and relationships. Nancie takes particular comfort in the friends she has made in her LD-related travels:

I have this other group of friends that's really special to me and I don't get to see very often, my work-related friends who also have LD. From an LD perspective, they are my closest friends. They understand about being LD and won't minimize it or trivialize it or look at me and laugh. We're all in the same kind of boat. That's a whole other special piece that I didn't have before and that I don't think many people have.

## STRATEGIES TO ENHANCE RELATIONSHIPS

There are several strategies available to adults with LD/ADHD that can improve social relationships.

### BELIEVING IN PERSONAL POTENTIAL

To strengthen friendships and dating relationships, it can be very helpful when individuals with LD believe in their potential to attract friends and partners. A self-defeating attitude serves only to sabotage efforts to meet someone special.

### SETTING SOCIAL GOALS

Setting a goal of initiating social contacts on a regular basis, though difficult, may be helpful. One way to ease this process is to begin initiating social contact with relatively safe people, such as neighbors or others whom they already know. Building upon these first successes, their confidence will be boosted enough for them to consider approaching work colleagues and, later perhaps, to ask out a potential partner. It is a great accomplishment indeed when a person who has suffered significant rejection in the past takes the risk and puts himself or herself on the line to ask for a date. Brown (1979) noted that adults with LD/ADHD who choose to make the first move and ask another individual out display great courage, as doing so often represents a triumph over a history of failure.

Those who actively seek a positive peer group experience may choose to join clubs, participate in church activities, or get involved in the organizations that focus on LD. Allyssa has found a way to relate more successfully by taking a leadership role. She proudly relates:

> I have beautiful relationships with people [now]. I'm a youth leader. People from high schools all over the place call me up and say, "You know what? I'm involved in this crowd and they're doing drugs, and I need help. Help me."

## UNDERSTANDING AND EXPLAINING LD/ADHD

Adults with LD/ADHD must be able to understand their disability and to explain it to others. Raising awareness and understanding of LD/ADHD is critical in new relationships. Pat and her husband are among the many who conclude that early disclosure and early education are desirable. A firm believer of explaining LD in detail to new partners, Pat describes the direct approach she took during her very first evening with Weldon, who was later to become her fourth husband:

> Before we ever went on our first date, we had a cup of coffee, and the cup of coffee lasted 5 hours. During that time I spelled out what I could and couldn't do, and he spelled out what he could or could not do and would not have, so before we got into this relationship, we had an understanding that there were things I could not do.

Weldon adds:

> When I met my wife, I knew absolutely nothing about learning disabilities. But by the time I met her, she knew what the problems were, and she knew how she could deal with them. We had this cup of coffee, and we sat down for 5 hours! There is no one that is married

who, after the first 5 years of their marriage, knows any more about their partner than she and I did after we finished this one cup of coffee. We got into details, specific details. One of the first things that she told me and explained to me about was her learning disability. It was important for her to do that so I would understand. I learned a lot about learning disabilities, and part of what I have learned is that you have to admit that there is a problem, which she did right up front during this conversation. She admitted it, said what it was, made me understand it. That built a foundation for us to work through problems that developed all through the years.

As part of these efforts toward education, it is important that the individual with LD/ADHD teach the new friend or date how to step back and help him or her without fostering learned helplessness. Nonnie describes how one friend learned to handle her:

[My friend] Helene learned that if I lose something, she shouldn't get involved. She should somehow close her eyes and walk away, and somewhere along the line I'll find what I'm looking for. She shouldn't enable me because enabling a person will make them dependent and will make them feel defective. You can show somebody once, you know, but you can't think that you're part of this saving them.

Yet, good friends do provide mutual support; thus, it should be comfortable for the adult with LD/ADHD to seek assistance from friends when it is needed. For example, when Terry was asked by friends to live with them in college, she reports that they responded positively when she replied:

I would like to live with you, but I'd like you to know that I need an editor in my life, so could you do that for me? I need that kind of help, and I am going to be asking for it. Is that something you're comfortable with?

## SELF-MONITORING

Adults with LD/ADHD can enhance their social development by setting a goal of developing the ability to self-monitor. It is particularly important for adults who tend toward impulsivity to learn to monitor their behavior. Those with a tendency to interrupt others may find it helpful to keep a pad of paper handy to jot down ideas so that they feel reassured that they can access the thought again when the other person is finished speaking. Those with a tendency toward angry outbursts may find that it helps to count silently to 10 before responding. In either case, if the individual has been diagnosed with ADHD, medications such as Ritalin may further help with impulse control.

It is also important that individuals with LD/ADHD monitor themselves when they are anxious and find that they are over-reacting to what would normally be minor stress. Many people find it helpful to use positive self-talk. For example, a person who acknowledges that he or she is feeling particularly anxious might save himself or herself from additional stress by thinking, "I'm upset, but I may be overreacting. I can handle this." To self-monitor effectively, adults with LD/ADHD can check others' reactions. Directly asking such questions as, "Have I said this before?" or "Have I been talking too long?" can help keep such behavior in check and can communicate to others that doing so is an important personal goal.

## ASKING FOR HELP

Admitting when symptoms are out of control and asking for help can make the difference between a positive and a negative interaction. Likewise, it is important to tell people when LD/ADHD symptoms are starting to interfere during an interaction. As Nonnie notes:

> A suggestion for the ADHD person whose mind is flying and thinking of 10 things at once—who's not really listening, not receiving what the other person is saying—is to ask the partner, "Could you please repeat that again? It's important to me, but it was too fast." You're not going to hurt the person.

Adults with LD/ADHD should feel comfortable asking for any needed assistance in self-monitoring. Telling someone, "I know I tend to talk too loud, but I'm not always aware when I'm doing it. Would you please let me know if I'm having that problem when we're talking?" or "I sometimes ramble. Please let me know if I go on too long" signals that working on these areas is an important priority.

## OBSERVING OTHERS

There is great advantage in observing the behavior of others. Dale Brown recounted that she was considered weird as a child and went off to college, hoping for acceptance. There she observed people, analyzed their behaviors, and imitated them. She watched others' reactions to her and learned how to time her comments so she would not interrupt. She learned the value of establishing eye contact before starting a conversation and practiced "leader" and "follower" body language: "I made a disciplined effort to make friends. I kept a notebook of people's names, classes, and other information, and I reviewed the lists each night. I learned to tell whether I was speaking loudly or softly by holding a hand to my throat" (1983, p. 21).

## RECOGNIZING TOXIC REACTIONS

Adults with LD/ADHD should learn to recognize and to avoid toxic responses whenever possible. It is important to recognize when people are offering "toxic help," assistance "that is harmful even when given by someone in the process of helping you" (Solden, 1995, p. 255). Adults with LD/ADHD rightfully feel demeaned and misunderstood when family members, paid helpers, or so-called friends make comments such as, "I thought you were on medicines that were helping you with this!" It is helpful either to confront such people or to avoid them rather than to internalize the negative feelings.

## DEVELOPING COPING MECHANISMS

When possible, adults with LD/ADHD should develop coping mechanisms for times when they feel they have deficient knowledge due to LD. Nonnie follows world events by watching 20/20 and other television news programs. She also has an informal understanding with friends who, knowing she does not read, keep her informed about the latest books they have read. Thus, she manages to keep current on a variety of topics.

Many years ago, Terry chose to "fake it" when asked about current issues:

> I remember once my husband, then to-be, and I were traveling in Turkey, and we bumped into some people. They started telling us something that had gone on in the news, and I was talking to them as if I knew what they were talking about. When they walked away, he said, "How could you know about that? We haven't seen a newspaper in 2 weeks?" and I said, "Well, I don't, but I figured maybe I did, so I just sort of played along to find out more information." That's sort of how I would cope with those kinds of interactions my entire life.

More recently, though, Terry has opted to honestly share her difficulties:

> In the past if someone would say, "Have you read this book?" I would think, "Well, gee, I could have. Who knows?" and I used to say something—not a yes or a no—to try and get more information out of the person. But now that I'm more comfortable with my LD, I'd say, "You know, it's so hard for me to remember the names of books that I've read. They just fly out of my head. Tell me about the characters, and I'll remember." So, I feel more honest about that, whereas before I actually got in a lot of situations by really faking my own knowledge because I felt like maybe I did know what they're talking about, but I didn't want to say I wasn't sure.

## Seeking Emotional Support

Betty looks for emotional sustenance where it can be found and feels that her many friendships are the source of a great deal of support and many hugs. She further fills her need for nurturing with a nontraditional partner. She explains:

> I'm Irish Catholic. [As a divorced woman], I'm pretty much committed to a celibate sexual life. I do have a very warm, very supportive relationship with a Jesuit priest who is quite celibate and keeps within himself. I think we're in a safe relationship, frankly, for both of us.

I want to put my energies more into society and changing society than being with another person and dealing with somebody else's needs. In many ways I live almost a nun-type lifestyle. I use that spirituality to give meaning to a lot of these struggles and to have the energy to get out there on a daily basis and fight for the poor. Sometimes after a long day at work, I've come home so thankful at night that I don't have another relationship to deal with, and yet I have my very loving priest friend who's a phone call away.

## SUMMARY

Friendship and dating relationships are often affected by the symptoms of LD/ADHD. Low self-esteem and the various characteristics of LD/ADHD can create barriers to the development of healthy and satisfying relationships. A major social concern of adults with LD/ADHD is the issue of whether to disclose to new friends or partners. Those who do decide to disclose must choose when and how to go about doing so. Many fear being misunderstood, pitied, or rejected.

Adults with LD/ADHD are advised to believe in their potential to attract friends and partners; initiate social contacts; learn how to explain their disability to others; learn social behaviors through observation; monitor their own social behaviors and the reactions of others; ask for help when necessary; and develop coping strategies for socially demanding situations.

# Partnerships

Although adults with LD/ADHD often enjoy long-term relationships that are stable and satisfying, many struggle with challenges that can overpower the romance and lead to separation and divorce. Characteristics of LD/ADHD listed in the previous chapter as significant influences on dating relationships and friendships are certainly very powerful in long-term partnerships as well. Many of the issues present during courtship continue: poor memory still leads to forgotten birthdays; impulsivity still leads to uncensored comments that can be hurtful or rude; and language difficulties still make it very hard for the partner with LD to express his or her most deeply felt emotions.

## RELATIONSHIP DYNAMICS

Several factors contribute to the relationship dynamics between adults with LD/ADHD and their partners.

### JUDGMENT PROBLEMS

Many adults with LD/ADHD have difficulty making decisions and using good judgment. The individual with self-esteem issues is especially susceptible to lapses in judgment when selecting a long-term partner. Self-derision may lead him or her to gravitate toward exactly the wrong kind of person. As Glenn explains:

According to *Driven to Distraction* [Hallowell & Ratey, 1994], if there is one mistake that you see a person with ADHD make over and over again in choosing a spouse, it's that they marry someone who is a caricature of a bad fifth-grade teacher, someone critical, unforgiving, inflexible, taunting, petty, demanding—someone who anticipates the next mistake, not to help or correct it, but to triumphantly point it out and ruthlessly foretell when it will occur again. They marry someone who relentlessly hovers, picking at this and that, finding fault here and there, giving dour predictions of the future and grim assessments of your endless culpability. They marry a specialist in the fine art of killing self-esteem. Why do they do that? Because they need such a person. They think that is what they deserve. They often actually think they are lucky to find such a nitpicker of a mate. They buy into the notion implanted since the fifth grade that they are no good on their own, that they are crippled and need constant supervision and assistance and should be grateful for anyone who has the patience to put up with them.

Panic can wreak havoc with judgment as well. Pat tells how she slipped into a loveless marriage with the first of four husbands out of alarm that she was terminally ill:

Weldon is my fourth husband. Does that tell you something? I had my children by my first husband. My LD is so severe that [in the 1950s, when few professionals understood the nature of this problem] they thought I was brain damaged and predicted I was going to die within a year. I made an LD decision to have a baby. I looked around and married my husband because he was the best thing going—he was smart, musical, and was able to support the kid after I died—but love was not involved.

For some adults with LD/ADHD, judgment is clouded by poor reasoning. Abuse of alcohol or other drugs further limits the ability to reason, making it even more difficult to weigh out the pros and cons of a particular romantic match. Nina laments that alcohol was a significant contributor to bad decision-making in her case:

My [failed] marriage is a case of somebody with attention-deficit disorder who used alcohol as self-medication. Alcohol impairs your judgment, so I had all of these things that fed into making that choice [of a partner].

## COMPATIBILITY ISSUES

A second challenge to relationships for adults with LD is lack of compatibility in the way each partner approaches life. Although this is an issue for adults in general, it becomes especially significant for those with LD/ADHD who have successfully compensated through an inflexible routine or a particularly rigid mind-set. Jule could not accept the incompatibility in style that surfaced in her marriage:

> We got married and went up to Chicago to Northwestern. When he didn't make the grades he wanted and I didn't make the grades I wanted, what I did is I worked harder to get better; he just settled. I would push; he would do things half-assed, and it didn't bother him. But it bothered me. I couldn't let him do his thing. I think there is a personality style that goes along with the ADHD. You don't settle. You don't give up.

## ANGER ISSUES

Difficulties with anger management can be very destructive to a marriage. Poor tolerance for frustration, mood swings, and explosive reactions all significantly interfere with the communication necessary to a healthy relationship. Nancie attributes many of the problems in her first marriage to her uncontrolled anger:

> I really don't think I was a very good wife in my first marriage for a variety of reasons, some related to the LD. Some were related to the anger management issues, to not understanding why and who I was and what was going on and why things were happening.

Andre also considers his argumentative style an important factor in his failed relationship with his first wife:

> I have a very short temper. I did not know how to deal with emotions [in my first marriage]. I didn't have maturity enough to understand her. When we started arguing, I would explode and then leave. I argued so much and wouldn't hear her side of the story.

Anger can become an issue for the partner without LD/ADHD as well, a byproduct of the persistence of symptoms of LD/ADHD, such as poor time management, which results in missed appointments, late arrivals at concerts, burnt dinners, and other disappointments. It can also rise out of the partner's resentment with continually having to rescue the spouse with LD/ADHD. As Terry notes, "The things that I have trouble with don't seem to ever disappear. It's sort of like anything in a marriage—things that are annoying don't actually ever go away. And so it's something that he copes with."

Unfortunately, the anger can become ugly and mean-spirited. Lilia describes a devastating scenario in her marriage:

> The one thing that used to really, really hurt me is that [my husband] knew I couldn't write a note. If the kids were late or something happened with the homework that they couldn't do it, I would go up to him and say, "Could you please write this note to school?" He'd mutter, "You do it," and he knew I couldn't. That hurt. "You do it. You friggin' do it." That hurt, very much so. It can break a marriage. It did mine.

## ISSUES RELATED TO HOUSEHOLD RESPONSIBILITY

The partner without LD/ADHD may become bitter when it is up to him or her to bear the responsibilities of keeping the family together and maintaining order within the home. In Nina's marriage, her husband harbored particular resentment over the issue of disorder:

> There's no way that there could have been a successful marriage there. Other couples that I know who are a mix of clutter people and more organized people—one of them takes over, and if it's the guy, he will usually start doing the cleaning, or they hire somebody to do that stuff. It was very confusing to my husband. One of the things that he always would say to me was, "I can't believe you don't get this—you're so smart!" and I would look at him and I would say, "I have no idea why I can't." He would set up this whole orderly system for us, and I would say, "Oh, it's great." I even had input. I'd say, "Look at how well it works if we just do XYZ," and he'd agree. We'd really set up a wonderful system. I never could follow through, but not for lack of trying.

In Andre's first marriage, tension developed concerning the money management that keeps a household afloat:

Financially, my money was mismanaged, and, of course, it caused severe problems. She [my first wife] had problems too, but I think, had I known what I know now, we'd probably still be married because I would have dealt with some issues more maturely.

Indeed, poor money management skills can plague a relationship. In some cases, the partner without LD/ADHD will gladly take on the necessary budgeting and financial record-keeping; however, in many cases, these spouses feel cornered, believing that they have no choice but to assume what is for them an unwanted responsibility.

### CONTROL ISSUES

Control issues often have a negative effect on committed relationships, particularly among those adults with LD/ADHD for whom being in charge is an overriding concern. Nancie's need for control has been an ongoing issue; she describes how she clearly specified her priorities and asserted control when she remarried:

The second marriage has been interesting. When I married the second time, I told my husband there were some priorities in my life. The most important thing was, and still is, my children. The second was my career and who I wanted to be, and he could be third. If he could agree with that, we could probably get married. Other people might look at that as being selfish. Twenty years ago, I might have thought that was selfish, but I think those were appropriate things to say, and they worked for me.

The extraordinary flexibility of her second husband and his full concession to her authority have been major forces for survival in his marriage to Nancie. Although she recognizes the inappropriateness of this imbalance of control, she has only recently begun to address it:

I would not be married if I didn't have an extremely flexible, bendable husband, plain and simple. We've been married 17 years. He basically does everything and anything I want. He's the one who gets the brunt of all the anger. He gets the tone of voice. The last 4 or 5 years I realized that's not the way life should be, and I've tried to do some changes.

In Jule's marriage as well, control was one of the major destructive issues. She simply could not tolerate deviation from her way of approaching tasks:

> There's a control issue all the way through. In my marriage, when something wasn't done, I would go and do it. When he got out of school 2 weeks early and I was still working and we weren't packed up, I couldn't understand why he hadn't packed up. I would get frustrated and would not just stay to my own business.

## CO-DEPENDENCY

An all-too-common issue in marriages involving a partner with a disability is co-dependency, which often centers around learned helplessness. For much of their lives, individuals with LD/ADHD are told what they cannot do and are discouraged from even making a passing attempt at many tasks. As a result, they soon come to believe that they are helpless in the face of challenge and that they must heavily rely on others, including their spouse, for assistance in nearly all arenas of adult life. This affects the dynamics of a relationship. Feeling self-important and in control, the spouse without LD/ADHD may emotionally benefit from the neediness of his or her partner, who often functions even more poorly when expectations are low. The result is a destructive cycle from which it is hard to disengage.

Nonnie's husband overprotected her for their entire married life, to the extent that when he died at a relatively early age, she found herself unable to handle even the most basic of adult responsibilities, such as banking or navigating the 3-hour drive to their vacation home of many years.

Harry describes how he and his wife slid into an unhealthy co-dependency:

> When we got married, I had a spouse that loved to talk. I didn't like to talk—it was difficult for me to do that. So it was very easy for me to kind of sit back and be the quiet one, be bashful, not have much to say, and let my wife be my spokesman. It ended up

becoming rather dysfunctional because I didn't do the things I needed to do, and I didn't get practice doing the things that would help me with my language. Even within our relationship I didn't do much talking. When things got difficult or if we had an argument, believe me, I was no match. I weighed 100 pounds more than she did, and I stood a foot taller, yet she could lick me any day of the week in an argument. There was no contest. So, we ended up being quite dysfunctional.

## LACK OF UNDERSTANDING

Another destructive factor in long-term partnerships is a lack of understanding. Difficulties arise when the spouse does not understand his or her partner's LD/ADHD, particularly in cases when the diagnosis was made later in life. Nonnie recalls how, unaware for years that her problem had a name and qualified as a true disability, her husband was chronically bewildered by her wide-ranging symptoms. He simply did not know what to do about the symptoms of her LD, including the fact that she was, as she described, emotionally "strung out."

Nancie's husband has also been confused, particularly in the face of the differences in their styles:

> I'm very, very verbal. I don't like to write anything down, don't like to read, don't like to do any of that kind of stuff. [My husband] likes to read a lot. He doesn't communicate as much, and he's not as verbal. I don't remember things in specificity—I'm very global, and he remembers a lot of details. There's a big difference in how we process and how we think about things.

She recognizes that he is baffled at times, not only by her verbal nature, but also by her sudden mood shifts. He cannot understand why she can be furious with him one moment and suddenly shift to being happy and cheerful when a friend unexpectedly comes over. She appreciates that he "rolls with the punches" but wishes he would understand why she so often feels overwhelmed. Although she has given him books to read about LD and ADHD, she feels he has yet to come to a real understanding of her day-to-day challenges.

It is often particularly mystifying to spouses to observe the inconsistencies in the skills of partners who have LD/ADHD. Glenn describes the confused reaction of the woman who was later to become his wife:

> I met the woman of my dreams, and she found it very, very hard to believe that I was as dysfunctional as I was in many areas, especially in reading and writing, because I was articulate, I was capable of doing things I knew, I absorbed so much. But to give anything back in a traditional role was impossible. There was the whole issue that many persons with LD are not necessarily cognitively conscious or tactilely aware of a lot of things like dirt on dishes. It's an important part of transition into marriage—you're being helpful and kind and washing the dishes, and you miss half the dirt on the dishes, and she says, "What the hell is going on here? How come you can't do this? Are you being lazy?" On some levels I was dashing, exciting, and intellectual—if I do say so myself—and attractive with this dynamic force, which is where a lot of the ADHD comes in. Yet, on the just very day-to-day interpersonal things taken for granted, I was very dysfunctional.

Even given some level of understanding by the partner without LD/ADHD, the issues can become destructive. Glenn continues:

> What is valued in a long-term relationship is consistency, reliability, steadfastness, ability to handle crises, being there—and those [qualities] were extremely difficult for me. My partner was working very hard to do all this because she loved me for a lot of other reasons, but the whole inability and discoordination of my life was very problematic. So it became a very unhealthy relationship for a lot of reasons. You compound that by anger management issues and all this other kind of stuff, and it became a very bad relationship.

Lack of understanding often gives rise to frustration. Andre recalls his wife's dismay at his drive to be in continual motion and at the ADHD-related constancy of his physical activity:

> [My wife] didn't know why I would get out there at 4 o'clock in the morning before I would go to work to ride my bike, lift weights—and when I got home, I would start doing other things, and then before

you know it, it was time to go to bed. She says we didn't do anything together. I was so hyper and so active, and she didn't understand. It was very frustrating.

A related source of frustration is the extremes in energy level of the partner with LD/ADHD. Nancie's energy peaks and plummets. She explains, "I'm very, very high energy, but when I'm ready to drop, I drop. It's all or nothing, so that takes away from the intimacy."

Seeking a spouse's understanding is natural in a good relationship. In Lilia's marriage, even after more than a dozen years together, her husband could not have understood her LD, largely because she did not dare to disclose her illiteracy:

I've been married for 15, 16 years and for the longest time, I was so embarrassed that I did not tell my husband. I would just say to him, "Could you please read that for me? I'm busy right now. Could you fill this out, 'cause I'm busy right now?" It's an unbelievable feeling. You feel like a criminal because you feel as though you're the only one in the world that cannot read and can't write. You feel like you've done something wrong. So that takes all your self-esteem.

Sadly, her fear of reprisal was well-founded; when she did finally disclose to him, he refused to understand, and she was subjected to intense verbal abuse that further eroded her self-confidence:

Then when I did tell my husband I was unable to read and write, that's when the abuse comes in—"Well, you're so stupid." And then you start to believe that, *Well, I am dumb. I am stupid because why can't I do this? Why can't I spell? Why can't I read this?* So it does take your self-esteem away. And when you don't have confidence in yourself, there's not much you can do because you're always doubtful.

## SOCIAL SKILLS DEFICITS

Weak interpersonal skills can contribute to tension within a long-erm relationship. The partner without LD/ADHD is often exasperated by such behavior as lack of eye contact. Harry describes how this particular problem served to amplify his difficulties in expressive language:

> On top of my verbal problems, I had a real eye contact problem, and I couldn't look at my wife when I was talking with her, particularly if we got into a conversation that was difficult or something that I had to give thought [to in order] to get the language out. I don't know how many times she yelled at me, "Look at me when you are talking to me!" That extra pressure on top of my struggle with language made the thing even worse. I went from poor to nonexistent sometimes in language.

## INTIMACY ISSUES

When there are significant problems in a marriage, the couple's sexual life is generally negatively affected as well. This, of course, holds true for those with LD/ADHD as well as the general population. Lilia describes how being demeaned by her husband turned her off first to sex and, ultimately, to the relationship itself:

> When you're married to someone you love and you think, in turn, they love you and they call you dumb and they call you stupid, that does affect your sexual life. I mean, you don't feel sexually romantic to[ward] that person because of the names he just called you a couple of hours ago. You forgive, but you can't forget. Five years into the marriage, day after day, "You're dumb, you're stupid, you're dumb, you're dumb." And, you know, it takes a little bit of love, takes a little bit of love, takes a little bit of love—and you end up hating the person because here's the one person that you expect to give some of the support you need, and he's not supporting you in any way. How can you feel? He has taken all your self-esteem away.

There are a variety of intimacy issues that may develop related to an adult's LD/ADHD. Although there are some who judge intimacy as inconsequential in relation to work and the other strains related to their disability, the implications of LD/ADHD on sexuality and intimacy can be quite serious.

## TACTILE SENSITIVITY

Some individuals with tactile sensitivity find that they overreact to touch and experience even a light caress as abhorrent; others disdain the light stroking that most find affectionate and sensual. As Glenn describes:

> Tactile issues play a lot into the levels of sexuality. Many people who are LD have confided in me that their hypertactile nature is such that they can't stand to be hugged. If they get touched, they are very uncomfortable. I tend to be hypotactile in many ways, which means I need much firmer touches. So I can be kind of a rough lover because I am looking for firmness and touch because if I don't, I don't feel it. My partner used to come to me and give light kisses on the cheek as a form of affection, and it would drive me nuts because it was like static electricity. She always thought I was angry at her because I was not accepting her affection. In fact, it had nothing to do with anger—it didn't feel good. So, you either need to find partners who are willing to adjust to you, or you leave a lot of partners out, because how you touch is very important.

There are times when those who have tactile sensitivity cannot bear being touched at all and react to physical contact with a "fight or flight" reaction, a distressing adrenaline rush. This is true for Nancie, who describes how she and her husband have learned to work around her hypersensitivity over the years: "Dick has learned the cues of when it's appropriate to hug and when it's not, and I've learned to say, 'I can't handle a hug right now,' and he's okay with that. It's not a push away."

## DISTRACTIBILITY

Distractibility is another characteristic of LD/ADHD that can have a significant negative effect on intimacy. Nina jokingly conveys the upside of the sexual issues that accompany distractibility and a short attention span by quipping: "Women with ADHD are perfect partners for premature ejaculators because we can't pay attention long enough to figure out if they were great or not."

However, the fact is that for most people distractibility is hardly a laughing matter. Many find that the short attention span that plagues them during daytime activities is no less disruptive during lovemaking. It is difficult to make another person the object of one's most intimate feelings when the individual continually loses focus and becomes distracted. Unfortunately, as Hallowell and Ratey (1994) noted, there are many adults who worry that they are sexually inadequate or bored when they are, most likely, merely distracted. As one woman with ADHD asked, "How could I feel so sexy, look sexy, dress sexy, be married to an incredible man—yet think of tomorrow's shopping list as he's making love to me?" (Hallowell & Ratey, 1994, p. 118)

Some who are distractible find they need total quiet in order to concentrate during sex, that even the ticking of a clock can be disruptive to their concentration. This may be incompatible with the preferences of their partners, who may enjoy music or talking during intimate moments.

## HYPERACTIVITY

Although some may find themselves so distractible as to avoid sexuality altogether, the excess energy that others with LD/ADHD put into their physical relationships can create tension as well. Indeed, some have a hard time simply slowing down to the extent needed to establish an intimate level of communication. Andre, who earlier described his wife's dismay at his constant activity, notes that his hyperactivity clearly affects intimacy within their relationship:

> Attention deficit affects my marriage because I'm very hyper sexually. It can cause a problem, especially with your wife because she can't keep up, and she fears you're going to have affairs and things like that. Once I started educating her, she understood, but at the same time, I'm still dealing with the problem. That's another reason I exercise and read so much. I have to do something else with the energy. Sometimes she just felt like I wasn't there, and it bothered her. [She would ask,] "Who are you thinking about, because you're definitely not paying me any attention?" even though we were making love. Those things were a problem. I have to make sure that she's comfortable, because that's the person that I love.

## LANGUAGE PROBLEMS

An additional complicating factor arises when an individual has either an expressive or receptive language disorder; difficulties with communication lead to misperceptions that further deter intimacy. Janet poignantly describes the loneliness she felt as a result of Harry's expressive language difficulties:

> When you're in a relationship where there is no language and no talk, it is very lonely. He didn't talk, and he didn't feel, and he didn't feel very comfortable with my talking and my feeling, and in my sick way I went along with that. There was no real intimacy. I think communication between two people might be very difficult at best, but where there are language problems in the relationship, it becomes impossible. Also, I never received a letter from my husband—maybe five notes, no more than that. There was just no communication, and there was great loneliness.

## TIME MANAGEMENT PROBLEMS

Difficulty with time management indirectly interferes with intimacy as well. Nancie's poor planning often leads to days that stretch until 2:00 or 3:00 A.M. Thus, with little time to spare, there is not enough opportunity for intimate contact.

It should be noted that for some adults with LD/ADHD, there are symptoms that actually enhance their sexual experiences. For example, those with neurologically based balance problems report a "floaty" or "dizzy" feeling associated with lovemaking; some find this pleasurable, yet others are disconcerted by the alien sensation. There are adults with LD/ADHD who, rather than being distracted and losing focus during intimate moments, are able to hyperfocus and experience intensified reactions. Jule notes, "What I can do is sort of just let it go, say 'Go for it,' in a sense, and have the freedom to just be able to thoroughly and intensely enjoy it."

## STRATEGIES FOR ENHANCING LONG-TERM RELATIONSHIPS

There are a variety of ways for individuals with LD/ADHD and their spouses to strengthen their long-term relationships.

## SEEKING COMPLEMENTARY STYLES

It is important for people with LD/ADHD to look for partners whose strengths and weaknesses complement their own. A couple should try to take advantage of the strengths of each partner. As the pair plans the division of household chores, for example, responsibilities may be allotted according to each individual's strengths and weaknesses. Thus, the partner with weak math skills may avoid being saddled with the responsibility of overseeing the checking account, and the poor speller can relinquish responsibility for most correspondence. The partner with LD/ADHD may choose to assume routine tasks that require attention on a regular basis and can be written in a daily planner or on a household calendar; the partner without LD/ADHD can then take on intermittent tasks that must be attended to on an as-needed basis, such as scheduling house repairs or doctors' appointments.

This division of responsibility works especially well in Harry's relationship with his wife; each takes advantage of the other's strengths. Harry reports:

> It happens that I am real strong in mathematical logical areas. I am also very strong in spatial areas. Now, when it comes to the computer, I have a wonderful time setting computer programs and loading the computer and setting up files, getting everything all ready. However, I cannot write, and my wife will do that part; so, between the two of us, we do quite a job with computers. We are usually quite relaxed when we do that, and it works out very nicely. In other aspects of our life, we do the same thing, and I think we have ended up with a lot more respect for each other, a lot more understanding of each other, and we have put together a real working partnership. I think that we have to not only understand the *disabilities* but we have to understand the *abilities*—I think that's just as important.

Rich appreciates the complementary qualities his wife brings to their partnership and gives her much of the credit for maintaining reason and keeping their marriage on an even keel when difficulties arise:

> My wife has had a huge influence on my life. She's had the tolerance, patience, honesty and all the rest of the characteristics which we

need to stay on track and not be self-abusive or go off on wild tangents.

Terry also appreciates the healthy equilibrium in her marriage:

> In the case of my marriage, it's interesting. Here's a guy who's a National Merit Scholar, the only kid in his high school class to go to Harvard—basically all these awards and super-dooper bright. His achievements are in the places that are just the worst for me, whereas he really lacks in being able to do the stuff which involves [my strengths, such as seeing] the big picture and all the little details. We balance each other in that way.

## UNDERSTANDING LD/ADHD

Both partners in a relationship should work to understand LD/ADHD and its manifestations. Education regarding LD/ADHD is a critical factor in the health of long-term partnerships. When the spouse understands the LD/ADHD, he or she is in a better position to offer crucial support. The husband who understands that his wife is only able to read in silence can avoid making a telephone call or turning on the television set in a room where she is reading the newspaper. The wife who understands that her husband is more likely to have difficulty with symptoms of LD/ADHD when he is tired can plan accordingly when she needs to discuss weighty issues or review important papers with him. All partners can develop the understanding that it is absolutely unproductive to ask their spouse with LD/ADHD to "just try harder." Andre appreciates his wife's support, which has evolved from her growing understanding of his disability:

> My wife is very supportive, though originally she wasn't, because she didn't understand. After I got diagnosed and started to educate myself, I told my wife very carefully about my ADHD. It strengthened me when I told her. She said, "I don't care," and at one point, I felt like I was on top of the world. For the most part, if you're not truthful, you can run but you can't hide all the time. Now she wants to get more involved in what I'm doing.

Many couples experience a sense of relief when they understand that the LD/ADHD has been a contributing factor to their ongoing relationship problems. For example, at one time, Janet was regularly annoyed with Harry because she did not understand that his difficulties with short-term memory were not simply a matter of carelessness. Harry recalls:

> I have short-term memory problems, and I was always getting into trouble with that. For instance, I was supposed to go to the store and pick up a few items. I would come home, and there would be one or two items missing. Before we understood about these short-term memory problems, we didn't know how to deal with them, and my wife would be impatient with me, and I'd feel pretty dumb. Anybody could go to the store and buy a few groceries, but somehow I just couldn't seem to do that.

Fortunately, both learned that the simple strategy of making a written list would resolve this issue. Thus, with knowledge came tolerance of symptoms that had once interfered. Harry explains how this was also true in other aspects of their relationship:

> I think it is probably [the limits of] my verbal expression that [have] had quite a lot of effect on our relationship. I picked a mate that was extremely linguistic—she loves to talk and does a good job at it. She can write and even now, when I have to have written material for the kinds of work I do, we sit and she runs it up on the computer and we edit it and it goes along quite nicely. Long before we understood the issues we were dealing with, we kind of did the same things, but they were usually accompanied with a lot of loud language. We didn't have a good handle on what we were doing, and it was difficult for us to cooperate. As we both grew to understood about the learning disabilities, we were able to function very differently.

Rich agrees:

> I think that as my wife and I work through issues and she has a better understanding of what's up, we do okay with my ADHD. I really didn't talk to her about my attentional issues or dyslexia until after I got this job [running a school for students with LD] because I didn't think it was significant, although to her it was, because all of a sudden things made more sense. She had a label

for it. She started attending some of the LDA conferences with me, talking and meeting with some of the other adults. I think it made more sense to her at that point. She knows [that when I'm impulsive] it's not something which is deliberate. It's easier for her to understand my need to run or to have exercise and to stay busy all the time.

Support from the spouse without LD/ADHD must be available as a matter-of-fact aspect of the partnership and not perceived as a favor because a sense of indebtedness on the part of the partner with LD/ADHD certainly has the potential to compromise the health of the relationship.

### BEING PATIENT

It is important that partners work together to avoid falling into unhealthy, co-dependent, enabling patterns. Sometimes this may entail letting the partner with LD/ADHD approach a task in what seems like a needlessly complicated manner. Mickey describes how frustrating this can be in his relationship with Nonnie:

She can sometimes misplace something. I may know exactly where it is, and she says, "Leave me alone. Let me find it my own way. Don't help me. Don't enable me. Don't tell me where it is. Don't look for it with me." It takes a lot of patience to sit back and see her tearing the house apart when I know exactly where the item is that she's looking for.

### TAKING TIME TO COMMUNICATE

General principles of good relationships certainly work for those with LD/ADHD as well. For example, it is very helpful if a couple can regularly set up a time for talking to each other about how the day has gone or about issues that have come up. Mickey discusses what he has learned from Nonnie:

I learned four things primarily from my association with her, and I think these are the key to our good relationship. I've learned to exercise a lot of patience, honesty, trust and frequent communication. Very early on, we learned that we could confide in each other and discuss anything that came to mind or that affected us without any hesitation. If one of us says something to the other, we just rely on it completely that this will be truthful and straight-forward and there's nothing to fear as far as any consequences are concerned—no game playing, no mind games.

It is important to give partners with language issues time to process what they hear and to make their own points. Mickey describes this challenge in his relationship with Nonnie:

Sometimes she has a way of telling me things in a very circuitous manner. She can wander off, and I'm trying to think what the heck this has to do with what we're discussing, but she eventually does come back to it. I just have to wait until she decides she's ready to make the full circle.

One person with expressive language difficulties explained that he likes to sit at a word processor and write what he is thinking and feeling, particularly at times of emotional turmoil. This helps him sort through his thoughts and feelings and helps him prepare to express them more fluently to others.

Couples should also take time to talk about sexual concerns. Intimacy issues can be minimized if the partners are able to discuss each individual's needs and preferences. Frank talk about such matters as timing of sexual relations, types of touch enjoyed, and preferences regarding atmosphere will help the couple achieve a more satisfactory level of intimacy.

## DEVELOPING STRATEGIES TOGETHER

Couples should work together to develop strategies for dealing with friction. It is very helpful to have a clearly planned strategy for how to cope with antagonism. The partners may choose to develop their own set of rules for conflict resolution. An example is an agreement reported by one woman with LD; her husband may verbally refocus her if she veers off on a tangent during an argument by cueing with a simple, "Let's get back to the issue." This neutral phrase keeps the discussion going without making the woman feel criticized. In a similar vein, Weldon and Pat have instituted their own strategy for moments of conflict, a "time out" until both partners feel that they can productively discuss the issue at hand. This plan has been implemented with considerable success over the years. Pat explains why such an arrangement has been necessary in their marriage:

> Oftentimes, I didn't know when I was angry, or when I got angry, I didn't know why. My pat answer was, "If I knew what had made me angry, I wouldn't be mad." We came up with a solution to that— whenever I was angry I could say, "That's enough," and back out of the situation, and he would leave me alone long enough for me to figure what it was that was wrong. We could come back and talk about it, but we didn't argue about those things when I didn't know what was wrong, and it was okay.

Weldon notes that, as in all relationships, in partnerships involving a spouse with LD/ADHD there is a need for both openness and patience:

> I feel that one of the most important things is that spouses be open to express or talk about any problems that they have. Don't lie. Don't hold back. Be open. Be willing to discuss them. I don't mean argue about them. If my wife and I get to a point that we are not able to communicate, we can say, "That is enough," and it doesn't matter what is happening at that point, whether we're in the middle of a word or a sentence or an idea, it stops right then. No "just one more point," no finishing the sentence, don't even finish the word. Stop until both people can get back to the point where they can communicate and discuss it. This is the thing that has kept our marriage running as smooth as any I have ever seen. We have this openness, and we know when we can talk about things. We know when to stop.

### MAINTAINING A SENSE OF HUMOR

There are many aspects of long-term partnership that are challenging for any couple; however, LD clearly does add an extra wrinkle or two. It is my observation that partners who maintain a sense of humor and can laugh together fare better through the stormy moments in their relationships. Janet and Harry have candidly shared their challenges, yet each has also been able to look at their life together with an eye for the comical. For example, Janet laughed when she told an audience of conference attendees that, although there are clearly difficulties associated with Harry's many challenges, she has recognized a humorous aspect of his LD:

> One thing about being married to my husband—I could feel fairly certain Harry was never going to have an affair and not get caught. He just couldn't handle the logistics of that. I could also be fairly certain I could have five going on at one time, and he wouldn't know it!

## ESTABLISHING A SUPPORT SYSTEM

It helps when partners can make a joint effort to create a healthy mutual support system, working out the degree to which each can meet his or her own needs and what kind of help each expects from the other. One person explained that her husband lightly squeezes her arm to signal when her voice volume is inappropriately loud in public. In Terry's marriage, the support is more technical; she and her husband long ago agreed that he would regularly provide proof-reading services for her written work. Although this responsibility sometimes tries his patience, Terry feels strongly that this arrangement was "part of the deal" when they committed to a long-term future together:

> The things that I have trouble with don't seem to ever go away. And, so, it's something that [my husband] copes with because I have to use him as an editor, a checker, whatever. I'll say to him, "I've got to do these reports, and I'm going to be asking for your help. Which night of this week are you not going to be busy, when you'll be willing to help me?" I think [it] sometimes is a problem— it feels like I expect this from him. I don't think he has a choice. I think it's part of the deal—it was for better or for worse, and this is my worse. Maybe he'd like to just say, "Go ask somebody else," but I don't feel that I'm willing to accept that.

## SEEKING OUTSIDE SUPPORT

Some couples need the help of a third party, through couples therapy, to help unlearn behavior patterns that have been destructive to the relationship and to acquire more productive methods of relating. The spouse may learn how to encourage the partner with LD without nagging; the individual with LD/ADHD may acquire new ways to compensate for the weaknesses that tend to surface and interfere in their relationship.

## SUMMARY

The dynamics of long-term relationships are often affected by LD/ADHD. Poor judgment may lead an individual to select a mate unwisely. Compatibility issues may arise, particularly relating to anger and moodiness. Tensions typically mount over issues of control, management of household responsibilities, and lack of understanding.

Intimacy issues are not uncommon in relationships involving a partner with LD/ADHD. Tactile defensiveness, distractibility, hyperactivity, poor time management, and language deficits are several of the factors that can impede the development of intimacy in long-term partnerships.

In order to maintain a healthy relationship, couples are advised to take advantage of each partner's strengths; work to develop an understanding of LD/ADHD, its manifestations, and its impact on their relationship; develop strategies for dealing with friction; demonstrate patience; commit time for communication; and maintain a sense of humor. In cases where significant issues persist, couples are encouraged to seek outside therapeutic support.

# Parenting

Most adults with children find parenthood to be both highly stressful and deeply rewarding. As might be expected, the demanding roles of motherhood and fatherhood are further complicated by LD/ADHD. Despite additional challenges and stresses, parenting with LD/ADHD can still be profoundly satisfying. This chapter will explore the effects of LD/ADHD on the experience of raising children.

## BENEFITS

Most mothers and fathers with LD/ADHD are very loving and caring and are somehow able to manage the multiple tasks inherent in parenthood. Indeed, the same LD/ADHD characteristics that often cause difficulties may at times present advantages.

### HIGH ENERGY

An extreme need for activity can be an issue for the hyperactive parent if the result is an overinvolvement at work that keeps him or her from home and from interactions with the children; however, it can be a plus when it becomes the force behind high-energy activities with the children. Rich explains this dichotomy in his life:

I think that my LD and ADHD have probably been more difficult for [my kids] because they've had to put up with me and my workaholic nature and always being busy. I'm really kind of a high performer, so I think it's difficult for them to try to measure up to that. From that point of view, I think it's been tough on them. At the same time, when they were younger, I was their coach for softball and soccer. We've done a lot of things together, field trips and camping and canoeing and white-water rafting, that probably came out of my need for a sense of excitement. They've gone along and had a good time. By and large, I have pretty good relationships with the kids.

## CREATIVITY

Many adults with LD/ADHD are notably creative, a characteristic in parenting that can be highly beneficial when channeled to the children's advantage. Glenn remembers with both pleasure and pride one particularly delightful activity:

Often my daughter and I would do amazing things in the areas of creativity and education, with her learning about stuff through tactile means because that is how I do things. So, we would turn the living room into the universe and have all the chairs be planets. There are all kinds of things we would do all the time that were wonderful.

## STRONG MODEL FOR COPING SKILLS

The very act of coping can be a positive in parenting, as the child sees his or her mother or father modeling the process of strategizing, compensating, and tenaciously pursuing goals. Lilia is pleased that her children have been able to observe and to benefit from her steadfast efforts to learn to read:

There's so much more that I can help them with now [that I've gotten help and learned to read]. I could not read my daughter a bedtime story before, so, to me, being able to now is a big accomplishment—a big, big one, because not only have I benefited, but my children have too. I think that my going back to school is an *example of good role modeling, helping my children see, "Look, if Mom can do it, why can't we?"*

## CHALLENGES

How adults with LD/ADHD experience their roles as parents is directly affected by their symptoms.

### LOW SELF-ESTEEM

Those with low self-esteem, for example, may direct negative behavior toward their children as a defense, a means of concealing the difficulties they themselves face on a daily basis. Glenn describes with regret how he approached parenthood in the years before he understood and came to terms with his LD:

> As Hallowell [and Ratey] says in *Driven to Distraction*, people with ADHD often marry a specialist in the fine art of killing self-esteem. The LD person who grows up and becomes a parent often models that behavior as a parent. They become the one who hovers about, nitpicking and attacking the self-esteem of the child, often as a way of masking their own issues. That is what I did a lot.

### EGOCENTRICITY

Parents who are egocentric are often rigid and may have difficulty responding well to the rapid transitions that occur throughout the life of a child. Many are particularly needy and may unconsciously vie with their children for their spouse's attention and affection. Glenn regrets that this was the case in his family. He was unable to offer adequate parental support, in part because of a self-centeredness that made it difficult for him to understand his daughter's perspective:

> Seeing my daughter's viewpoint and understanding it was difficult. [Self-centeredness] also trickled into lack of support for her in educational settings because [dealing with her studies] brought on shame for my failings. A lot of the major problems my daughter

has with me are a direct manifestation of my LD—my inability to support her in certain levels; my inability to be sensitive in certain levels; my inability to control anger and frustration at certain levels; my inability to relate to her on her needs.

## TACTILE DEFENSIVENESS

Tactile defensiveness can lead to difficulties with parental bonding. If the mother is tactilely defensive, she may shy away from touching her children or may recoil from their loving hugs. If she has difficulty modulating the firmness of her grasp, she may inadvertently inflict bruises on her children, ultimately making them fearful of her touch.

## DISTRACTIBILITY

Poor concentration can make it difficult for parents with LD/ADHD to spend extended time doing one activity with their children or to listen attentively to what they are saying. One mother reported with sadness that her son often has to remind her to focus on him when they are talking. Andre expresses regret that his concentration difficulties interfered with his parenting in the years before he started taking Ritalin:

> I think the biggest problem I had previously was when they said, "Daddy read me a book." I could read myself because I was interested in the material, but reading to them, I'd get it over with very quickly. They didn't actually say it out loud, but their look said, "Daddy, you didn't care," because I did not have patience. I wasn't interested in sitting there and reading to them.

## DISORGANIZATION

Disorganization can be the root of significant stress for the parent with LD/ADHD. Women in particular feel handicapped by organizational difficulties, as they experience societal pressure to run a household efficiently and to be the overall general manager of family life. As one woman lamented:

> If I don't plan for the weather, my kids go to school without appropriate clothing. So it's snowing, and they don't have boots

to wear at recess. But I don't have boots on either—I just never manage to listen to the weather report along with the million other things that have to get done every morning.

Some mothers with LD/ADHD feel so overwhelmed by the simple goal of trying to survive that they question whether they can successfully manage to meet the complex requirements of parenting. Nonnie sadly tells the tale of her early days of motherhood:

> I didn't have the faintest idea of what it meant [to be a parent]. The emotional part of having a learning disability that I didn't know about was interfering, and it was too overwhelming to have a child. There were so many things that one had to do. It wasn't an enjoyable experience. Having a learning disability and trying to survive, you almost can't do anything. It's almost like a child having a child.

She found that being so chronically overwhelmed made it hard to bond with her children:

> For me, a person with a learning disability, cooking and diapering and all the things that one had to do was an overload. You try to survive getting up in the morning, getting dressed, finding the things you have to—and then you're married and are supposed to make a meal. I did the things that one has to do as a parent, like feed the person so they don't die, diaper the person. But I couldn't do the touch part. I cut off the feeling because I was so scared . . . I couldn't bond with my children. It's a terrible, terrible sadness that I have, but you can't look backward.

Because many who are now adults did not know that they had LD when they were raising their children, they had no insight into why they were so stressed, so overwhelmed, and so angry. Nancie mourns:

> I wish I had known about my learning disability—I would have been better with my children. Emotionally, I was really strung out. When we had children at home, and [there was also] work and school— I realize that sounds like a fistful to manage anyway—I managed it very poorly. I, basically, just bitched everybody out and said, "I

don't understand why you don't keep the house clean. I don't understand why you don't do this or why you don't do that." Anything that I couldn't control or that I couldn't get done that I saw as my responsibility, I just basically shoved on somebody else. Cooking and getting the kids off to school and managing lunches and getting them to the doctor were all somebody else's responsibility. They either didn't get done or they'd get done after I'd gripe and scream and say, "It's not my responsibility. I can't be responsible to do it all," kind of thing. Even though I could direct in other environments, I would never say, "Okay, let's organize this." It would just be, "Oh, shit, we've got to do all this stuff and I can't do it all."

## LANGUAGE DISORDERS

Expressive language difficulties limit the effectiveness of communication between a parent and child. Harry describes the undiscussed "secret problem" in his family:

I was so ashamed of my language difficulty. I kept that a secret. I didn't talk about it; our family didn't talk about it. "Daddy doesn't read much, but we don't talk about it," that kind of thing. We couldn't solve any of our problems because I couldn't participate in good verbal exchange.

## IMPULSIVITY

Parents who are impulsive may react too quickly in anger, may make hasty decisions regarding child care without due consideration, or may chronically interrupt their sons and daughters. Nina offers an example of how her symptoms can be trying to her son:

The other day a close friend called. I said "Do you want to say hi to [my son] Matt?" They started talking on the phone, and as they're talking, I'm thinking about these things I want to tell my friend. I yell to Matt, "Tell him that blah blah blah. And tell him that blah blah blah," and Matt leaves the room with the cordless. When I got on with my friend again, I said, "Did Matt tell you . . . ?" My friend said, "You've got to let him talk on the phone if you want him to talk on the phone." I said, "All right, all right, but I wanted to tell you all this stuff," and he said, "You were going to have time to tell me all that yourself."

## PERCEPTUAL IMPAIRMENTS

Perceptual impairments can interfere in a variety of ways. Glenn reports that his **difficulty with depth perception** surfaced in even the most basic activities of early parenting. When the baby came along, he had trouble changing the diaper without pricking her skin with the pins. **Visual discrimination difficulties** can make it hard for the parent with LD/ADHD to pick up the many messages children communicate through body language. This impedes their ability to monitor how their children are feeling and, thus, interferes with their ability to offer appropriate support. **Auditory discrimination difficulties** undermine the parent's ability to hear the differences between the kinds of cries of an infant or of a preverbal toddler and make it far more difficult to determine if the child is hungry or angry.

## SKILLS DEFICITS

Skills deficits significantly affect the parenting experience as well. Parents with serious **reading difficulties** are at a distinct disadvantage. They are persistently challenged and frustrated by the expectation that they will be able to read such everyday items as notices from school and medicine labels. Unable to decode and understand the many excellent and widely available reference books and magazines on childrearing, they do not have access to these resources for answers to the many questions faced by all parents as they assume the challenges of raising children.

Many parents find themselves reacting with considerable sadness, embarrassment, or, in some cases, defensiveness when they realize that their reading difficulties reduce not only their own but also their children's access to the written word. Lilia found it excruciating that she was unable to read even a simple bedtime storybook to her little girl. She would make excuses, such as, "Honey, Mommy's too tired," and then would feel humiliated and saddened by her inability to fulfill what she considered to be a basic responsibility of parenthood. Glenn, too, found himself in this position. He describes the dynamics with his wife when it came time for him to read bedtime stories to his young daughter:

> How does the dysfunctional LD parent affect the family dynamics in the house? If they are undiagnosed and have a lot of other issues going on, they will be very defensive around the child's education. Before I was diagnosed, I was extremely defensive about reading to my kid. I couldn't read, but my partner always thought I was just being passive-aggressive by refusing.

**Writing problems** can also present challenges. Terry describes how anxiety-producing it can be for someone with severe spelling difficulties to write off-the-cuff notes to her children's school:

> Writing a note to the teacher if one of my kids is sick feels very stressful, and I feel that I don't have access to my coping mechanism of the spell check or the grammar check or even being able to see it as a whole printed piece. There are very few things that I write that I don't write over again if it's handwritten. I've become too dependent on my computer. Sometimes I have actually gone and written something on the computer and then copied it from the computer printout in my own handwriting.

She continues, describing how dealing with something even as basic as an extracurricular sign-up sheet can be an embarrassing experience:

> I put myself into positions where I feel I've shown myself not to be very smart, and it feels embarrassing to me. An example of that was recently we had to sign up at the Little League to work at the concession stand where you're supposed to write your name, the name of your kid's team and your phone number. I had written down "Red Sox" and I wrote "Red Socks." Later that evening, my husband said to me, "Oh, by the way, 'Red Socks' is S-o-x." I asked, "What did I write?" And he said, "S-o-c-k-s". I said, "And you didn't change it? That sign has been up on that wall all day on Saturday, and everybody else that wrote on it had a chance to see me write 'Red S-o-c-k-s' like that?" That just felt so demoralizing to me. Who

knows—probably nobody even noticed. Even if they did, maybe they didn't care. But those kinds of situations just take me aback.

Terry reports that panic invariably sets in whenever she is asked to fill out forms at the doctor's office. She worries that her misspellings will be so outrageous that the doctor will wonder what is wrong with her and will think she has had no education. Lilia, too, has faced humiliation at the doctor's office. She recalls:

I'm going to tell you one time I'll never forget. Oh my God, I was so embarrassed! I had taken my son to his doctor. He needed to have his throat checked out because he needed his tonsils out. I went up to the receptionist and I said, "We are here." And she said, "Fill this out." I filled it out the best that I could do. I had just started [my literacy classes], and I said, "This is the best that I can do." I didn't want to ask my kids, "Can you help Mommy with this?" I don't know, I just felt embarrassed, even with my children. I went up to the receptionist, and I said to her, "Could you please help me with this? I don't know how to spell it out." There must have been a good four or five people in there, and she looked at me and she said, "You can't fill this out?" Oh, I wanted to die. I just wanted to cry, I felt so embarrassed! It felt demeaning. I just wanted to cry because there are people who understand, and there are people who never had a problem in school, so they don't understand.

**Weak math skills** can have many financial implications for parents with LD/ADHD, but on a day-to-day basis with regard to parenting, difficulties in math primarily surface when they are unable to help their children complete their nightly homework assignments. Lilia, who strongly feels that it is a parent's job to help children with their schoolwork, describes the scene at her house:

I have a 15-year-old and a 12-year-old who both had to stay back because of math and English. It's hard when a child comes home and says, "Mommy, help me do my homework," and you have to say, "Jesus, I don't understand it either." So that child goes in, and the homework is not done, or he got half of them wrong—he's affected by it. I went into the school and I told them, "Please, it's not his fault. I don't have the knowledge to help my son with his homework." The school's response was, "Don't blame yourself." I had to blame myself.

## CHILDREN'S REACTIONS TO A PARENT'S LD/ADHD

Children's reactions to a parent's LD/ADHD vary across age groups. Certainly, those who are very young rarely notice or care about a parent's struggles. However, as they grow older and more aware, children often find it baffling to see a parent's weaknesses when they are conscious of so many of his or her strengths. This is true of Lilia's children, who dismiss her assertion that she has LD: "My kids say, 'Mommy, you don't have a learning disability.' I don't even want to hear that. Maybe [they think that] because they see what I'm capable of, all that I'm doing around the house." Terry describes the similar confusion felt by her elementary and middle school–age sons:

> There are ways that it comes up that are kind of shocking to my kids because I know they see me as an extremely capable person. They see me as the person who was in charge of this, in charge of that, and sort of can get everything to happen. I have a very strong presence in their life as a leader. So it's kind of a funny thing when they see me make what seems like a simple error in spelling or pronunciation.

Indeed, in their confusion, children may mock the parent's symptoms, feeding feelings of shame. Terry sighs and reports that her sons' joking comments have at times been hurtful:

> In recent years, my children have actually made fun of me, and I've talked to them about that, that I don't think it is fair. For instance, my son who's in third grade now has words on his spelling list that he can spell and I can't. He just thinks that's a big hoot that he actually knows something that I don't. I said to him, "You know, I think it's great that you're a good speller, and I'm so happy you're a good speller. This was really hard for me in my life, and it's terrific this is not a problem for you. But you can't make fun of me. That's not fair. That's hurting my feelings." My son was

laughing, but he said, "I know. I'm sorry. I didn't mean to hurt your feelings."

Older children may feel disconcerted by the parent's symptoms, mortified by the fact that their parent with LD/ADHD is a "space cadet" and often forgets to do things like wake them up for school or make their lunches. Nina's son feels this embarrassment and has at times been reluctant to invite friends over for dinner. She explains:

> I saw that my son was embarrassed to have his friends over. If he did, he would shut the door to my office. A lot of [my getting help to be more organized] is because it would be hard when my son would say, "I don't want my friend to stay for dinner because I don't know where we're going to eat." I'd say, "Well, we'll just make a space here on the dining room table," and he'd say, "Mom, you know, most people eat on the dining room table without mounds of papers."

Some children mimic their parent's LD/ADHD symptoms, not because they have a disability themselves but as a result of role modeling. Nina came to realize the full power of her modeling one day when her son was in primary school:

> The biggest parent issue for me is the whole thing about being my son's primary role model. When my son was in second grade, his teacher said, "I want you to look at his desk," and opened it up. I said, "Oh, that's my desk." It hit me that because I'm his only role model, [his father's not much in the picture], he feels disorganized. When he has trouble organizing for a paper or something like that, he'll say, "Do you think I have ADHD?" and I'll say, "No, I just think that you've watched me do these things [and have picked up my disorganized style]." He doesn't have the disorder. My disorganization and anxiety that this is how he sees an adult living her life made me really work on things a lot, much harder than I think I would have had I been alone.

## PARENTING STRATEGIES FOR THE ADULT WITH LD/ADHD

There are several strategies that can help parents with LD/ADHD.

## Learning About LD/ADHD

It can be very helpful for individuals with LD/ADHD to educate themselves about their disabilities. Nonnie did not know anything about LD and was, therefore, at a distinct disadvantage 3 decades ago when she had her children. She describes with regret how she missed the signs of her son's difficulties:

> I believe now that my son has a learning disability, though not like my daughter's. He was bright but hypoactive; he was quiet, withdrawn—those were the symptoms. He stayed in his crib until he was 6. I had no knowledge of developmental steps, of what you were supposed to do, because I didn't know my own developmental steps, even though I was 30.

Her son has had many social difficulties in life, both with peers and on the job:

> Do I think it was my fault? Yes, I think it was my fault on an intellectual level. On an emotional level, I don't—I did the best that I could do at the time because I didn't know about anything. It was like we were two children, one bringing the other up. When my daughter was born, she was hyperactive and never slept. It was a disaster for my son. If I had had one child it would have worked. My daughter made her mother famous because she was the "Ritalin kid." She was the reason I developed programs and taught classes about LD. My son was the forgotten child. He was quiet and withdrawn, and she was hyperactive and all over the place, so the focus was on her when the focus really should have been on him. There was no individual that could say to me, "Don't have a second child." If I could have done it again, although it's hard for me to say, I would have had only one.

Armed with knowledge about LD/ADHD, parents are able to develop an understanding of their own strengths and weaknesses, are in a better position to explain them to their family, and are prepared to watch for telltale signs of the disabilities in their children. Andre suggests to parents with LD/ADHD:

> First of all, get yourself educated and get yourself some help, because if you don't get any help yourself, you can't help anybody

*else. You can't help your kids and you're doing them a great disservice and you're not giving them an even field to play on because they deserve to be armed with as much knowledge and [as many] advantages as anybody else.*

Andre's relatively new self-understanding helps him be a better parent to his children, who have LD and ADHD. They appreciate that he is learning about his disabilities because his new knowledge helps him understand their learning difficulties as well.

Terry feels that her children benefit from the knowledge she has gained, not only about her LD, but also about learning in general:

> I came to understand my learning disability just by finding out more about the whole idea of how people learn and the idea of multiple intelligences. It sort of came home to me. I can say to my son, who was getting annoyed with himself because he has a lot of trouble with how to build three-dimensional houses and how to do crafts or even fine motor kinds of things, "You know, this is how I'm smart. Don't be upset because I thought of the answer, and you didn't. You can do so many other things that I can't. This is how I'm smart, and I now understand that. I don't just see it that I stunk at school, and I like to do this stuff, and that's sort of my hobby. This is how I'm smart." When I say that, I think that's really helped [both my sons and] me in terms of self-esteem because [we all know that] I can "this," I just can't "that."

### Teaching the Children About LD/ADHD

Parents with LD/ADHD can begin early in their efforts to teach their children about the disability. Nina urges parents to disclose and to explain their LD/ADHD as soon as their children are able to understand. Over time, she reports that her son has become more and more able to comprehend her difficulties. Terry agrees. Believing that children value truth and often react with empathy when a problem is presented candidly, she notes, "The important thing is to be honest, because there isn't anybody who doesn't have things that are difficult for them."

Lilia, too, sees advantages to talking with children about LD; however, she waited until she was ready to return to school to tell them about her learning issues, feeling that they would then receive a positive message about empowerment:

I feel comfortable with my children. I talk to them about my LD. The reason that I can actually talk to them about it is because I'm in school [now]. I don't think I could say, "Well, I have a learning disability. That's why I can't learn, so why bother?" My oldest daughter, she gets distracted easily and so does my 8-year-old son, and I'll say, "You know what? Mommy's like that too! I understand. I know what you mean. You need quiet. Let's go in your room. We'll do the homework in there."

## SELF-ADVOCATING

Parents with LD/ADHD should use self-advocacy with service providers such as doctors and teachers; it is legitimate to ask them to speak slowly or to write down key points when they are offering medical or educational information.

## USING MEDICATION

Some parents who have both LD and ADHD may want to consider taking medication to calm some of the symptoms of ADHD. Andre has found that Ritalin noticeably increases his tolerance of the more difficult aspects of childrearing and helps him focus on what is happening with his children: "[Parenting is] 100% different with medication. The medication definitely helps me be more receptive to what's going on with them. Now I can see very clearly what is going on. I can take in a whole lot."

## TAKING ADVANTAGE OF TECHNOLOGY

Many individuals use technology to help them cope with some of the demands of parenthood. Using a computer's spell-check program has been a lifesaver for many adults plagued by weak spelling. Terry depends on her Franklin Spelling Ace for the situations in which she has no time to pre-write notes on her computer and then copy them by hand: "At the doctor's office, I carry a spell-checker, and if the spell-checker is not good enough, I carry a spell-checker with a dictionary, because I don't even know the word that I think is the right word that I need."

An automatic scheduler is a popular and readily available tool for noting important dates, such as birthdays and appointments. Those who tend to forget telephone numbers or reverse the digit sequence and frequently call wrong numbers find it very helpful to use telephones with an automatic dial feature.

## SECURING SUPPORT

Being resourceful will help parents secure support. Parents with LD/ADHD who are worried about their inability to help their children with homework have several options. Rich notes:

> Parents need to trust in their own gut feelings that the kids need to get information or training from somebody else and do their research and find the people they trust out there and let them do it. At a certain age, the parents can't do it all anymore. Don't beat yourself up about that. Get outside resources to do it for you.

Teachers can be asked to provide after-school tutorials. If that support is not available, parents may opt to find a teacher-in-training to help their child wade through daily assignments. It can also be beneficial to set up a cooperative program with other parents, trading child care or other services for academic support from others who are more capable of providing help with school work. In other areas where support is needed, friends and neighbors are often willing to lend a helping hand. Terry reports:

> I call a neighbor if my husband's not there and ask him or her to look at a note to the teacher because I am very immobilized by the thought that somebody's going to look at this and just be so shocked at the level of communication that I have.

## BEING SENSITIVE TO THE CHILDREN'S POTENTIAL LD/ADHD

Because LD can be genetic, parents with LD/ADHD must observe their children closely. They can engage the help of their children's teachers and alert educators to watch for signs of LD and to help their child learn the organizational skills that they may feel unqualified to teach. Nina found teachers open to her request that they observe her son for signs of LD or ADHD:

> If you get married and have kids, knowing you have ADHD or a learning disability, start looking at ways to work on [checking the kids out for the same problems]. Even talking to your children's

teachers [can make a difference]. That was the thing that really helped. Now I [tell my son's] teachers that I have ADHD and I'm dyslexic. When he was in sixth grade, I asked them to keep their eyes open for it—I had not been as aware up to that point that these problems tend to be genetic.

### Seeking Assessment When Needed

It may be necessary for parents with LD/ADHD to push for diagnostic assessment of their children. Lilia found she had to fight for the testing she believed would diagnose LD and ADHD in her children:

> Listen to your child. I mean if you have a learning disability and you see yourself in your child, when your child is saying, "I can't concentrate. This noise is bothering me. I don't understand what this is saying," listen to him. And if you have to, go into the classroom and talk to the teacher. If you have a problem and she says, "Well, he doesn't sit still and he's not paying attention," and you know what your child is like at home, have him tested. Seek help, because, even if your child doesn't have a learning disability, he doesn't have to go through life saying, "I'm stupid. I'm dumb. I don't understand."
>
> With my 8-year-old, I would say, "How was your day?" and he'd say "Mommy, bad. I couldn't concentrate because they were all talking." I went to the school and told them I wanted him tested, and everybody said, "Oh, no, he doesn't have a learning disability; he just doesn't want to pay attention." I saw what my kid was like [at home]. If I had my child in a room where he could do his homework with no TV on and no noise, he was good, but the minute he got in the classroom with 28 children, it was hard for him to concentrate. I had him tested. He has a learning disability.

### Becoming Informed About Services and Treatment

When fully informed, parents are in an optimal position to participate in decision-making about recommended services or medications. Although Andre feels he is adequately informed, he struggles to help his former wife understand the potential benefits of medication for their young son:

> My son just turned 6. He's dyslexic and has ADHD also. I think my ex-wife is still a little bit afraid—maybe she just needs somebody

else to explain the medication to her. She calls me up and says, "He's doing this, he's doing that." I say, "I want you to understand, I'm not making excuses for him, but you're asking him to climb the stairs in a wheelchair, so to speak. That's what you're doing to him. You're crippling him at the same time. You're condemning him. He needs to be on meds."

### Providing Structure

Parents need to provide lots of structure for their children who have been diagnosed with LD/ADHD. Betty advises tightly structuring their days and their nights: "Make sure they get 8 hours of sleep at night. Make sure they get up at the same time, eat meals possibly at the same time. I think that we don't understand how much circadian rhythm affects kids." Children also benefit from structured homework time and a planned approach to performing the regularly occurring tasks in their lives.

### Providing Energy Outlets

One helpful tip is to provide energy outlets for children with LD/ADHD in order to help shape reasonable behavior in public places. Nonnie shares a strategy that helps her hyperactive grand-daughter:

> I don't believe other people should be annoyed by your child. They [go to restaurants] to relax. So, before we sit down to dinner, I let [my LD granddaughter] run in the hall. This is the game, and I get some of her energy out. In the middle of dinner, I say "Okay, we're going back, and we'll play another game and run in the hall again." It's a good idea to order ahead in restaurants, if you can, so there's less sitting-around time. Also, I teach her restaurant manners. If she doesn't listen, I ask the waiter to pack up the food, and we eat it at home. I've done this two, three, or four times. Through the repetition—not of talking [since they tune you out], but of demonstrating the consequences—they eventually get the message. And this happens without saying they're bad, they're wrong. The nonverbal message is what they remember for the next time.

### Being Patient

Children with LD/ADHD may have emotional difficulties at times. Parents should remember to be patient with them. One woman advises, "Parents should realize that their kid is not struggling on purpose—the LD is something that they have no choice about. Patience is critical." Parents must also try to understand the underlying reasons for any anger their children might show. Betty suggests that parents "analyze the child's behavior. If the kid is being oppositional, you need to take a look at how the learning disability affects him or her."

### Reducing Causes of Stress

Another option is to reduce causes of stress in the child's life. Betty explains the rationale: "Try to take the stress off the kids as much as you can. These kids are stressed out when they come home from school. Find positive ways that you could see their heart and their soul."

### Modeling Positive Attitudes and Behaviors

A positive step that parents who have LD/ADHD can take when their children have difficulties similar to their own is modeling ways to compensate. Betty notes the value of role modeling, "I think the critical element for a lot of this stuff is self-knowledge and teaching the kid how to cope with and compensate, saying 'Well, look, Mom can't spell but she's got a spelling machine.' "

Parents with LD/ADHD are also in the unique position of being able to model the necessity of trial and error in learning. Terry explains:

> I think that it's very hard for kids in general to not be able to do things. For instance, the idea of having a model of something and then they try and do it, and it doesn't look good—they want to have it be right. So I think it's important to be able to show how you haven't [always] done it right. It's important for kids, so they understand that it's all about taking risks and trial and error.

Parents can also model feeling okay about their own strengths and weaknesses and the importance of planning how to capitalize on strengths and work around weaknesses. Terry lays out the hard realities of school life versus some of the choices adults can make to avoid regularly confronting their areas of weakness:

> [We need to] say, "This is not easy for me, and I'm trying hard to work on these things, but the truth is that I don't like them, and

if I can avoid them, I will." The problem is that when kids are in school, they can't avoid them. What I tell my kids is, "You have to do this at this point in your life. This is part of what you have to learn. When you get to be older, you get to choose the thing that you love and that you're good at, and you could go with that, and that could be your dedication, your life's work. But right now, you need to try the hardest you can on whatever you're doing."

Parents with LD/ADHD are in a unique position to teach their children to take responsibility and not to use their disability as an excuse. This may involve working with children from their positions of strength. Rich urges parents not to treat their children with LD/ADHD as if they're disabled, but instead to use their strengths as a jumping-off point and offer lots of praise and affirmation. Betty suggests:

Praise the kids to the hilt whenever they do something right. Look at what they can do, not at what they can't do. Find ways of loving them to death. Sometimes these kids are pretty hard to love. Find and talk about the positive aspects with these kids. Affirm them. Find some areas where they can succeed. When I was failing out of high school, I was doing really well in leadership skills in Girl Scouts. I was succeeding at something—so while my self-esteem was being adversely affected by failing, it was also being built up in areas where I could succeed. I give my parents credit because they were always looking for some area that I could excel in.

### Reading to Your Children

A final way to nurture children with LD/ADHD is to read to them throughout their childhood. Although reading aloud is important for all children, those who have LD may need help discovering the wonderful world of books. Parents with LD/ADHD who lack confidence in their ability to read aloud well may take their children to storytimes at their local library or may borrow books on tape to play on tape recorders at home.

### SUMMARY

Although adults with LD/ADHD tend to bring much love, energy, and creativity to parenting, many find they must also contend with a variety of disability-related challenges in the process of child rearing. Defensiveness, rigidity, lack of focus, disorganization, and impulsivity are problems faced by many parents with LD/ADHD. Further issues develop when parents have skills deficits or difficulties with expressive language or perception. Children tend to have mixed reactions to their parents' LD/ADHD. Some take little notice, while others are confused or embarrassed.

It is important that parents with LD/ADHD learn as much as possible about their strengths and weaknesses and explain them to their children. They should watch for signs of the disabilities in their sons and daughters throughout childhood, seeking the assistance of their children's teachers in observing and diagnosing any difficulties that do surface. Parents can help their children who have LD/ADHD by providing structure and energy outlets for them; reducing sources of stress in their lives; teaching them to take responsibility; and being patient, understanding, and affirming.

# Day-to-Day Living

Research tells us that adults with LD tend to live at home longer than their peers (e.g., White, 1992). A contributing factor to this trend is that adults with LD are often unemployed, underemployed, or poorly paid (White, 1992). This was certainly the case for Jo Ann, who reports that she was not ready to step into independence until she was 35, when she decided to apply for subsidized housing:

> When I saw the ad [for apartments] in the paper, it said, "senior/disabled," so I called them up and said, "Do you mean seniors with disabilities, or did you mean two populations?" And then I said, "Well, what do you mean by 'disabilities'? Do you mean people in wheelchairs? Or are you including people who are blind or deaf people that don't need any specifically major modifications in the apartment?" They hadn't really thought much about that, so they said, "Just put your application in." I didn't even bother to say "learning disability" because I figured they might not know what it is. Because of my involvement in the community, many people had known my struggles, including ministers and counselors who were on the board of this project, that there was enough clout for me to get in. That was my first ticket to independence.

In addition to her financial constraints, Jo Ann's chronically low level of self-confidence and her persistent fear of failure slowed her progress toward an independent life. She continues:

There was a lot of scaredness about it, of course. I wasn't gonna be that far away [from] my folks. I always wanted to be independent. I'd always felt I was inadequate, a failure. I kept looking at my peers and thinking, "They're doing this, and I'm not doing it, and I'm still sitting here." I still get that feeling. I mean, here I am, almost 50; I thought by this time I would be making a comfortable salary, not worrying.

Too often, a further obstacle for the young adult with LD/ADHD who feels ready for independent living is parental overprotection. Some parents weigh the disability too heavily and presume that their son or daughter is incapable of taking on even the most basic of adult responsibilities. Those who over-manage their child's life promote the development of a learned helplessness that is far more incapacitating than the disability itself.

Wise parents foster independence from an early age, promoting self-determination and confidence to take risks in learning skills required for adult life. Years ago, I was struck by the disparities in the personal histories of two young women, both 19 years old and recent high school graduates, both scoring similarly within the low–average range on measures of intelligence. One was energetic and outgoing and had led an exciting life during her teen years. She had a driver's license, had held several part-time jobs, and enjoyed spending her salary at the mall, where she often went with her many male and female friends. She did her own laundry, made her own lunches, and occasionally cooked simple suppers for the evenings when she was by herself. Her history stood in stark contrast to that of the second young woman, whose parents admitted to being "a little overprotective." This second woman had never been expected to assume any responsibility for chores at home and had, in fact, never even made herself a sandwich. She had never held a job, had neither a license nor friends. Even on her bicycle, she was always restricted to the block on which the family lived. She had been denied the opportunity to blossom. The striking fact, however, was that as soon as she had the opportunity to learn independent living skills, she grew enormously. Clearly, she had been ready for quite some time to move toward an independent adult life; her major constraint had been not the disability itself but the attitude of parents who had cultivated an unnecessary dependence.

Although she was nearly middle-age when she finally did strike out on her own, Jo Ann believes she benefited from prudent parenting. She expresses gratitude that her mother was wise enough to foster her independence and prepare her not only for the normal responsibilities of adult life, but also for the immense transition she ultimately experienced in her forties, when both parents died:

> One of the things that I thank my parents for is that over the years, my mother [who never had a college degree] did things instinctively that were just smart moves on her part. For example, when I was in my twenties and they would take a vacation and I was working, she would make a list of the bills that had to be paid and checks that I had to write, and she showed me her system. Sometimes I'd go, "Oh, I don't want to do this, I don't want to do this." If you go do something over and over, eventually a little bit more sticks, and it did.
>
> Because of that, when my mother died, I was able to take care of Dad and handle all the affairs and all of the things my mother always did; it was a real challenge managing a checkbook, managing the house, hiring the gardener, and getting the income tax preparations ready to take to the taxpayer, taking care of my dad, and cooking meals, all while I was trying to run Puzzle People [an organization for LD adults]. Also going with my dad when he had to go in for medical purposes, talking to the doctors, and trying to understand what I was supposed to do and being able to say, "I need this in writing because I have learning disabilities, and I really want to make sure everything is done right." It was a real, real challenge. The biggest challenge was in 1995 when I was at the National LDA Conference in Florida with my dad, and he died there. So that was a huge change for me.

Adults with LD/ADHD often feel pressured by the demands of daily life, finding it difficult and frustrating to contend with what many would judge to be the simplest of activities, such as getting dressed or running errands. They struggle in new settings, such as unfamiliar grocery stores, where they cannot locate regularly purchased items. They suffer similarly even in familiar markets when stock has been rearranged. Some cope with the associated stress by becoming more rigid. One woman provided an example of this reaction when she disclosed that she continues to frequent a smaller but familiar grocery market rather than risk becoming overwhelmed by the enormous superstore in town that is known to have lower prices and an impressive range of food and other goods.

Women in particular are vulnerable to stress, because the day-to-day responsibilities related to the classic role of homemaker typically call for a high degree of organization. Those with LD/ADHD who have poor organizational skills are at a great disadvantage when they attempt to meet perceived cultural demands of American womanhood. Linda Weltner (1998), a *Boston Globe* columnist, aptly described the extent of the disorganization that adds great stress to her days:

> Certain habits have me in their grip today as tightly as any falcon ever grasped a rabbit. . . . Some of it is disorganization. I write messages on scraps of paper. I can't seem to put Jack's mail in the same place every day. I always think of one last thing to do before I leave the house. I misplace the portable phone almost every time I use it. I never completely empty my car of junk. (p. F-2)

In addition to the responsibility of coordinating an abundance of unrelated tasks in their own lives, women are generally held accountable for managing family matters. Many feel overwhelmed by the expectation that they will organize their children's lives along with their own (Solden, 1995). As Sari Solden noted, however, this level of demand, though stressful, can actually have positive repercussions as well:

> As a result of their struggles, they often develop a reservoir of strength, perseverance, and determination. The creative problem-solving ability that they have developed as a result of not being able to do things "'the regular way'" can be of help when strategizing about effective solutions to their difficulties. (1995, p. 51)

Indeed, creative problem solving and persistence serve individuals well as they face the challenges of day-to-day life with LD/ADHD. This chapter describes many of those challenges, particularly focusing on self-care, housekeeping, managing money, and getting around. Suggested strategies will be offered in each area.

## SELF-CARE

Looking presentable and maintaining one's health are basic expectations of responsible adulthood. However, LD can sometimes present a barrier to meeting these fundamental goals.

### Hygiene and Grooming

Characteristics of LD/ADHD can interfere with good personal hygiene and grooming in a variety of ways. Perceptual issues, for example, can lead to a generally slovenly appearance. The **visual discrimination problems** of one adult I know make it difficult for him to match his clothes well. **Visual–motor problems** explain why it so often happens that his tie is askew, his hair is messy, and his shirt is untucked. They also make it difficult for him to fold garments, which is why he generally resorts to stuffing his clothing into his bureau drawers. Because he has never mastered ironing, the end result is a rather disheveled effect. Glenn notes that challenges in this area are far from atypical:

> My house is in chaos usually, and my life is in chaos usually, and the way people perceive me from the outside is chaotic. One of the classic signs of young males with LD is blood on the collar because what they do is nick themselves shaving. They do not realize it. They flip their collar up to put the tie on. They get blood on the tie, and then they go off into the world and people are staring at them. You see it all the time, this lack of self-perception. Now that I don't have much hair left, I keep whatever is left cut very short because I almost never have to take care of that kind of stuff. This disheveledness is part of the nature of LD.

**Time issues** may contribute to poor appearance as well, when a man with LD/ADHD rushes to get ready and misses a spot while shaving or a woman brushes her hair too quickly, leaving tangles. One woman told me that she once lost all sense of time when she was giving herself a permanent and left the lotion on too long. The result, she groaned, was hair that turned out "looking like a Brillo pad."

**Tactile defensiveness** may also contribute to issues related to hair care. Nancie explains:

> As a young woman, I went to have my hair done one time and realized that I didn't want anybody to touch my head. Now I've found a woman that I've used for the last 25 years—God forbid she ever dies, because I don't know if I'll ever have my hair done again. I think I probably trust her. She engages you in conversation. It's like all of a sudden it's done and it's over with, and it's okay and it's not like just sitting there.

She cites ADHD-related impatience as the reason for her disdain for dealing with beauticians; they simply require too much time and too much sitting still:

> I think part of it is the ADHD of just sitting there and having your hair done . . .or having anything done for that matter. I don't do my fingernails, I don't do my toenails. I don't do any of that stuff. I can't stand to put my makeup on in the morning.

### Strategies for Effective Hygiene and Grooming

Maintaining hygiene and grooming can become less challenging for individuals with LD/ADHD if they use these helpful strategies.

*Finding a Trusted Hairdresser*    Finding a trusted hairdresser will make going to get a haircut less stressful. Tension can be further reduced by keeping hair in an easily managed style and consistently having cuts by the same good stylist.

*Using an Electric Razor*    Men with fine motor difficulties often find it easier to shave with an electric razor. They should always double check with their fingers to make sure that they have fully shaved the intended area.

*Asking For Help with Makeup*    Women with fine motor difficulties who struggle with the application of lipstick find that it is easier to avoid "mistakes" when they use light lipstick or gloss. Women may also find it helpful to ask a clerk at a department store makeup counter for a lesson on application.

*Asking for Help with Clothing Selection*    Getting dressed can readily be simplified. Many adults with LD/ADHD who have visual discrimination difficulties find it beneficial to establish an arrangement with a trusted friend or relative to advise about clothing matches. Making charts of matching outfits and coding labels of clothes can help a person remember which garments work well together.

*Allowing Sufficient Time*    Adults should allow themselves plenty of time for self-care, so that potential obstacles can be more easily overcome. Many find it helpful to get up early and allot ample time, keeping routines simple.

*Following the Weather*    Finally, one should try to lay out accessories and clothes appropriate to the next day's activities and local forecast of weather conditions.

## HEALTH MAINTENANCE

There are a variety of ways that characteristics of LD can interfere with personal health care. Some adults with LD/ADHD find that **disorganization** creates obstacles to good health maintenance. Failing to follow up on the latest forecast, they cannot organize themselves to plan weather-appropriate attire, and they often find themselves without an umbrella in the rain, without boots when it is snowy, and too bundled up on the early warm days of spring, thus putting themselves at risk of illness.

Many people with LD/ADHD do not reliably schedule appointments for regular medical and dental checkups. Even those who do make the appointments may fail to follow through and attend. This is due to a combination of **disorganization** and **memory problems**, which may also contribute to difficulty keeping track of questions to ask the physician or dentist.

Poor memory interferes with treatment compliance as well. One young woman complained that she felt overwhelmed but too embarrassed to tell her dermatologist that she could not remember oral instructions. She was only able to recall the full prescribed treatment plan when she finally asserted herself and asked him to write down the several steps that he expected her to take to contend with her chronic skin problems.

**Language disorders** can also be an impediment to health care. People who struggle with **expressive language** often have difficulty explaining their symptoms to a doctor or accurately conveying their medical history. Those with **receptive language difficulties** may find it challenging to follow the doctor's discussion of symptoms, the diagnosis, and course of treatment. I once accompanied a young man with LD who was in severe abdominal pain on a visit to an emergency room. He was awash in both physical agony and acute embarrassment as the doctor asked him rapid-fire questions that he had no time to process, to which he had few useful replies. As his advocate, I asked the doctor to slow down and simplify the inquiries; once this request was honored, doctor and patient were able to move efficiently toward a diagnosis of kidney stones and on to treatment.

**Skills deficits** can produce a variety of obstacles when it comes to health care. Limited ability to read makes it difficult to follow directions on medications and challenging to read nutritional labels. Limited ability to write makes filling out medical forms a very stressful task. Difficulty doing math leads some to calculate dosages of medications inaccurately or to take the medicine at incorrect intervals.

**Perceptual impairment** has implications for health care as well. People with poor visual discrimination are at risk of mistakenly taking look-alike pills, again with serious health implications. Visual–motor difficulties can keep patients with LD/ADHD from properly using special medical equipment. One example is the difficulty one woman reported when she had to learn to effectively use a humidifier prescribed to help control persistent respiratory infections. It was a struggle for her to learn how to manipulate the knobs to turn the machine on and to adjust its vapor discharge.

### Strategies for Effective Health Care

Several health care strategies have been proven successful for individuals with LD/ADHD.

*Keeping a Calendar*    Adults with LD/ADHD often find it helpful to maintain a calendar and mark when they are due for checkups. They sometimes find it easier to remember annual checkups when they are regularly scheduled around their birthdays; likewise, twice-yearly dentist appointments may be remembered if they are tied to the beginning and end of daylight savings.

*Making Notes*    People with LD/ADHD often find it helpful to prepare written or tape-recorded notes of symptoms and questions to ask the physician during their appointments. They may find it useful to maintain a written medical history that can be updated as needed and brought to new doctors. They may also benefit from bringing a tape recorder to each doctor's appointment to record and later review any discussion of symptoms, diagnoses, or treatments. Those who choose to disclose their LD/ADHD to their medical doctors tend to be more willing to ask that their diagnosis and treatment plans be simply stated and written down. Many find it useful to repeat the treatment plan back to the doctor in order to ensure that all directions have been fully understood.

*Asking for Advice*    At the drug store, pharmacists are available to advise people about correct dosages of new medications and to help plan exact times when pills should be taken.

*Marking Medicine Bottles*    Individuals with LD/ADHD who have poor visual–discrimination should take special care to mark similar looking bottles clearly so they can be readily differentiated.

## HOUSEKEEPING

Many adults with LD/ADHD are daunted by the challenges of maintaining a household, a set of complex tasks that entails a great deal of decision-making, problem-solving, initiative, judgment, and organization. They struggle with each aspect of keeping house, having difficulties in areas ranging from shopping to food preparation to cleaning. Nina reports that her daily challenges in this area corroborate that LD is more than an academic matter: "The household stuff has really made me see that this wasn't just about work or learning or my academic success or lack of it. My whole life has been affected."

### SHOPPING

Shopping presents its own set of issues. For example, the grocery store, with its large array of choices, is overwhelming for many adults with LD/ADHD. Even the process of getting to the store can be a major challenge, involving getting dressed, finding the house and car keys, putting together a list of needed items, and finding cash or the checkbook. Upon successful arrival, the shopper must contend with the chaotic environment of the market, cope with the checkout line, and, ultimately, organize purchased items in the kitchen cabinets at home (Solden, 1995).

There are a variety of ways that characteristics of LD/ADHD can interfere with shopping for food and other items. **Skill deficits** complicate the process. Reading labels is a challenge, as is the process of writing up lists. Of her visits to the market, Lilia sighs:

> Shopping list? I do not write out a shopping list. I wish I could, but I can't, so I have to memorize—"Okay, I need this, I need this, I need this." Then I get home and I say, "Oh, I forgot this and I forgot this and I forgot this."

Math difficulties make it challenging for people to calculate the price when an item is marked "25% off" to estimate how much they are spending and, thus, to maintain a food budget.

When they arrive at a store, individuals with **poor memory** often have trouble recalling which items they had intended to buy. Some who do make a list are hard-pressed later to remember where they put it. **Visual memory problems** may also make it difficult for them to remember the layout of shops and where frequently sought items are shelved; thus, they require extra shopping time for repeatedly checking the map of the mall or individual store directories.

People with **visual discrimination difficulties** find it a challenge to distinguish between ripe and overripe bananas, between a nectarine and a peach, or between other foods that are similar in appearance. **Visual figure–ground issues** can further complicate shopping tasks; for example, a cookie aisle with hundreds of varieties can overwhelm the shopper seeking one specific kind of animal cracker. Nancie equates this phenomenon in the grocery store with the challenge of renting a video:

> I can't go to a video store to pick out a video. One of the kids will say, "Mom, we need to watch X movie," and I'll go in and ask for it by name, or I'll have my husband get it. Same thing happens in the grocery store. I can grocery shop, but can't buy the soup if I don't know exactly where it is. I'll come home and say, "I didn't get the soup. You have to get the soup when you're out." Anything that looks the same is totally overwhelming.

In fact, Nancie feels so overwhelmed by shopping that the crowds and the multitude of choices tend to make her snap:

> I've always had anger management issues—can't handle crowds, noise, can't go shopping in the malls during the peak seasons. I'm

the one who will look at the sales clerk and ream her out because of something that wasn't her problem at all. It's not what I want to do, but it comes out. It's just totally overwhelming. I don't do well in the grocery store if it's crowded. I'm better off just to stay in my car and go home.

**Distractibility** presents major challenges to the shopper with LD/ADHD. *Boston Globe* columnist Linda Weltner describes an incident that occurred one day when she was out buying food. She was in line at her neighborhood market, waiting to be checked out, when a woman behind her commented that she was 12 items over the 8-item express line limit. Weltner apologized and explained with embarrassment that she had never made this mistake before, whereupon the woman complained that, in fact, she had observed Weltner doing so on a regular basis. Weltner was stunned. In reflection, she faulted her ADHD, realizing that, because she is so vulnerable to distraction, she forces herself to hyperfocus as a compensatory strategy when she shops. Thus, she actively avoids reading magazine covers or tabloid headlines or any signs that could distract. Unfortunately, this clearly includes the express lane sign. She wrote, "If I don't screen out everything extraneous, it can take me hours to buy a can of soup" (1998, p. F-2).

### Strategies for Shopping

There are several ways to make shopping less of a challenge.

*Frequenting the Same Stores*    Going to the same store regularly helps shoppers become familiar with the layout and eases stress associated with the process of finding desired items.

*Using Lists*    While at the store, lists can guide shopping excursions. Harry finds that, beyond ensuring that he will bring home needed items, a grocery list has the added benefit of helping him avoid conflict with his wife:

If I go to the grocery store now to pick up a few items, if there are three or more to get, I go with a little list and I come home successful, and my wife doesn't get impatient, and it works very well.

*Avoiding Crowds*    For many people with LD/ADHD, anxiety levels tend to rise in chaotic environments, so it is wise to plan shopping excursions during off-peak hours. Nancie describes further shopping strategies:

> When I shop, I start in one spot and go up and down all the rows. I don't take a shopping list or anything. I shop by orientation to the picture on the shelf reminding me or the item on the shelf reminding me. I don't do well in the grocery store if it's crowded. I don't do well at all, so I avoid that.

*Using a Calculator*   A calculator helps shoppers who have difficulty with math to figure the price of sale items and to develop a sense of how much they are spending.

*Asking for Help*   People who have LD/ADHD should not be afraid to ask for help from salespeople. Those who struggle with the confusing space of big stores benefit from asserting themselves by asking for help to find the items on their list. Andre benefits from this tactic:

> Usually I have a list of what I need before I get there. If it's too time consuming, I won't hesitate to call some salesperson and say, "Do you have any of these items on this list here?" and then cut down the time greatly.

Jule, too, feels free to call upon the help of store personnel:

> I like to go to the same grocery store regularly, because when it's a new store, I don't know where things are. Or when they revamp the grocery store, I then will go up to the counter, and I will say that I need someone to show me where these things are.

*Keeping Back-Up Supplies*   As "insurance," it is a good plan to have back-up supplies on hand at home. Jule uses this strategy to help control tension and to avoid a crisis if an item is forgotten on her regular trips to the grocery store:

> I usually will write down a couple of things, essentials like milk, but I always go up and down every row to see if something is a trigger, if I see something of interest. If I [forget] something, then I usually have a back-up. Like if I forget the milk, I have the Cremora. If I'm out

of the Cremora, then I usually have a can of that evaporated milk that you can store.

## COOKING

Cooking presents a number of additional challenges to people with LD/ADHD. Again, a lack of basic skills can get in the way. Those with **reading disorders** have difficulty decoding recipes and the ingredients they call for. Those with **math difficulties** have trouble measuring. **Visual discrimination difficulties** translate into difficulties discriminating between look-alike items, such as a teaspoon and a tablespoon, or look-alike foods, such as zucchini and cucumber. Individuals who struggle with this may cut too short a piece of aluminum foil to wrap the chicken sufficiently or may have difficulty choosing a food storage container that is the right size for the dinner's leftovers.

Those who, like Glenn, have a **poor sense of space and time** tend to misplace ingredients and needed utensils. More often than not, they burn the food and have great difficulty coordinating preparation so that all parts of the meal are ready to be served together.

### Strategies for Cooking

A number of easy cooking strategies are available for individuals with LD/ADHD.

*Using Picture Recipe Books*    Many people with LD/ADHD find it helpful to use one of the several cookbooks on the market that incorporate pictures in the recipes. The photos help them by showing what is expected.

*Color Coding Measuring Spoons and Cups*    It can be a fun and useful project to color code measuring spoons and cups. Some people find it helpful to use permanent markers to mark the $1/4$ teaspoon and $1/4$ cup with red and the $1/2$ teaspoon and $1/2$ cup with blue, and so on. This provides an additional visual clue to help them differentiate while cooking.

*Creating a Schedule*    Finally, some people find it helpful to plan ahead and create a schedule of exactly when each part of the meal should be prepared and cooked. This eliminates the need for on-the-spot decision making.

## CLEANING

Because LD/ADHD affects individuals in all areas of their lives, equal opportunities for untidiness develop in the home, in the office, or in the automobile. One man reports difficulty with maintaining order in his car:

> I just throw cans and wrappers on the car floor when I snack while I drive. It's embarrassing when people ask for a lift and I have to clear the debris for them to have room to sit, but I do it anyway.

He also feels tense when he is invited to stay as someone's house guest, fearing his sloppiness will surely be exposed. Indeed, many adults with LD/ADHD share his struggles with the process of cleaning. Nina describes her challenges in this area:

> My house has always been a mess—and I mean a mess! My house-keeping was a big sore spot in my marriage. The way that my house looks has affected my relationships because people have a hard time living in chaos. It's a very natural state for me. If I can get to the point where I can clean something up, I make it so much better because I do think very creatively and think about how things could be arranged or should be arranged to make much more sense. But maintaining them that way has been an issue.

A variety of factors contribute to the difficulties people with LD/ADHD may have in cleaning. Those who are **disorganized,** for example, find it difficult to formulate an effective plan of attack to clean the house, the office, or the car. When confronted with a significant cleaning task, they cannot prioritize what to do first. Nina struggles to control clutter:

> I have this long, wonderful counter space. It's kind of 1950s Formica pink, and I love it—it's a little kitsch. But for the first 2 years I lived at my house, there was a mound of paper so big on the counter that you didn't even know the counter was there. I moved into this house because it had an incredible amount of counter space, cabinets and drawers. I wanted a bill drawer. I wanted a junk drawer that could truly be a junk drawer and not every drawer being a junk

drawer. But it's taken me 2 years to figure out a system. There's a pile still on the counter, but it's smaller now. It's funny, when I go through this stuff, I don't even know what half of it is. I really don't. Now I don't care as much about the paper that I'm throwing out, whereas 10 years ago I still would have kept everything because I would have thought for some reason it was important. But I can't remember why it was important now, so I can throw it out.

Organizational issues contribute to losing things as well. Nina describes how her difficulty in this area exasperated her husband and led to real tension in their relationship:

The kind of paradoxical thing is that I have a very good memory for things that have happened, but the day-to-day functional stuff I've always had difficulty with, like losing my keys. My ex-husband and I argued about that issue so much that before we would leave places, I'd be in tears. He'd say, "How could you do this? This happens all the time. What's wrong with you?" That's very much my family pattern, too. "I can't believe you lose things like this." Then when I would find them, I'd have this sense of relief but also shame—how stupid!

Although Nina did develop a system of sorts, she recognized that it failed to meet social standards, and she often felt embarrassed when it was subjected to the scrutiny of others:

When I would have people come over to work with me, I had this sense of them looking around, and you could see it on their face that they were thinking, "How could she work like this"? And I don't *know* how I could work in those conditions.

Others, like Nancie, develop systems but recognize with disappointment that they fall short of meeting even their own standards for household order:

I'm a pile person. I make piles for a long time, and when the piles get too big, I go clean them up. I'm not a messy person, but I never kept my room clean at all. I'd shove everything under the bed because I was supposed to have a clean room. I used to be really stressed out about it—I'm a wife and a mother; I'm supposed to have a clean house.

Some individuals attribute the lack of order in their lives to their **time management issues**. Allyssa explains:

Cleaning? Organizing? I'm a mess. My room—if you saw it, it's perfectly neat and there's no dirt or anything like that, but open the drawers, and they're a mess. I don't know if this is rationalization or whatever, I just don't have time to straighten up my drawers. I'm too busy living, so I just throw things in my drawer and that's just the way it is. It doesn't bother me. I just got a bill in the mail for my beeper. I'll look for the checkbook for hours and realize that I left it on my bed. So, it's like under the sheets, and I made the bed, and it's been there for weeks. That's how I am. But I do find the checkbook.

Individuals who are **impulsive** tend to leave their belongings here and there, which inevitably results in a cluttered environment. Rich comments, "Organizationally, I can impact the house because I just come in and drop stuff." Impulsivity may lead to laundry fiascoes as well, when people who are impatient throw light garments in the washer with dark items, resulting in clothes ruined through color bleeds.

**Distractibility** is a further factor that can interfere with an individual's ability to clean. The man who starts to tidy his living room but gets distracted by the magazine that he finds on the floor and begins to read may never finish the job. Nor may the woman whose vacuuming is interrupted by a telephone call. Even when they do manage to stay on task, adults with LD/ADHD may take an inordinate amount of time completing their chores simply because of the extra time that has to be factored in to contend with the many distractions that surface during any one cleaning task.

**Perceptual impairments** interfere with cleaning as well. Perceptual–motor problems make it difficult for some adults to use tools to make minor household repairs or to be thorough in washing dishes. Spatial issues add to the challenge of not only dishwashing, but also sweeping, vacuuming, dusting, or raking leaves; inevitably, spots are missed. People with these problems most likely also have trouble organizing their drawers and cabinets because they fail to stack dishes according to type and size or to group foods by category. Those who have visual memory problems tend to lose things on a regular basis, even within their own living space. Glenn describes this phenomenon in his own life:

> If something goes away into a drawer, I don't remember. In order for me to recall it, it has to be right in front of me. I have to touch it, feel it, multiple times. I have to keep it in front of me because if I don't, it's gone. In a household, you get all this stuff all over the place all the time, because once out of sight, out of mind. To some people it is chaos, but to people with LD it is order. Other people with LD come over and say, "My, how this looks like my house or my desk or my car," but it is not socially accepted.

### Strategies for Cleaning and Other Housekeeping

There are a number of tips that help adults with LD/ADHD manage their housekeeping responsibilities.

*Establishing a Master Calendar*    Using a monthly calendar to clearly schedule routine tasks, such as setting out the garbage, laundering clothes, and paying bills, provides needed structure and gives the adult a visual sense of any free time that will be available throughout the month.

*Using Lists*    Many benefit from planning and posting a list of daily tasks and find it very satisfying to physically cross off items as they are completed. The key is to focus on only one listed item at a time. Further, complex housekeeping tasks are to be tackled in this same step-by-step fashion.

*Establishing Specific Spaces for Items*    Many people strategize about consistent places to keep belongings. They benefit from establishing specific spaces for specific items, even specific places for clutter. One woman has designated a chair in her room on which she feels free to throw her clothes. Each Saturday morning she tackles the pile, hanging and sorting the garments. This tactic has reduced the tension that formerly existed between her and her husband about clutter in their bedroom.

Some adults with LD/ADHD find it helpful to actually label drawers and cupboard shelves and draw up a master plan of where items should go in each. Because for many people with LD/ADHD, "out-of-sight" means "out-of-mind," it can be very helpful to use open shelving both at home and at work. When everything is where it can be seen, it is more accessible to the individual's memory and, thus, more available for use when needed. Jule explains:

> If it's not in front of me, I don't see it. I have nothing in the drawers in my office. Everything is on the surface, because once it's there in my drawers, then it's gone. I have to be so incredibly well organized that it's almost boring.

Nonnie finds that open crates serve the same purpose as open shelving and, further, make an excellent portable filing cabinet:

> I can't put things in a file cabinet. I have to lay it all out on one table and as long as I see it on top, I'm fine. I'm better now because my clients (I guess my clients love me) bought little crates, a filing cabinet that you can carry.

It is also very beneficial to establish specific places where often-needed items, such as keys or glasses, are to be kept—whether it be a hook on the wall at home, a corner of a desk at work, or a particular pocket in a purse or backpack. Nina reports how she became accustomed to using consistent "parking spots" for her keys:

> I have a hook on the inside of my front door, but I decided there's a small window ledge as I walk up the stairs, and it's better if I just put the keys there. I actually had to train myself. I put a sign on the door for awhile that said, "keys on the sill." Then I got nervous that burglars would see it and come in, but for the first week or so, I had a Post-it right on the steps, "keys on the sill." So it was a training thing. I lose them less now.

Many people who just cannot seem to hold on to their keys find it helpful to carry extras. Jule chuckles as she explains that one extra set of keys may not always be adequate:

> I carry four different sets of keys, because one time I was traveling, and I locked my keys in the car with my purse, which had my extra second set of keys. I also carry an extra set in my briefcase, which was in my car. So the next time I went to buy a car, my mother was with me and advised me to get a car

that can only lock from the outside. You have to build in safety nets.

*Over-Organizing*    Many feel comforted and in control when they are very tightly organized. Jule counts herself among those ranks. She reports that she over-organizes, double checks everything, and is always figuring out the most efficient way to accomplish a task. At times Nancie has also used this type of hypercontrol as a means of coping:

> I used to be this fastidious housekeeper when the kids were young. Everything had to have its place, and I knew how to clean everything. Organization—if anybody came in, and something got out of order, I was cleaning it up almost to the obsessive point.

*Imposing a Tight Structure*    Structure often serves to relieve tension. For example, when Jule closely structures her day, she feels an added sense of control:

> You have to impose an incredibly tight structure. There is no question about it. If you have something to do, you have to write it down, and then you have to check it off, and you have to follow it through and make sure it's completed then and there. You don't delay. It's like with my briefcase—when I finish preparing a case, I immediately put it back in my briefcase. When something is completed, it is completed and then put where it's supposed to be. It's not a matter of being able to say, "Well, I'll put this up in the morning." If I don't do it right away, it's forgotten.

She also finds that laying out clothes and needed items nightly for the next day can be very helpful. Indeed, she has routines for many aspects of her life:

> You have to set it up where you're efficient. Saturday mornings are when I clean the house, and if I'm not too tired, Friday night is when I do the laundry and change the linens. Actually, I find it relaxing. But if I'm too tired, then I do that on Saturday mornings.

Readying herself for a work day involves a tight routine, which she clearly has down to a science:

When I get up in the morning, I set my clock in my bedroom 30 minutes early because then I let the alarm go off and I hit the set button so that I can sleep 10 extra minutes. And then I say to myself, "Now it's 6:30," but really, it's only 6:00 and I've gotten that extra 10 minutes. Then I go in, and I immediately make the coffee. I brush my teeth, and by the time I've done that, the coffee's ready. After I make the coffee, I take out the pancakes, so they're thawed by the time I finish putting on my makeup. It's a very efficient routine. It's not like I go in and brush my teeth and then make my coffee, and then after I finish doing that, then I go defrost pancakes. I do it so, within a certain amount of time, I go in and I accomplish four or five different things.

*Using Cues*   There are a variety of ways to create reminders of tasks that need to be tackled. Jule reports that she uses objects as cues. When she knows that the next day is trash day, she pulls the garbage can out from where it is kept as a cue, so that "the only way I can get into the kitchen to make the coffee is to run into the trash can." She also writes herself notes:

Then if there's something that I really must not forget, I take [the note] and I put it right over the dial part of the phone, so the only way I can get to the phone is by seeing it. If you don't do that, you're still going to screw up. I put the laundry in front of my door and still end up walking over it.

Nina, too, finds notes to be helpful as cues:

Some of [becoming organized] is just things like putting a Post-it up saying, "When you walk in the door, put the bills in the bill drawer, put the junk mail in the trash"—having notes everywhere. I still have the notes up because I'm still doing that quite a bit.

*Securing Support*   Support for management of day-to-day responsibilities is available through a coach or a professional organizer who can specify where books, socks, light bulbs, and other household objects should go. It is also important to have help maintaining established organizational systems. Nina receives this support from her therapist/coach:

I guess the main strategy for me is having a therapist who I'm very comfortable with as a coach, too, who stays with me so that I can work out the kinks of this thing. That's the biggest strategy, getting the support.

*Jotting Notes*  An excellent tip for people with weak memory or distractibility is to always have paper available for random important thoughts. Jule finds notepads invaluable: "I keep a little notepad next to my bed because I'm always thinking. As I think of things that I need to do, I jot them down."

*Dividing Responsibilities*  People with LD/ADHD need not feel as though they must do it all alone. They can benefit from coordinating with others in the household to divide responsibilities according to abilities. One set of roommates I know cooperatively divides household responsibilities in a manner that minimizes the potential for trouble; the individual with LD/ADHD does routine tasks, which he is more likely to remember, and his roommate handles those that need doing on an as-needed basis, such as starting and stopping newspaper deliveries.

*Keeping Self-Attuned*  Finally, it is important to keep self-attuned. By tuning in to their own thoughts and feelings, adults with LD/ADHD can learn to recognize when they are beginning to feel overwhelmed and to use a range of strategies to regain control. Betty notes how she copes when panic sets in:

I know when the symptoms are getting rough. I know when to get some extra sleep and think, "Okay, I'm cutting it too short." I know when I come into my apartment and it's a disaster area, I think, "Okay, it looks like an ADHD apartment. Well, let's do this one thing at a time tonight. What small thing can be done [first]?"

## MONEY MANAGEMENT

Adults with LD rank handling money and banking the most difficult among the problems most often encountered in daily living (Hoffman et al., 1987). This seems to be the case regardless of intelligence; despite her master's degree, Nonnie struggles to integrate the many steps of bill paying and banking:

I have a hard time understanding what a bill says, so I have to read it out loud. That takes energy, and then I have to figure out the check, and then I have to go to the bank and put the money in, and then I have to put the check with the bill in the envelope, and then I have to usually go to the post office to buy the one stamp. Some days, that's all I can do. There are some days that I feel exhausted from having a learning disability.

Many adults with LD/ADHD struggle with poor money management skills even when they conceptually understand financial matters. Some, like Glenn, cope through avoidance: "For years I never had a checking account. I couldn't handle the checking. I did everything in cash because I didn't know how to keep the account. I didn't want to."

Nina, too, at one time coped through avoidance. Despite an expensive history of regularly bouncing checks, she was reluctant to ask for help:

One year I must have spent a couple of thousand dollars in bounced check fees, and I don't make that much money! I got into a real hole because of that, and I was too embarrassed to say to them, "You know, I'm really in trouble here." I actually am going to leave the bank that I'm at now because they said they no longer will provide me special accommodations.

When she finally did reach out, she was appalled at the lack of understanding of bank personnel:

The first time I went to the bank, I cried. There was a woman that kind of struck me because she's not anybody who's had training or even exposure to LD. She said, "Well, what do you mean you can't add?" It was painful to have to go through it—"You know, when I see a 7, it looks like an L to me, and when I see this, it looks like that." And then she responded, "Oh, really!" There should be some kind of information that goes out to institutions through the ADA [Americans with Disabilities Act] about learning disabilities.

Some adults with LD/ADHD find themselves being "protected" by well-meaning folks, sheltered from having to master important money-related skills. Allyssa describes how this happened in her family:

> A lot of people tried to enable me in my life. There were people that had good intentions to help me but really held me back from growing by doing things for me. For example, I have a checking account now and my mother really wants to help me. She felt bad for me, so she put money in the checking account 'cause she knew it was empty, and I'd written out a check. I love my mother with all my heart, but I really don't want help from people, and I don't mean that in a bad way. I mean that I'm an adult, and I should be able to take care of my checking account by myself. If the check bounces, guess what? It bounces. And you know what? I'm responsible for that, and I'm gonna have to pay the penalty, and I want that. I want to be able to take the consequences and be an adult about things, because my whole life I was protected. People would say, "Oh, you know, it's not her fault. Let it go. She has a learning disability," stuff like that. I'm sick of it, and I don't allow people to shelter me or do things that are not healthy for me anymore.

Problems in this area, as in the others discussed in this chapter, are often tied to various characteristics of LD/ADHD.

**Impulsivity** may lead a person to charge purchases without thought to his or her current account balance, to exhaust his or her savings before the rent is paid, or to fail to record checks and ATM withdrawals. All of this makes it impossible for the individual to monitor his or her checking account balance. Nancie describes her own related difficulties:

> I have very poor money management skills. Somebody can give me $50 for a birthday gift, and I'll spend the same $50 16 different ways. I understand the concept. I understand when you don't have any. I've been in both situations—I've had none, and I've had some.

**Time management issues** can be a complicating factor behind poor money management. Nancie admits that she puts off all the bill paying until the very last moment. She reports that she has a chronic history of being late in payment but that she still has good credit because "everybody knows that I'm good for it."

**Disorganization** comes into play as well when people have difficulty gathering all the items necessary to reconcile their checkbook—the monthly statement, the check register, a calculator—and cannot remember where they left the stamps as they get ready to send off bill payments.

Some adults with LD/ADHD are so disorganized, stuffing their cash in various drawers and pockets, that they are unable to account for cash on hand at any given moment. A young woman emptied her pockets in my office one day and had several dollars individually crumpled, with no order at all. She easily could have dropped a few bills and would never have noticed her loss because she certainly had no idea how much she was carrying.

**Conceptual difficulties** may stand in the way as well at times by limiting the individual's understanding of the relationship between math symbols and money concepts (Posthill & Roffman, 1991). One young man I knew did not understand the concept of credit. When he received his monthly statement with a balance marked *CR* for a returned item, he promptly made out a check for the listed amount. When the figure doubled the following month, he again paid the listed sum. This continued unnoticed until his credit totaled $1,800, and he began to bounce his checks because all of his funds had been diverted to this "bill."

**Skill deficits** affect money management. Reading disorders make it difficult to contend with signs in stores when shopping and bank notices and statements when managing checking accounts. Weak math skills interfere with account reconciliation, making it difficult to perform necessary calculations. Writing difficulties cause stress when an individual must write a check and spell numbers correctly. Faced with this challenge, Christopher Lee recalled:

> I was standing in line at a surf shop when I realized I was going to have to write in front of somebody. My palms grew sweaty, and the adrenaline began to flow. It was the worst feeling in the world . . . Not only was I faced with the problem of writing, but also with disclosing my inability to another person. The check was for $35. I pulled out one of my oldest tricks and wrote so messy that the spelling problem could not be recognized. I found out that this trick did not work with check writing when the clerk asked me to rewrite it. I got very shaky. I couldn't spell *thirty*, much less the name of the store. I concentrated on the things around me until I found the

name of the store written on a pad nearby. To this day, I don't know if I spelled *thirty-five* correctly, but they took my check. (Lee & Jackson, 1992, p. 16)

**Memory problems** may keep a person from regularly recording transactions. **Attention difficulties** can challenge the individual's concentration as he or she proceeds through the rather tedious process of reconciling the checkbook. Difficulties with **visual perception** can cause the individual to misalign numbers in the columns of his checkbook, resulting again in computation errors. Visual–motor problems can also be the cause of number inversions; the person who means to write *61*, but writes *16* is going to make an unavoidable error in his or her calculation. The person with weak visual figure–ground perception faces monthly challenges as he or she tries to read individual lines on bank statements that look like a hodge-podge of numbers and text.

## STRATEGIES FOR BETTER MONEY MANAGEMENT

There are several strategies for money management that are beneficial to people with LD/ADHD.

### Self-Advocating

Some strategies, such as learning to self-advocate and asking for needed help, are more challenging than others. Nonnie finds this an effective strategy:

In terms of everyday problem-solving, I'm learning to function as an independent person with a severe LD. I've been my own advocate. For example, I went to the bank drive-in, and I had four different transactions. There was a big sign that said you could only do one, but I can't transpose money, checking to cash. I was going to do one thing at a time, get it back, another thing, then get it back. That takes time. People behind me were losing their minds. So I decided to go into the bank and talk with the manager. I introduced myself and told him I'd been banking there many years, that my husband had died, and that I couldn't understand any numbers, that I was responsible for my children and my bills, that I had a learning disability. I asked if I could have a card stating that I had a problem in this area that would permit me to do my four transactions, back and forth, back and forth.

So, now I come into the door, and they all jump up. I made a friend because I was honest enough to go into the bank and ask for help. After I learn [a new skill], I pull back and don't ask for the same service, but I'm not afraid of asking.

### Using an Explanatory Letter

An explanatory letter from a physician or therapist can help an individual work through disputes about paying for missed medical or dental appointments or for bank overdrafts. Nina found this effective:

> I work it out with my doctors and dentists, but that's only been in the last 2 years. I have my coach write a letter that says I'm being treated for ADHD. I had to have it for the bank because of the amount of checks that I bounced. Basically, I've said to them that I am a person with a diagnosed disability, and customer service ought to learn the ADA stuff. But that's been very recent, just kind of standing up for that.

### Using Direct Deposit

There are regular services such as direct deposit that adults with LD/ADHD can use. Having a salary directly deposited in their checking account simplifies the process of banking by at least one step. It also protects the impulsive spender from the temptation of having ready access to large sums of cash.

### Pre-paying Bills

People who become anxious about forgetting to pay bills on time can pre-pay. In anticipation of being late sometimes, Jule finds it reassuring to do so:

> When I pay my bills, I'm always afraid that I'm going to forget, because I put them in a drawer. At the beginning of every month, not only do I write my bills, but I pay a month in advance for health insurance, car insurance, rent, answering service, accountant, all the ones that I know are standard. When I do forget, which is occasional, I'm a month ahead so I don't get in trouble.

### Setting Up a Home Office

One useful habit to establish is for an individual to be ultra-organized in dealing with his or her checkbook. Adults with LD/ADHD should consider setting up a home office at a desk or at a table where they can keep all the items needed for successful money management (Posthill & Roffman, 1990). This home office should include the usual desk supplies—paper, pens and pencils, tape, a ruler, paper clips, a stapler; an accordion file, where important papers may be filed under separate headings, such as "bills paid," "receipts," or "bank statements"; a budget book in which they may record expenditures and realistically estimate expenses; and a calendar, which can be used to note the receipt of monthly bills and to record when each is due.

### Using a "Crib Sheet"

Another strategy to ease money management is to have a "crib sheet" with correctly spelled numbers tucked into the checkbook for easy reference when writing checks.

### Using Carbon Checks

Carbon checks help avoid the many difficulties that arise when transactions go unrecorded. Nancie sings their praises:

> The first thing that my husband and I did was buy checks with carbon copies because the checks were written wrong. Not too long ago, I wrote the check out for the office manager for her salary and missed several words in the amount, and she couldn't cash her check. So, when I know I don't have enough time to do it, I just sign them and have somebody else write them out.

### Maintaining a Cushion of Money

Many people leave a cushion of extra money in their account to avoid bouncing checks. As Betty has experienced, this practice can be helpful in anticipation of future errors: "I can pretty well balance my checkbook, but I make sure that it's at least $70 or $80 off, and it has been for years—as a cushion, in case I reverse numbers or forget to put in things."

### Using Home Accounting Software

Making use of home accounting software is also a popular strategy for those who are computer literate. Once acclimated to its use, adults with LD/ADHD may find checking software to be highly valuable in account management. Those who learn how to make effective use of such programs will find that they ease the process of record keeping.

### Using a Budget Envelopes Book

People who are uncomfortable with computers or who cannot afford accounting software can use a budget envelopes book. This inexpensive and handy tool, available in most stationery stores, has separate envelopes for specific budget items, such as food, transportation, rent, and entertainment. Budgeted sums of cash are placed in each envelope at the beginning of each month, and the individual makes a commitment to spend the allotted funds only for the stated purposes.

### Dividing Responsibilities

As with housekeeping, in money management it is a good idea for people with LD/ADHD to coordinate financial responsibilities with their spouse or roommate, each assuming responsibilities that match his or her strengths. In Pat's case, this means that Weldon deals with their checkbook. He explains the logic:

> My wife can sit down and do any mathematical equation you want done. She can sit and work out complicated problems, but the drain it takes on her is so severe that by the time she gets through with it, she is a basket case for awhile. Bless her heart, she can do all of this, but it is not worth all the effort to balance the checkbook. I balance the checkbook. I don't mind. It is no problem. She can, but why put her through that aggravation and turmoil to accomplish that when it doesn't bother me?

## GETTING AROUND

People with LD/ADHD often have difficulty arriving at their chosen destinations. They chronically lose their way, have trouble using public transportation, and struggle with driving-related issues. Challenges may be related to poor time management, spatial problems and perceptual impairments, conceptual issues, or difficulties with eye–hand coordination.

With all of its complexities, driving can be of particular concern to individuals with LD/ADHD. Challenges vary and can develop for a multitude of reasons. For example, people may find it difficult to train their right foot to recognize the difference between the accelerator and the brake and, on manual transmission vehicles, to train their left foot to work the clutch simultaneously. They may find it challenging to develop a working understanding of the reactivity of the steering wheel, which must be turned only so much to pass another car but must be turned even more when it is time to round a corner. They may struggle to interpret what they are seeing in the rearview mirror. On cars with manual transmission, they may have difficulty moving from one gear to another, particularly to reverse, which generally requires an additional thrust. Further, they may have considerable difficulty learning how to parallel park. Indeed, many struggle in their efforts to meld the many separate aspects of car handling into one coordinated driving experience. Glenn lists some of his many driving issues:

> I still can't drive a stick because I have no hand–eye coordination. So I drive automatics. No one ever wants to drive with me because I have very poor depth perception, I cannot tell left from right, and I never know how fast I am going. I am a fun person to drive with if you are into thrills.

Added to his issues is his preference for fast driving, which is not unusual among those who have ADHD, with its associated attraction to risk-taking. He tells us:

> I also love to drive at relatively high speed for long distances because it actually gives me a sense of power and common focus. When you are driving, you are actually having to focus—it forces you to focus.

Problems with getting around may stem from several characteristics of LD. **Poor time management** may be a factor. Because time is an abstract concept, the many adults with LD/ADHD who are concrete thinkers may have difficulty conceptualizing how long it takes to get somewhere. They tend to lack internal monitors regarding how much time has passed. One woman admitted that on several occasions she returned late to work from her lunch break because she had gone for a workout; although she knew that the aerobics class was only an hour long, she had failed to factor in time for showering and changing her clothes.

**Disorganization** represents another obstacle to getting around efficiently. The individual who is disorganized has difficulty pulling together needed items for a given appointment. For example, one man described his struggle to gather his résumé and references along with the appropriate jacket and tie for a job interview. These difficulties led him to feel overwhelmed, and he unintentionally arrived late.

**Attention problems,** such as distractibility and hyperfocusing, often lead the individual to get sidetracked. One woman reports, "I was on the subway, had plenty of time to get to my exam but got distracted studying my notes and missed the stop. I ended up being 20 minutes late."

People with **spatial problems** struggle with the concept of self-in-space, which may lead them to bump into things, to appear clumsy, and to become disoriented when they must approach familiar territory from a less familiar, alternate direction. For example, one woman described getting lost in Macy's just because she entered through the mall entrance instead of through the side door that she customarily used. Many people with difficulty in this area also find it extremely hard to read and follow maps.

**Directionality issues** also significantly affect ability to distinguish east from west and successfully arrive at desired desti-nations. As Nonnie notes, this can be devastatingly debilitating: "I have severe directionality problems. I cannot do map reading. I even get lost in hotels. After my husband died, I didn't know how to leave the front door."

Lilia's poor sense of direction has significantly limited her radius of travel to within just a few miles of her hometown. She regrets that, although she has lived in Providence since the age of 8, she still does not know how to get to Boston by herself.

Like several others I interviewed, Nina has a poor sense of direction. She chuckles as she recounts:

Everyone who drives with me knows that you have to say "this way" and "that way" instead of "left" or "right." [They say], "No, the other left!" when I go the wrong way. My favorite thing is people will put their thumb and index fingers up and say to me, "This is how you can remember the direction of L." And I hold my other thumb and index finger up and say, "So what's that? Honey, for me this is an L, too!" I could write L and R on the appropriate hand, but I'd have to have it tattooed. Even then, I'd have to make sure that that R was really prominent.

**Difficulty with depth perception** can make it dangerous for an individual to travel. Just walking down the street, they may have trouble dealing with curbs; or they may bump into people on a crowded sidewalk because they are poor judges of the distance between themselves and others. They are in danger of getting hit by cars when they cross the street because they misjudge how far away the cars are and how fast they are traveling. When driving, they may have difficulty gauging a safe traveling distance from the car in front and judging what is behind them based on the images in the rearview mirror. Glenn reports:

I have terrible depth perception, I don't know how close I am to the car as I am coming up, so I usually tend to stop a lot. I have compensated—instead of ramming into people, I stop a lot further behind people. I also have a horrible time parallel parking and parking near poles. I have actually taken a car and rammed it into walls in Portugal because I couldn't fit in the alleys. I have terrible depth perception, but I accept that in me—I am not a bad person. I just have terrible depth perception.

Those who have **difficulties with auditory processing** often confuse oral directions. They may mix up the sequence of instructions or forget some of the steps. Allyssa regrets that she is vulnerable to this type of error:

I was in Florida one time, and I wanted to come home early. I called up the airport in New York, and I said that I wanted a flight to New York from Florida, blah, blah, blah. And they told me, "We don't have a flight going into Kennedy. We have one going into La Guardia." I got it all confused. I thought it was the opposite. Because I'm dyslexic, I heard it backwards, so I ended up going to the wrong airport. Somebody was waiting for me there, waiting for hours, and I wasn't there, I was in a different airport. Stuff like that has happened my whole life, but I always just took a deep breath and said, "You know what, I'm not gonna get upset about it." I used to. I used to really be hard on myself, but I've learned not to beat myself up anymore.

People with **visual memory problems** find it difficult to remember landmarks, so they lose the advantage of feeling reassured by familiar sights when they are trying to find their way.

Those with **conceptual limitations** run into obstacles as well. A young man once told me he failed his first driver's test when he was told to take the next left and, in a very concrete and literal way, he turned into the next driveway. Allyssa, too, has struggled with concepts related to travel. She reports, "I just realized last year that to get back from someplace, you just reverse the directions. It was like a revelation to me."

### STRATEGIES FOR GETTING AROUND EFFECTIVELY

Adults with LD/ADHD can benefit from a number of strategies that will help them go from one place to another.

### Asking for Directions

Many find it helpful to ask others for directions. Often it is useful to supplement directions with a map.

### Avoiding Potential Distractions

Those with problems of attention should avoid potential distractions, such as driving in rush hour or using a cell phone while behind the wheel.

### Maintaining a Directions File

Keeping a directions file in the car is very useful. It is often a good idea to stick with main roads and avoid short cuts. Jule comments,

> If it's someplace I've been, I never remember how to get there anyway, and I always have to call up and get directions. Even when I go to the same place every year for Passover, I always have to call up and get directions. I write them down, and I have a directions file in my car. I have them draw it as well as write it out.

### Using Creative Problem Solving

Many adults with LD/ADHD who have been successful in getting places use some creative problem-solving about handling direction-related issues. Nonnie tells the inspiring story of how she overcame what seemed an insurmountable problem of not knowing how to drive to her weekend house when her husband, who had always driven there, died unexpectedly:

> I realized I was a prisoner—I had to learn how to drive there. I joined a group for phobics. I didn't have a phobia, but it was the only way I could get this social worker to teach me how to drive. Usually people who have phobias want to cross the street or use an elevator. I said I'd like to go from Woodmere, New York, to Massachusetts—that was the bottom line. She felt so much anxiety that she ran to her supervisor.
>
> That's the strength, my creativity to figure out how to do this. I just wanted to get a car on a highway without killing either myself or the other people. So, I had a tape recorder, and the car had a tape deck. I explained what I wanted her to do. I was a very good driver, because I have good motor control. First she taught me to merge the car on and then get off at the next exit. That was my homework for the week. After I did this for three exits, I said "Now I'm ready for the bridge." She told me the bridge is just an extension of the road, but my two legs were completely numb. I was scared, but that wasn't going to stop me.
>
> I had to get to Massachusetts. There's a certain drive, a certain extra survival instinct or something or other that ADHD people have. Sometimes it works for you, and sometimes it doesn't work for you. It took 1 year for her to teach me, one year of my life. I would pay the toll, and then I would go back west—that was my homework for the week. I got lost at Hunt's Point, and I had police escorts home. I got up one morning, had confidence, and said to my brother, "I think I'm going to try it now." I decided to try it for the first time in my life. The airports were closed due to fog, so I called my brother up, and he said, "Don't worry, it's only up in the sky." I called my daughter, and she said, "Call me when you get there." It took me 6 hours—now it takes 3. I was so excited. It was the practice and what I was doing for the whole year and not quitting. The idea of getting from one place to the other was secondary to the process of not quitting. It took a year—that's a long time in one's life. I cried because I had done something that I'd never done before.

Nonnie's success in achieving this major goal was related not only to her creative problem solving but also to her willingness to ask for help.

### Writing Down All Directions

Another strategy that Nonnie uses to help her find her way is writing down all directions, even when she is in a hotel. She carries a little notebook so she can write and remember her hotel room number and where to take a right or left to get to it.

### Going for a Test Run

Going for a dry run is very helpful, particularly for those who struggle with time management, as it offers a sense of how long a trip will take. Jule routinely plans to do what she calls a "drive-by" when she must find her way to a new destination:

> If I have to go somewhere really important, and I don't want to screw it up, and I've never been there before, I do a drive-by. Then I always will stop at gas stations along the way to check to make sure I'm going in the right direction. I get the address because if I can't remember to turn right or left, I start going one way and check the addresses and then can turn around. I build in enough time to do that so I'm not late. I'm very punctual because I put aside so much time to get there that I really allow for all of the problems. I mean you have to build in for all the problems.

### Maintaining a Sense of Humor

A final strategy for getting around is to maintain a sense of humor. It is always helpful to try to go with the flow and avoid panic or angry reactions when struggling with directional issues. Betty comments:

> People know I'm going to get lost. I've gotten used to the fact that getting lost can be kind of fun, and I embrace it. When I lived in a dormitory, Saturday mornings there used to be mystery tours— 9:00 A.M., and I'd have a full tank of gas and a cooler, and we'd go off. I'd invariably get lost and would start saying, "Well, where's the sun?" And they'd start realizing, "Oh, dear, she's trying to figure out where the sun is so she can figure out where the routes are." They began to get used to the fact that I'd always get lost. I've made a game out of it.

## POSTSCRIPT ON TIME MANAGEMENT

Time management is an essential ingredient to managing the responsibilities of adult life effectively, whether in taking care of oneself, housekeeping, managing personal finances, or getting around. Thus, it seems fitting to add a postscript for those adults with LD/ADHD who struggle in the management of their time. A number of strategies may be helpful.

### USING A PLANNING BOOK

Using a planning book is highly recommended. There are several things to consider when using a planning book to organize.

#### Using Only One Book

Maintaining one book for multiple purposes makes more sense than trying to keep up separate books for work and leisure. Nonnie regrets that she learned the hard way that it is too easy to forget to transfer information between the two:

> I lost a friend because I had two plan books. I forgot her birthday because I looked in the wrong book, and she was very upset. Now, I have one large plan book. I put clients, shows, social things, birthdays, everything in that one book, and I do it immediately. When I look at it, I think, "Oh, this is someone's birthday." Otherwise, I won't remember anything.

#### Writing Down Only Important Information

It is necessary to write only important information in the planning book. As Nina discovered, doodling on the pages undermines the book's usefulness:

> I always have had a schedule book and never used it. Actually, when I started [seeing a therapist/coach], I brought and opened up the book I had then to show her that I was actually writing things in it. My calendar was all doodles—all of it! Even if there was stuff written in here, I couldn't find it because I had doodles all over it. I would sit there, and I would write the same word over and over again to the point where you couldn't read it, just out of my nervous habit. I'd be

making plans with you over the phone. I'd write "lunch with Arlyn" and then, I would doodle. By the time I'd finished the conversation, it would be illegible. I still do it, but less. Now I doodle, but I do it outside the plan book. The book I have now has a place for addresses and a little compartment in the back with all these tabs on it that I labeled "music," "ideas," "goals," "meetings," "clients." And now, when I have a meeting at my job, I take notes in this one "meetings" section and then I make my newsletter for work from it. It's not like I never took notes, but it's all in the organization—before, I had random sheets of paper all over the place.

### Keeping the Planner in a Consistent Place

The planner must be kept in a consistent place. It will be much more valuable if it is readily retrievable from one particular pocket of a purse or briefcase. Also, as Andre discovered, the planner must be taken everywhere, even on vacation:

> If I'm not organized, I have no life. I have a planner, a computer, and it reminds me that this needs to be done on this day. I made a mistake when I went on vacation—for some reason, I thought I shouldn't take the planner. I wasted a lot of time and didn't see a lot of great places because I didn't take the planner and didn't plan my time while I was on vacation. So even when you're on vacation, [disorganization] can still affect you and hurt you.

### Using a Computerized Planner

Adults with LD/ADHD who are comfortable with technology can also try a computerized scheduler to help keep track of appointments, addresses, and phone numbers.

### ALLOWING EXTRA TIME WHEN TRAVELING TO UNFAMILIAR PLACES

It is always a good idea to allow extra time to get to unfamiliar places. It is helpful for people with time management issues to build in a cushion of at least 15–30 minutes to arrive at their destinations. Betty recognizes the value of doing this. Because she has a strong tendency to get lost, she accepts the fact that if she is going someplace new, she always needs to plan an extra hour to find her way. Nonnie does the same, but also finds it helpful to strategize around landmarks because it is difficult for her to read maps: "I will always get to places a little earlier as a compensating strategy. If I don't know the place, my friends and supports give me the landmarks. Landmarks are very important."

### SETTING TIME LIMITS ON ACTIVITIES

People who have a tendency to hyperfocus should set limits on time allotted for an activity. An alarm may be set as a cue to end an activity; a watch alarm is particularly handy for this purpose.

### AVOIDING OVER-PLANNING

Finally, to keep from becoming overwhelmed, people with LD/ADHD should avoid planning too many stressful activities for any one day or weekend. Some find it helpful to restrict their social activities to either Friday or Saturday night, as overplanning strains their schedule and leads them to feel pressured.

### SUMMARY

Day-to-day life can be challenging for adults with LD/ADHD, particularly in the areas of self-care, including hygiene and medical care; housekeeping, including shopping, cooking, and cleaning; money management; and getting around. The characteristics of LD/ADHD interfere with each in varied ways.

Specific strategies can be very effective in easing the stress in each area. Time management tends to be an overarching issue for many adults with LD/ADHD who often benefit from maintaining a time management system involving calendars, planning books, deadlines with cushions of extra time built in when possible, and avoidance of overplanning.

# 8

## Learning
## Beyond High School

Postsecondary opportunities have changed considerably since the 1980s for students with LD/ADHD. Those who wish to continue their education after high school have more choices than at any other time in history. Perhaps the greatest catalyst for change has been federal legislation designed to protect the civil rights of individuals with disabilities. Two laws in particular have helped to ensure equal opportunities in higher education.

**Section 504 of the Rehabilitation Act of 1973** is a civil rights statute that prohibits colleges and universities that receive federal financial assistance from discriminating against any individual on the basis of a disability. As a result of this legal mandate, postsecondary institutions are required to provide support services and reasonable accommodations to allow "otherwise qualified" students with disabilities to access the full range of educational programs and activities available on campus.

**The Americans with Disabilities Act (ADA),** passed in 1990, has broad societal implications for the rights of people with disabilities, who are ensured equal access to learning opportunities within the postsecondary environment. Under the ADA, it is the postsecondary student's responsibility to identify himself or herself as having a disability to a Disabled Student Services (DSS) officer or counselor, to consult with this individual regarding any appropriate reasonable accommodations, and to complete all assigned work. The DSS counselor writes an accommodation agreement letter, which the student may present to faculty to communicate that a disability has been documented and that the particular accommodations have been deemed reasonable; however, DSS is prohibited from disclosing the specific nature of the disability itself without the student's permission. Indeed, all disability-related information is treated as confidential and kept in a secure file.

Students with LD/ADHD who have chosen to continue their learning in colleges and universities after high school have benefited enormously from these pieces of legislation. Glenn's account of his academic history illustrates the difference made by these laws:

> When I was coming out of high school in 1968, I had never heard of LD. I had no idea what dyslexia was, but I knew that I was pretty dysfunctional. My LD dramatically affected what happened after high school. I had gone to school in San Francisco in the 1960s; all my teachers were hippie wanna-bes, so they were allowing me to do collages instead of writing papers. I ended up graduating functionally illiterate, reading at best on a second- or third-grade level and writing worse than that. I misspelled my own name on job applications—how are you going to get hired if you do that? You cannot go to college very well. When I tried to go a community college, it meant going from a protected, isolated, supported high school environment into English 101 in college classrooms with 600 people. There was no way that I could function. I didn't make it even halfway through the first semester when I left and descended rather rapidly into a nonliterate world.

After years of academic failure, Glenn found that the accommodations made available through the new laws provided him with his first opportunity to excel:

> After I was identified, at age 37, I [finally] transitioned into college [successfully]. Going through college then for me was not just a personal vindication of the failures that I had as an illiterate person all along; it was also a major testing ground for my new tools for understanding LD as a disability. I was able to use that designation to go through college as an accommodated person, so I never took a test in the classroom. I never had to handwrite anything; as far as exams went. I had extra time, I had isolation, and I had note-takers supporting me. The university and the college program I was in all accepted me as a person with disabilities. I was entitled, and

I had it all worked out to the right accommodations. Once I got identified, I got my associate's, bachelor's, and master's [degrees] in 3 1/2 years.


## OPTIONS AFTER HIGH SCHOOL

There are a number of options for adults with LD/ADHD who wish to continue their learning.

### COLLEGE-BASED PROGRAMS

Hundreds of **4-year colleges**, ranging from moderate to high in selectivity, are listed in *Peterson's Colleges with Programs for Students with Learning Disabilities, Fifth Edition* (Mangrum & Strichart, 1997). At more selective colleges, applicants must meet certain academic criteria set by the school itself, such as strong personal qualities, high grade point averages (GPAs), rigorous academic preparation during high school, and high standardized test scores.

Students who wish to begin with a 2-year course of studies may choose either a **junior college or a community college**. In either case, credits earned toward an associate's degree may be transferred to a 4-year college. Publicly funded and nonresidential, community colleges are attractive to many students with LD/ADHD as a low-cost educational alternative. With open admissions to any high school graduate older than 18, they require neither standardized college admissions tests nor a roster of college-track courses during the high school years. Community colleges tend to offer a wider array of courses than junior colleges, with classes ranging in focus from vocational to liberal arts. Credits may be transferred to either a vocational school or to a 4-year college.

Until the 1950s, students with severe LD/ADHD who wished to continue learning but who did not meet the intellectual standards of most postsecondary institutions were closed out of the college experience. Since then, several college-based **nondegreee options** have opened, offering students with LD/ADHD and intelligence measured in the low-average range the opportunity to continue learning and to experience campus life. Programs offered typically are 2–3 years long and focus on preparation for independent adulthood through a series of practical courses and experiences that promote development of vocational skills, apartment living skills, consumer and money management skills, meal planning and preparation skills, and social skills. Most incorporate transitional support for graduates as they meet their goal of moving from campus life into both the community and work world.

## COMMUNITY-BASED PROGRAMS

A growing number of offerings focus on the same skills addressed in the college-based, nondegree programs but are less academic and are situated in the community. These programs are often apartment based and focus on development of community living skills along with work preparation. Some of these programs maintain an affiliation with local colleges, and students may travel to those schools and take postsecondary courses as part of their overall program.

Many adults with LD/ADHD receive additional training through their local office of the Department of Rehabilitation. The focus of such training varies somewhat but largely targets development of skills related to obtaining and maintaining employment. Reflecting on the experiences in high school that led her to a particularly beneficial rehabilitation program, Allyssa recalls, "I was told my whole life that I would never amount to anything. They grabbed my dreams from me and just yanked them away." She reports that in high school, "My life was a mess. It wasn't about school—it was about, 'My friends are here, and I'm gonna be cool and hang out.'" Allyssa got heavily involved in drugs and regularly skipped class. She admits that when she did attend, she rarely bothered to listen. But at age 18, she began to change:

> I stopped hanging out with my friends, and I cleaned up my life. When I graduated, I was making major changes. I didn't even go to graduation, to the actual ceremony. I was trying to straighten out my life. I knew I wanted to work with people. I was working with handicapped adults at the time, and I knew that I got pleasure out of working with disabled people, and I was gonna pursue that. I didn't think that I needed to go to college. That was my attitude.

She returned to school, attending Learn and Earn, a rehabilitation program at Queensborough College that helps people with disabilities develop vocational skills. She describes her experience there and her appreciation for the individual attention offered:

They teach you how to have confidence in yourself and how to get a résumé together, asking for letters of reference, and all that kind of stuff that I didn't know how to do. In the beginning, when I first came into Learn and Earn, I didn't show up. Guys from this program called me and said, "What's going on with you? What are you doing sleeping until 12 o'clock?" I was sleeping [so late] because I had so much fear my whole life of becoming the person that God wanted me to be, and I was so comfortable being a mess. Learn and Earn pulled me out of that. The people in this program have been awesome. For them to call me up, it goes beyond their job. A lot of times I felt like I was slipping into a pit, feeling sorry for myself, and they didn't allow me to do that. They're always reaching out their hand to me.

In Learn and Earn they gave a lot of different help. I had a lot of good professors. One professor said, "You know what? I have a learning disability, and I know how you guys feel. I'm here to tell you that if you put in the effort, you could be what you want to be." I was like, "This guy's nuts. He doesn't know what I go through." Then he told me that he did, and I was, "Wow, I'd really love to do what he does. I'd love to give people hope. That would be the best." And I'm doing it, and it's awesome. When I went to graduation, I was remembering all those things they taught me, like, "Believe in yourself," and "Don't drop out of school." I had a great time in those classes.

The Office of Vocational Rehabilitation (OVR) may also pay for college courses if they are required to address the employment goals targeted by their clients. Such funding was essential in Glenn's case, as he was not in a position to finance his own continuing education. He fought long and hard and, ultimately, was approved for OVR financial support of his further schooling.

The percentage of students with LD who graduate from high school and continue on to college is very low, a fact that is certainly related to the shocking reality that 35% never manage to graduate from high school at all (Wagner, 1992). The percentage of individuals with LD among those attending adult basic education classes is suspected to be high (Sturomski, personal communication, March 15, 1995). Indeed, the National Adult Literacy and Learning Disabilities (NALLD) Center estimates that 60% of adults with severe literacy difficulties have undetected or untreated LD (Podhajski, 1994). Recognizing the significance of this issue, NALLD has launched an initiative to provide training for adult literacy providers to help them more effectively assist people with LD/ADHD.

Among the ranks of those being served is Lilia, who is refreshingly forthcoming about her history of school failure and her determined efforts to achieve both literacy and a general educational development (GED) diploma. The eldest child of Portuguese immigrants who spoke no English and could offer their children no help with school work, Lilia began to experience academic difficulties during her elementary years. She remembers that she was never able to understand what was being written on the blackboard and that she lived in fear of being called on by her teachers. Soon she was regularly truant. She recalls, "I would pretend I was my mother and I'd say, 'Lilia can't come in today. She's sick.'" One day in middle school, she decided to drop out:

> My last grade was eighth. And don't ask me how I even got that far—they just pushed me up because of my age. Three years ago, I went back to school to get my GED. As far as work qualifications, I have work experience. I know how to work with people. I have a lot of good qualities, but the qualities that I need to get a good paying job, I don't have—that's my reading, my spelling. . . . I haven't finished my GED—not yet, because of my learning disability. It's heartbreaking, because I see girls that go in there for 3 months, 6 months and, boom, they're out of there. And I see women who have been in there for 5 years and are still there. I've been there for 3 years. It just takes me longer to understand what they're teaching me. It doesn't make sense to me. I can't remember it. In order to learn, it has to make sense—it's almost like I've got to feel it, I've got to taste it, I've got to touch it.
>
> When I started with Dorca's Place [the GED training center], my reading level was at fifth grade, and it went up to 11.5. So, I have regained some of my self-esteem because it feels good to be able to open up a letter and read it. Not that I can respond to it! That's

another thing—you lack confidence. You have that in your head, that you can't do it, so why even try. A lot of times I'll try, and I'll surprise myself and think, "Oh, God, I did it!" and my eyes fill up with water because I can't believe I did it. I'll go around the house like a little child, somebody who just got a new toy. It feels so damned, damned good! So that's why I feel a lot better today—thanks to Dorca's Place. It's taken me a lot longer, but if it hadn't been for them, I would have been maybe still at a fifth-grade reading level.

Family Literacy Centers also help adults learn to read and prepare for the GED exam. Joni Krantz wrote about her experience in such a program, which she joined when she realized she was unable to help her children with their homework:

One day my daughter brought a flyer home from school about a program called Even Start. I learned that I could go to school and take my 4-year-old son with me. While I was in class, he would be in class with kids his own age. The program offered free breakfast, lunch, and transportation. . . . When I first started at Even Start, I had to work on my self-esteem. Eventually, I gained confidence in myself, and before I knew it, I had passed three GED tests. I was so excited about learning that my family thought I was going nuts. . . . It's been a year since Andy and I graduated. . . . Now Andy is in first grade. . . . He is the top reader in his class. . . . (1996, pp. 12–13)

After Joni Krantz completed her Family Literacy program, she attended and graduated from a local community college with a 3.74 GPA and became a travel agent.

## EFFECTS OF LD/ADHD ON POSTSECONDARY LEARNING

Students moving into postsecondary learning environments today tend to have been diagnosed much earlier in their lives than most of the individuals interviewed for this book. Many have benefited not only from early diagnosis, but also from special services throughout their school years. Nonetheless, their LD persists and continues to present challenges in a variety of ways.

## PERCEPTUAL IMPAIRMENTS

Perceptual impairments affect learning experiences. Students with **auditory attention issues** find themselves challenged by fast-paced college lectures. Requiring extra processing time, they generally have a great deal of difficulty taking notes and absorbing information delivered through a lecture presentation format. Those with **visual figure–ground problems** have trouble tuning in to any one item on a crowded blackboard, map, or overhead projected image. Those with **visual–motor difficulties** often have handwriting that is illegible, sometimes even to themselves. One person complained, "Whenever I have to take notes, I write so fast, it ends up like a scribble in my notebook. When it comes time to study, I can't read my own writing, so the notes are just about useless."

## LANGUAGE PROCESSING DISORDERS

Language processing difficulties affect postsecondary learning as well. Those who have **receptive language problems**, for example, may find themselves confused by written test items or by oral directions. Jule thinks it is ironic that when she was in college, she tutored people for exams, yet would often earn lower grades than they did because she had misunderstood the test questions. Students with **expressive language difficulties** may have trouble finding the right words to convey their thoughts, synthesizing their ideas, formulating their answers to questions in class, and expressing themselves precisely. Dale Brown (1981) recalled an uncomfortable pattern in college, when she would want to speak up in her courses; she would stop to think through her answer thoroughly, but by the time she formulated her thoughts, the conversation typically would have moved on.

## SKILLS DEFICITS

Skills deficits can cause tremendous obstacles for students with LD/ADHD. Students with **reading disorders** are at a significant disadvantage when notices are posted or distributed with the expectation that they will be widely read and understood. These students feel particularly burdened by the heavy reading requirements in many areas of study, such as literature or history. For example, Betty reports that it was the reading in graduate school that ultimately "did her in." She recalls being pressured into pursuing further studies when she was doing well in her master's program. She intuitively knew this was the wrong route to take:

> They said, "All right, you've proven yourself. You've done very well here." Meanwhile, they didn't know I wasn't reading. I write very well, and I could pull together like a weaving a lot of different ideas from a lot of divergent areas. They guilt-tripped me into a Ph.D. program. I was sitting there screaming, "Ph.D.'s read. I don't! This is not what I want to do!" And they said, "You're denying your abilities." All the second semester was focused on getting me into the Ph.D. program. I applied and was accepted. I managed to make it through [for a while], but I was having a lot of stress. The Ph.D. program was a lot more reading, I was taking statistics and research courses, and the demands were just so heavy. I bailed out with my master's degree and four courses on my doctorate. Everybody's hopes were kind of dashed.

**Difficulties in writing** include the physical act of penmanship, problems with spelling, and trouble organizing written language into a logical sequence of thoughts. Some students manage to compensate for their writing difficulties outside of class but crumble on essay tests when time limits raise their anxiety levels.

Students with LD/ADHD often find it painful when faculty do not understand the challenges they face when writing. Nina recalls one such incident at a state university:

> I took an English class, and the teacher said to me, "You know, it's a good thing you can talk. From what you wrote, I would think you're totally stupid." I still have difficulty with that—I know that I think it and say it better than I actually write it.

In an effort to avoid such scenarios, students with poor writing skills use a variety of methods to mask their difficulties. For example, those with serious spelling problems may limit their word usage to only the vocabulary that they can spell correctly, a practice that significantly constrains their ability to communicate. They may hide behind poor penmanship, making it difficult for people to read their writing and discern the true limits of their spelling ability. Or they may resort to cheating. Terry recalls that she successfully hid her disability for years by cheating through whole courses:

> I hid what I couldn't do mainly through cheating. I got good at that. My friends gave me help editing, letting me copy notes. I was not and still am really not able to listen and write at the same time. That was always very difficult for me, so I would have to study from somebody else's notes. I got through an entire science course by copying off a friend. They gave the final, and when my friend wasn't there, I basically couldn't take this test. It was really an awful experience for me, because the teacher came up to me afterwards and said, "You've done so well this year. I don't understand. Is this test too hard?" I just said, "You know what? I never studied. It's the end of the year—I just don't care." But it's kind of a shame, a missed opportunity. I mean, you don't learn [when you cheat].

**Math** can be troublesome for a variety of reasons. Students with language processing problems often find it difficult to grasp math concepts due to their confusion with the words. Students with perceptual impairments cannot easily move on to more advanced concepts when they misalign numbers in their calculations or invert digits, such as 2 and 5.

For many students, their new independence as college students creates a math-related challenge when they find themselves in charge of their own money for the first time. Thus, in addition to being expected to perform in math-oriented courses, they are rather suddenly obligated to master "real-world" money management. This expectation proved particularly burdensome for Betty. Recognizing that with her significant math problems she was at risk of making serious financial errors, she speculates that it was only her father's establishment of a bottomless checking account in her name that averted a personal financial crisis during her college years:

> One of the major things that affected my transition to college was that I had never managed money. I don't know how to subtract, and this was prior to the days of handheld, easy-to-manage calculators. My father had a slide rule and tried to teach me how to use it, but that was beyond me. When I went to college, he knew

I couldn't subtract from my checkbook, so he simply contacted the bank and said, "Look, she has a problem. If she runs out of money, give me a call." And through 4 years of college, I never subtracted. So I didn't have to worry about managing money.

## TIME MANAGEMENT DIFFICULTIES

Time management issues intensify organizational difficulties. The student with temporal problems has little sense of the time required to complete a task, tends to have inefficient study habits, and often assumes an impractical approach to required work. It is not unusual for students with poor time management to end up "pulling all nighters" in order to meet deadlines. Nancie recalls:

Time management was an issue, and time issues were a real detriment. I went to school part time and worked full time. I studied a lot. I really worked at it. I worked until the middle of the night and early morning. I know that if I could have done it differently, I could have done it better. What I've always known is, because of the time issues, what I do produce is not as good as what I could produce. And that's probably one of the bigger frustrations. If I could fake myself into believing that [the paper was due soon and that] the time crunch was a week or 6 weeks, then I had a deadline, and I could do better.

## DISORGANIZATION

For many students with LD/ADHD, the sudden shift from the tightly organized days of high school to the relatively loose structure of college life is challenging and stressful. One student reports:

I never appreciated the structure of the school day until it wasn't there anymore. When I could sleep late, had only two or three classes I was supposed to be at, and was suddenly responsible for productively filling in the hours, I just fell apart.

Navigating the several steps that must be taken even before classes begin can be a daunting journey in itself. Wading through the catalogue of course offerings, registering for classes, locating and purchasing required texts, finding the classrooms, and gathering notebooks and supplies specified for each course are individual challenges that arise even before the semester begins.

Moreover, once established in their classes, students with LD/ADHD find that organizational difficulties can be a considerable obstacle to efficient studying. Many find it challenging to prioritize their assignments, to break complex projects into a series of achievable short-term goals, and to choose the appropriate set of study skills to apply in each individual course.

In addition, organizational issues often spill beyond academics into students' living quarters, resulting in considerable disorder and conflict between dorm roommates.

## Distractibility

Distractibility has broad negative effects on students with LD/ADHD. The distractible student has difficulty completing an assignment and is challenged by such basic academic expectations as the requirement to listen to a lecture, observe a laboratory demonstration, or read dense material in a course textbook. One person expressed frustration:

> I can read the same paragraph over and over, and the meaning just doesn't sink in. It takes me forever to make it through one chapter, and by then I need a snack. After the snack, I remember a phone call I should make, and then I try to go back to the chapter, but by that time I've forgotten what I've read and have to start all over again. This goes on all the time!

Lilia considers her distractibility to be a significant problem; when she is trying to study, she finds herself plagued by an inability to concentrate:

> In order for me to read something, in order to do my homework, my kids have to be in bed—no movies, no noise, nothing because I get so easily distracted. [Even running] water will distract me! Isn't that sad? When it comes time for me to do my homework, I have to be in a room with the door shut, where I can't hear any noise, because the minute the kids say, "Mommy," that's it.

Distractibility is particularly troublesome in graduate school, where classes meet less frequently but for longer sessions, often for 3 hours at a time. One woman expressed dismay at the contrast between her ability to take short-term and full-semester courses:

> Since I left [graduate school], I've always taken a lot of workshops and short-term seminars—I don't know if that's kind of an instinctive way for me to continue my education. I probably take between 5 and 20 workshops per year. My problems don't affect me so much in professional development classes. It's not as bad there, because they only need my attention for basically 2 hours a night for 4 weeks or for a weekend.
>
> When [a course] goes for a longer session, I get scared. When I took a whole-semester class, I had a really hard time staying with it. What generally happens is, I'm afraid I'm not going to be able to do it; then, because I get scared that I won't be able to keep focused, I start to short circuit sooner. I can perseverate on that one thing—"I'm not going be able to finish"—to the extent that I almost sabotage myself. The emotional stuff interferes.

### IMPULSIVITY

Impulsivity can be troublesome as well. Like many of her student counterparts with LD/ADHD, Jule struggled throughout her school years with impulsive reactions to assignments, rushing without forethought, often sacrificing quality for speed of accomplishment. She recalls two painful experiences which, although they occurred early in her academic life, indicate how an impulsive approach can backfire:

> There are two incidents that I still have never forgotten. One of them was when I studied very hard for a test, and I got the highest grade in the class, [which was unusual for me in fourth grade]. But the teacher had said to skip a line before you wrote your name, and I didn't, so she took off 15 points. And then another, when I was in eleventh grade, and the teacher had said, "You have 5 minutes to take this test. Read it completely through before you do it," and I didn't want to waste the time reading it through. The girl next to me was just sitting there, and I thought how stupid she

was. I was quickly working as many of the problems as I could get, and I got to the very end of the test, and it said, "If you've read this test completely through, you will know that you will get an A if you don't do any of the problems." So there's a "ready, fire, aim" approach, a tremendous amount of impulsivity.

## SOCIAL SKILLS PROBLEMS

Social skills problems often lead to a deeply felt loneliness. Dale Brown, poignantly described her own difficulties in college:

> Social functions were lonely for me. The crowds and the noise were overwhelming. . . . People quickly formed groups, and I did not know how to join these circles. . . . Nobody approached me, and the wish to know people was so strong that I often approached them too boldly. I did not understand the need to make eye contact. . . . I didn't hear the sound of my own voice and didn't realize it was loud. . . . I would ask question after question and listen to their answers. My interviewing style made people very uncomfortable. (1982, p. 14)

Dale Brown's difficulty with interpersonal skills affected not only her social life, but her academic experience as well. She recollected an incident long ago when, in order to share a book, she sat too close to a college classmate who, in exasperation, ended up throwing the volume at her. She simply did not understand the concept of personal space.

## EMOTIONAL ISSUES

Students with LD/ADHD contend with several trying emotional issues.

### Shame and Low Self-Concept

Shame and low self-concept, rampant among students with LD/ADHD, are often unfortunate byproducts of inappropriately lowered expectations during high school. Contributing to further erosion of self-esteem is excessive hand-holding by parents and educators, to the extent that students develop learned helplessness and a lack of confidence in their ability to succeed independently in the classroom. Like successful dieters who continue to perceive a fat reflection in the mirror even after the achievement of their weight goals, many adults with LD/ADHD often retain these negative feelings about themselves, even when they succeed in moving forward in their studies. Jule recalls a paradoxical moment when her self-confidence wavered, even in the face of the ultimate academic victory:

> Before my orals [the last step in completing a doctorate], a friend of mine said, "When are you going to believe that you're really smart? You got the highest degree you can get, and you're still wondering if you're smart."

Nina reports that throughout her life she has been so consumed by a sense of shame due to her LD/ADHD that she has avoided several promising educational opportunities for fear of being judged. Shaking her head in regret, she reports why she chose not to take advantage of an opportunity she had many years ago to attend Yale University to study drama:

> Some of my decision to not go for the Yale Rep drama thing was because I thought that they would find out that I was stupid, and then I'd be humiliated. Actually, Meryl Streep was in New Haven at the same time I was, and I've often said over the years that at some point God looked down and said, "We need a young woman with strong features and a good voice and a strong personality to be a movie star." And I had to leave because I was too afraid that even He would find out that I was stupid! So then He gave the job to Meryl Streep. I often joke that she has my life right now. Anyway, some of the academic decisions have been out of fear of being found out, a sense of shame.

### Fear of Failure

For some individuals with LD/ADHD, fear of failure can be paralyzing. Pat describes the powerful effect fear had on her when she faced potential failure:

> By the time I was in junior high, nobody gave me any tests because teachers were warned, "If you give her a test she will faint!" [Later, when I got to college] the University of Arkansas didn't care—every time I fainted there, they sent me off to the infirmary and gave me the test [again] the next day. So, I transferred from there very

rapidly. When somebody asks where I went to college, I go through a long list of 10 universities.

It is important to tell you that I had no conceivable idea until after I got into college and began to find out what was wrong, that the reason I fainted was because I was going to have a test. When they evaluated me, they found out that I couldn't read and that I didn't understand enough. My comprehension was so low that I couldn't take the test. Only then did I pinpoint the fact that if I looked back, the pattern was there that I had fainted so I wouldn't have to take them.

## Pat's husband, Weldon, continues her story:

When I met her, she had her master's degree. She was doing talks all over the country—people were calling her for advice or consultation. I said, "Why don't you get your doctorate degree?" It took years of encouraging her. Finally, during one of our discussions, I said, "Look, you need the piece of paper. You are not likely to learn much of anything, but you need the piece of paper." Bless her heart, she finally consented and agreed to go back and work on her doctorate. Because she worked full time, she went to cluster sessions. The first night of the first session she went to, I got this phone call, and here Pat was basically hysterical crying, very despondent. She'd just found out they were going to give her a test, and she knew she couldn't pass out! It took hours talking long distance to convince her that that instructor was not going to ask her a question she could not answer. At that time if I had said, "You poor baby, why don't you come on home?" believe me, she would have come home in a heartbeat. But after talking to her several times and getting a horrendous phone bill that first month, she did go ahead and finish the class, and she did continue on and get her doctorate degree.

Some students with LD/ADHD become too frightened to take risks; when this occurs, their ability to benefit fully from continuing their education is significantly compromised. Glenn describes the terror he experienced as he approached a new learning opportunity after years of failure in elementary and secondary school classrooms:

This transition into college was one of extreme fear, because all of a sudden I was in this environment again where I had failed so dramatically before. There is no way that I can explain to you how fearful it was for me to even go near an educational setting. When I was school phobic, I literally had nightmares. I lived in Seattle for years and never went on the university campus, not once. I just refused to go anywhere on the university campus. The first time I went into the community college setting after I was diagnosed, I was [unbelievably] scared.

### Loneliness

Loneliness due to isolation is an important concern in the postsecondary life of individuals with LD/ADHD. Many students feel isolated as they struggle with academics beside classmates who have no sense of the challenges they regularly face. One student who found this true within her honors program in undergraduate school reports that her isolation was intensified due to self-imposed regimentation that was, and still is, her coping mechanism. Thus, even though she generally fares well academically, she remains socially isolated from her fellow students.

### FATIGUE

One final, ongoing issue that is worthy of mention for many students with LD/ADHD is the problem of fatigue. The extra effort required to cope with the continual social and academic demands of schooling can be chronically exhausting.

## STRATEGIES FOR ACHIEVING SUCCESS IN POSTSECONDARY ENVIRONMENTS

A great number of strategies for success in postsecondary learning are available for adults with LD/ADHD.

### CAREFULLY SELECTING A SCHOOL

First students should give careful consideration to school selection for their postsecondary studies, taking time to research and identify learning opportunities that will best fit their intellectual aptitude, interests, academic and social needs, and learning styles. Betty sought such a match when she applied for graduate school to follow her dream of becoming a social worker. She was admitted to the University of Maryland, but explains:

> I didn't fit the mold in social work. I was more of a community organizer than a clinician. I felt social work was a whole profession, that in order to be a clinician, you had to change the lives of people and systems. The University of Maryland and I had a different approach.
>
> I ultimately got thrown out because they said I [supposedly] had no aptitude for social work. At that point, I had a 3.8 [grade point average]. I can't spell, and I'm not sure what to do with periods, but they had overlooked a lot of that because the content of my writing was so good and because what I said in class was so cogent. I got a lot of A's, and the professors were enthusiastic about my being a social worker because of my creativity. [But] they saw [my tendency to be wired] as being inappropriate for a social worker. When I failed my first year of field placement, they had a hearing and threw me out—said I was not together enough, that I was pretty well nuts and should never consider social work as a profession. I went back [to work] full time. It was devastating.

Later she learned about a graduate program at the University of Pennsylvania that seemed a better match for her holistic philosophy of social work. She wrote the application, explaining her struggles as a person with learning disabilities and her history at the University of Maryland. In her own unique way, she was very straightforward during her admissions interview:

> I met with the Dean of Admissions who asked, "Why did you get thrown out of the University of Maryland?" I said I was a smart-ass, and I talked too much, and she kind of fell out of her chair. She said, "Well, you're honest. We accept you in the University of Pennsylvania on the basis that you'll keep your mouth shut and read books." I said, "You're giving me conditions I can't meet—if you want to accept me, you're going to have to accept the facts that, one, I don't read books and, two, I will never keep my mouth shut." She doubled over with laughter and said, "You've been accepted at the

University of Pennsylvania, and you are coming here. We're the only people that will put up with the likes of you."

Betty reported in our interview that she had no idea ahead of time that the University of Pennsylvania was an Ivy League school and left for Philadelphia the following September, "scared out of my gourd, thinking, 'I've already been thrown out of a program once. What's going to happen this time?'" However, once she was there, she knew she had found a school that fit both her temperament and style:

> Penn was the most incredible experience. The professors knew who we were. They knew exactly what I had done. They accepted my strengths and my weaknesses. They intuitively could teach us in a way we could learn. Penn had never asked for a formal diagnosis or documentation, yet [professors] accommodated all over the place. They were more looking at what I could do and what I had done and what they wanted me to do. I was a good writer, and they accommodated for spelling. They would overlook some things, but the content was always so good, and I got basically A's at Penn. I had phenomenal people there. I did extremely well in all my classes, and they had decided that I was gifted in social work.

For each institution being considered, students should investigate several things.

### Available Services

Beyond considering the school's reputation for its academic offerings, prospective students should research how the Disabled Student Services (DSS) Office works and the services it provides. There is no universal model of service delivery, and students at any one institution may find themselves accessing a relatively narrow range of services and accommodations or a broader-based LD program that provides a comprehensive array of support options.

Given appropriate documentation, schools typically provide auxiliary aids, such as taped textbooks, tape recorders, readers, and sometimes note-takers. Accommodations such as extended time on exams or distraction-free test-taking rooms must be available as well. Many schools provide an academic skills center that helps students improve study skills. Campuses with comprehensive support programs provide more in-depth services for students. Coordinated by full-time personnel with expertise in LD and ADHD, these programs use a diagnostic–prescriptive approach, providing individualized services, such as subject–area tutoring and developmental courses in math, writing, social skills and/or self-advocacy training (Brinckerhoff, Shaw, & McGuire, 1993).

### Policies Regarding Course Requirements

Prospective students should also investigate the school's policies, particularly its flexibility with regard to course requirements. Those seeking a college degree should inquire about the institution's stand on course substitutions for math or foreign language, particularly if either has been an academic obstacle during the high school years. Some colleges are willing to substitute culturally oriented courses, anthropology, or sign language for foreign language and logic, philosophy, or computer science courses for math (National Joint Committee on Learning Disabilities, 1998). Terry describes her own circumstances:

> I needed to go to a college that did not have a language requirement because I was not able to really ever accomplish French. I took French for 3 years in high school. I did not move out of the first level. Eventually the teacher passed me out of it. This is the God's honest truth—I made a Quiche Lorraine, stood up in front of the class, and named the ingredients for my final. It was just awful! I just wasn't capable of it. At Emerson College in Boston, there was no language requirement. I was interested in acting, and it just seemed like it was kind of a loose place that kind of accepted people to do their own thing. I was very interested in psychodrama.

### Teaching Styles

Programs and professors differ in their method of information delivery and in their expectations for students' output. Although a traditional lecture format continues to be popular, there are increasing opportunities for students to take a more active role in their learning. Terry benefited from one such opportunity. Years after being accepted to and transferring from Emerson College, she found herself again seeking a good educational match, an institution where she could embark upon master's-level studies and take advantage of her particular strengths. After conducting extensive research, she discovered a program that was a good fit. She enrolled, flourished, and was finally able to develop confidence in her ability to succeed in an academic environment:

> It took me 15 years to go back to graduate school, and I think that the reason that I did was twofold. First of all, I was comfortable with the computer. But also, I found a graduate program where I thought I could really present material in the way that I do well. This was Lesley College's Weekend Program in Creative Arts and Learning. It was so interesting for me to be in this room, basically with the same 28 people, for 2 years. Not only was I on an even footing, but I actually felt that I was superior to people in this classroom in that there were a lot of people that were taking it because they didn't see themselves as creative, and they wanted to add creativity to their repertoire. They had a lot of trouble letting go of the written word as the way they presented their output of their thinking, and for me, that was sort of the way I could do it. This was my place! Also, graduate school didn't have any tests. There were times that I did have to write papers to show my knowledge, but a lot of it was more my own thoughts with some kinds of references to books and reading and things like that. That wasn't a problem.

Nancie, too, found an academic environment that was the right match for her particular learning style:

> I went to Evergreen State College, which is a nontraditional state college, one of the top 10 in the nation. It's located in Olympia, and it runs a night school to meet the needs of a variety of nontraditional students. Classes meet three times a week in the late afternoon to early evening. The professors teach as a program faculty. You don't go to Class A, Class B, Class C—everything's integrated. Their process allows you to apply everything that you learned in two methods: one, in what they called "seminary," which is small-group discussion with your peers; and the other is in practical application. As I grew in my educational experience, I started to understand that people learn differently and that I learned differently. I was in my mid-twenties. My undergrad degree is in education and administration. The purpose of that direction was that I absolutely wanted to change education [policy]. I hated

my educational experience, so I was going to be a superintendent, and I was going to change the world.

### Academic Approach

When trying to match with the school that best meets their needs, students should also consider their learning style and how it will mesh with the institution's offerings. For example, it is imprudent for the person who flourishes in small discussion-oriented classes, where the professor provides individual attention, to apply to schools where lecture-style classes with 500 students are the norm. Further, students who have trouble with spatial concepts are wise to recognize the potential for problems in finding their way around very large universities and should choose schools that have smaller, more navigable campuses.

## BECOMING INFORMED OF RIGHTS AND RESPONSIBILITIES

Students with LD/ADHD must study their rights and responsibilities under the ADA and Section 504 and learn how to access support services on their campus. In order to take advantage of those services, individuals with LD/ADHD must disclose their disability to appropriate school personnel. However, students have the right to decide whether to do so, and some do choose to forego special services. Reluctant to divulge their problems for fear of a variety of negative reactions, they are determined to start college with a "clean slate."

Nina shares this concern, fearing that faculty will think she is using her disability as an excuse if she discloses her LD. She recalls a distressing experience when she disclosed her LD/ADHD to a college admissions officer:

> When I did talk to one college official about my learning disability, I was worried about the math stuff. There was a woman in admissions there who said, "Well, can you follow a recipe? If you can follow a recipe, you can do even more. That's algebra!" and kind of brushed off my concern and my fear and was very glib about it. I sat there thinking, "What an ass!" I didn't even think that had anything to do with me. It just makes me think that she's a jerk. In some ways, though, that's colored my actions. I don't want to

be brushed off. I don't want to go in and always feel like I'm making excuses for myself. I go back to that shame thing, being embarrassed about having these problems or having people feel like it's hogwash.

Nina explains that she wants very much to do the work and be successful, but that she would like to be able to confer with faculty to avoid falling into her old pattern of not finishing what she sets out to do.

Nancie managed to skirt the need to disclose to her graduate school professors. When she decided she was ready to pursue a master's degree, she interviewed a variety of schools and chose the one that would allow her to apply all of her knowledge to people with disabilities within business. She did not want special attention or any special notoriety in the rather traditional graduate school program in which she eventually enrolled; thus, she chose not to disclose her disability at all and never asked for any accommodations. As she explains, "I know people who have disabilities that go there who have disclosed, and it hasn't been easy for them."

Students should keep in mind, however, that they cannot expect to benefit from their civil rights protection under Section 504 or the ADA unless they do disclose and provide appropriate documentation of their disability. Because they have the same responsibility and obligation as any student to meet and maintain the institution's academic and technical standards, should they choose not to disclose and then do poorly on a test, there is very little that can be done at that point by support personnel to access additional time or other accommodations.

Those who choose to take advantage of support services on campus should keep in mind a number of responsibilities and rights that they have. They have the responsibility to identify themselves in a timely fashion as needing accommodations; to request specific services; and to provide documentation of how their disability affects their learning. They have the right to an equal opportunity to learn; to educational services without discrimination; to evaluation based on their abilities rather than on their disabilities for appropriate placement; to receive help both in class and during tests; to modifications or auxiliary aids, if needed; and to appeal the institution's decisions concerning accommodations (Andresen, 1997, p. 10).

## Accommodations

Students should become informed about the range of accommodations for which they may qualify and should be aware that the earlier in the semester that they request accommodations, the more likely it is that instructors will be flexible. Becoming knowledgeable about accommodations made a significant difference for Andre, who, after many years of grappling with what was for him an unnamed problem, was diagnosed at age 33. As he continues his studies, he is able to benefit from a variety of accommodations:

> I'm still in college—I have been off and on. I skipped around. I attended Morris Brown College, Tennessee State University, University of South Carolina. I realized that I had a problem but I couldn't pinpoint it. I thought the answer was to work harder. Well, that wasn't the answer. I finally found out I was LD and ADHD. I instantly set myself up with a counselor at the college who could set me up with tutors to help with any other problem in class or in school. Math is still a problem, but I have accommodations now to help me to get over some of those obstacles. I have extra time on math tests and things like that. The tests could be taken in isolation where you don't have a distraction, because we get distracted most of the time. If I request, I could get a certified note taker in class, things of that nature.

As Andre discovered, if a student has a need for reasonable accommodations during testing and if there is documentation supporting this need, a variety of accommodations may be arranged and provided on an individual basis, depending on the nature and severity of the disability.

*Time*    One of the more commonly requested accommodations is extended time tests (ETT), generally time and a half of the period allotted to other class members, but more if needed. Students may request rest breaks between test sessions or more than one test day for long exams or when multiple exams are scheduled on the same day. Some students request an early start when they know they will need extra time, finding it less awkward than finishing late.

*Space*    Many find it beneficial to be tested in a separate, distraction-free space. This accommodation is particularly important for those with ADHD in addition to LD. If such space is unavailable, the student may use other sound-suppression devices, such as headphones or earplugs.

*Technology*   Students should check whether technology can be made available for test taking. Word processors or calculators may be appropriate, depending on the knowledge being tested.

*Alternative Test Format*   Students may be able to request a test in an alternative format. For example, if their documentation supports such an accommodation, they may ask for an objective test rather than an essay exam.

*Comprehension Checks*   Students can request the right to clarify or rephrase exam questions as a comprehension check prior to initiating their response.

*Readers*   Some students perform best with readers to help them decipher the questions on exams.

*Alternative Grading*   Students may request that instructors give them a split grade, one for content and one for mechanics, with the understanding that the mechanics errors will be corrected outside of class and resubmitted for a revised grade (Garnett & LaPorta, 1991).

When Lilia is ready to take the set of five GED tests, she may take advantage of several accommodations, depending on her need and documentation of her disability. Possible accommodations include a taped edition of the GED tests with a printed reference copy and double time allowance; a large-print test edition with extended time; use of a scribe or a calculator; frequent breaks with or without extended time; or a private testing room (Latham & Latham, 1998).

Unfortunately, accommodations cannot be made for every aspect of the disability. Thus, limitations associated with LD/ADHD can restrict the direction some students with these disabilities might take. Glenn sadly reports that this was true in his case:

I had actual dreams of one day being a college professor in history. That is my true and wonderful love, history. I am quite a good historian and understand world history. The thing is that one of the prerequisites for getting a Ph.D. in history is learning three languages, because one of the essential elements of the job of being an historian is doing original-language research. I can't learn foreign language. I argued that they provide interpreters as an accommodation, and then I could handle it. I thought I could argue that point, but I lost. Thus, my LD has limited my capacity to fulfill my dream.

## PLANNING BEFORE THE SEMESTER BEGINS

Even before the beginning of classes, several steps can be taken that can result in a less challenging semester.

### Pre-registration

Students who have disclosed their LD/ADHD should take advantage of any opportunities to pre-register for classes. Some schools offer students with disabilities the option of priority registration, which allows a greater degree of planning in course selection and reduces the stress that is generally inherent in the registration process. Whenever possible, students should identify the time of day when they are able to work most efficiently and strategically plan their course meeting and study schedule prior to registration. Those who study best late at night should look for late sections of their courses and avoid registering for early morning classes, if possible. Those who are sharpest in the morning should make a practice of turning in at a reasonable hour of the evening to ensure that they will be fresh for their early start.

It is very helpful, when possible, to schedule breaks in between courses to create an opportunity to rest or regroup between classes. Even in the 1950s, long before her LD was diagnosed, Pat intuitively knew it would be beneficial for her to space her courses:

> I would schedule a course, and then I would make sure I had an hour free afterwards. I would take my notes and the gibberish that I would write, and I would immediately go to the library and sit down with a book and copy it out so I could remember it, because I couldn't take notes legibly enough to even go back and read. I had to have that extra time.

Special registration sets the stage for students to obtain taped texts ahead of time. Some schools also allow late withdrawal from courses without penalty, another advantageous policy for students who may have difficulty quickly determining their ability to meet the workload.

### Careful Selection of Courses

When enrolling each semester, students with LD/ADHD need to plan their course selection carefully. When Betty was entering college in the 1960s, she chose her courses, as well as her major, based largely on what she could not do:

> I went to my guidance counselor when I was 15. I was failing out of high school at that time, but I told her I wanted to go to college because I recognized that I couldn't make it in the traditional women's careers of the 1950s and 1960s—secretary, nurse, a clerk of some kind, or cashier. I couldn't be a cashier because I couldn't do math. I couldn't be a clerk because I couldn't spell or write. I told her I had to get beyond what I couldn't do, that you either go to college or become a custodian, and I knew I was too bright to be a custodian. So, this guidance counselor, my mother and my family looked all over for any college in the country that would accept me, and I got accepted in the local state university, Northern Illinois University in Dekalb, by a fluke of Illinois State law, even though I had a D average and was in only the 35th percentile. I went for the bachelor's degree in Education because I figured I could pass education courses where I would not have to pass a language. But there was something inside of me that intuitively said social work was what I wanted to do.

Since the early 1990s, the process of advisement regarding course selection has become more refined. Today, in order to plan a course of studies that both meets the school's requirements and matches the individual's interests, students with LD/ADHD are encouraged to seek the advice of someone who understands the potential impact of their particular learning style in academic settings. Most often, the best advisors are DSS staff members who can direct students toward appropriate courses and away from professors who have a negative attitude about providing accommodations. Terry describes one such professor:

> I did take a graduate course, maybe 5 or 6 years out of college. I wanted to give the level of work that I thought I was capable of. I remember going up to the teacher and asking if it would it be okay if I did all the work for this final project but presented it orally

because it was really hard for me to get my thoughts down in a written way that reflected my knowledge. She said no. So I thought, "Oh, jeez, this is bad. I'm not going to school unless every bit of this is 100% mine. There's just no point." In the end, I did do the paper, and I really worked hard. I spent an entire semester on it, a really ridiculous amount of time. A friend of mine typed it for me, but other than that, it was really 100% mine.

Further, DSS staff are prepared to help students understand policies and procedures relating to reduced course load; course waivers and substitutions; and special opportunities available at some schools, such as auditing courses before taking them for credit or concurrently taking two sections of the same course for the benefit of double exposure to the material.

Students find they can achieve the success that previously seemed unattainable when they carefully strategize and choose courses that call upon their learning strengths. Jule outlines the broad-based strategy that served her well in college:

The first thing I did when I hit the University of Texas was I identified the math, English, and chemistry departments because I was going be taking those classes, and I knew that I was going to have trouble. I also figured out how to get out of taking a foreign language, both for undergrad and graduate school. Then, as soon as I started my classes, I immediately tried to find a teaching assistant that would work with me when I ran into trouble. Because we had hundreds of kids in the classes, I also tried to sit in the front of the class so the professor would know who I was.

I'd try to find the professors whose notes on a previous test I thought would be in the sorority or where somebody else I knew really well was taking the class, and I would get their notes. The problem was that when I took notes, I learned my notes cold and they were inaccurate. I would also go and talk teachers into giving me a better grade—I usually could get them to raise it at least half a letter—because I could talk them around. If I said that Prince Charles was the Queen of England, I could explain why he was the Queen of England and by the time I was through, depending on the professor, they would give me some credit because it made such logical sense.

Selecting courses that tap into strengths is desirable when possible. Thus, a student with strong oral language skills may opt for a course on public speaking. Nonnie recalls, "I decided to take three art courses and one academic. So if I got an A and B in the art work but a D in the academics, with my personality they would probably pass me."

Terry found that, with careful course planning during her time at Emerson College, it was unnecessary for her to resort to the cheating she had felt was necessary in order to survive her high school years. As she explains, college focused less on rote learning and more on concepts:

> The college I went to was very interdisciplinary, and it suited me to a tee. That was very lucky. One course I took was oral interpretation, where you had to read things and then you had to actually act them out, play all the parts. It had to do with the way you held your body and the way you could use your voice. That was something that I was very comfortable with. What also helped me a lot was that much of my course work was hands-on.

Conversely, Rich unfortunately found that lack of careful course planning could prove very costly, both in terms of time and tuition:

> Part of my issues came back to bite me later on. As I was going to graduate school for my Ph.D., I more or less defined my own program so that I was taking courses from the medical school, clinical psychology, special education and education, and I didn't necessarily focus on certification. It came back to haunt me when I left the area and moved to Boston as the director of a school and didn't have my administrative certification. I ended up having to go back to school and, as a consequence, I have an equivalent of another whole doctorate in administration.

### Meeting with Professors

Many students find it helpful to meet with their professors prior to the first class meeting to jot down their office hours for easy reference when help is needed and to preview the syllabus and reading list. This gives them a chance to gain a head start on their studies, to plan their use of study time, and to develop a sense of the degree to which the professor seems sympathetic and flexible.

Those instructors who do seem flexible may welcome self-advocacy and may be more amenable to special arrangements, such as permitting a hyperactive student to sit by the classroom door so he or she may leave class and walk around for a few minutes every 45 minutes or so.

## COPING DURING THE SEMESTER

Several strategies are available to students with LD/ADHD for use during the semester.

### Self-Advocacy

Students with LD/ADHD will be more successful if they learn to become staunch self-advocates both prior to and during the semester. Although Betty attended college in 1964, years before she had been diagnosed and well before there was any widespread knowledge about LD, she instinctively knew that she should convey her needs to her professors:

> My first semester in college, in 1964, I nearly failed. That year I began to ask for reasonable accommodations for my handicapping conditions, although, of course, we didn't really call them "reasonable accommodations" back then. I went to every teacher the second semester of my freshman year and said, "I have a neurological disorder. I don't know what the name of it is, but please look at what I can do, not at what I can't do." I did manage to get off academic probation.

Betty's decision to ask for what she needed made an enormous difference in her performance and, ultimately, helped her turn a critical academic corner. Now, some 30 years later, the need for self-advocacy is as strong as ever. This is particularly true when students graduate from high school. Throughout 12 years of elementary and secondary schooling, the responsibility for advocating to meet the needs of students with LD/ADHD lies with teachers and parents. After graduation, however, the responsibility falls on the individual students themselves.

In order to self-advocate most effectively, students with LD/ADHD must understand how they process information and the strategies that work best for them and must develop the social skills to be able to communicate their learning style and needs to others. DSS staff can provide needed support as students develop self-understanding and self-advocacy skills.

### Maintenance of a Master Calendar

Students who find time management a challenge will benefit from maintaining a master calendar. Recording all obligations, academic and otherwise, on one master calendar, and color-coding items according to areas of life can be enormously helpful. For example, a student may record academic assignments and exam dates in blue; note deadlines for bills to be paid in red; list planned times for completing household chores, such as laundry and food shopping, in green; and use purple to note any appointments.

Blocking in planned study times along with class times and other obligations on a weekly calendar allows students to be more organized by providing a helpful visual sense of their weekly obligations and the time each requires. Here again, color coding can be helpful, with one color for classes, another for study time, and a third for free time available for leisure activities.

### Auxiliary Aids and Technology

Students should also know about available allied services that can supplement services offered by the university. Recording for the Blind and Dyslexic (RFB & D), the National Library Service for the Blind and Physically Handicapped (NLS), and other services provide books and magazines on tape. Thousands of students each year are able to make use of the services offered by these organizations. Some find tracking the printed text while listening to the words being read to be an effective multisensory approach. Nonnie considers taped texts to have been a lifesaver when she went off to Adelphi University unsure of how she could achieve her goal of becoming a social worker to help others with LD:

> I met the Dean. . . . I said, "I want to go to your school, but I don't think I could make it." I explained to him that I couldn't pass the work. He told me that maybe I could if I listened to all the books from the Recording for the Blind. I had never heard of that. To learn, I have to hear the written word, and that institution single-handedly got me through school because for the next 5 years, I was plugged in.

Many students find technology a valuable support. Low-tech options include carbonless note paper, Post-its, and highlighters.

Tape recorders can be highly beneficial. Many students find it helpful to tape record their classes and listen to them again while they do a variety of activities, ranging from cooking to driving to taking their daily run. Although it is time consuming to listen to an entire lecture a second time, there are students who find the tapes a worthwhile learning tool that can be used in a variety of more efficient ways. For example, some find it helpful to take notes or to obtain a copy of the professor's outline and mark in the margin the number on the tape counter where important points have been raised; this allows them to fast forward past minor material and to avoid listening to the entire lecture again. Others benefit from listening to the entire tape as soon as possible after the end of a class, rewriting any notes that were taken and highlighting key concepts.

Some students with strong auditory memory find it helpful to listen to the tape before ever reading the assigned material, as this helps earmark important points to note from the text. Nancie describes how this worked for her: "I listened to the professor and lectures first. I tried to take everything that they talked about, and then I went back and skimmed the text and applied it to structured content." Others find it helpful to read the text both before and after listening to a lecture. Students often find tape recorders to be a writing aid as well; dictating their ideas into a tape recorder before embarking on a writing project helps them organize their thoughts.

Another technological aid is the calculator. The model with a large keypad and enlarged number buttons is particularly helpful to individuals with fine motor difficulties. Talking calculators that vocalize data and calculations through speech synthesis are valuable tools as well, as they help reduce keypad errors among students who have strong mathematical ability but who struggle with the sequence of the digits within the problem they are trying to solve.

Other "talking systems" are available for those who have literacy issues. The Kurzweil Reader and other optical character recognition (OCR) systems can be very valuable for the weak reader, as they scan and read type and turn it into synthetic speech.

Assistive listening FM devices can be enormously helpful to students who are distractible or who have auditory figure–ground problems. The professor wears a speaker, and the student wears a headphone; this arrangement closes out competing sounds and allows the student to directly hear the lecture.

A computer can be an invaluable tool; it offers spell-check, a dictionary, grammar check, and a thesaurus as resources available at the click of a mouse. Christopher Lee wrote, "Before learning to use a computer, I saw writing as . . . simply a horizontal spelling test. The computer helped me to discover that there was more to writing than just spelling" (Lee & Jackson, 1992, p. 23). Glenn reports that his life, too, was changed when he discovered the computer's potential as an aid. After so many years of failure with the written word, he at last discovered his promise as a writer:

> More and more tools came into my life, and the tools helped me become more and more functional. The primary tool that came into my life was the computer. The computer was a tremendous tool that enabled me to reenter the world of writing for the first time since I became dysfunctional when I fell behind my peers in writing at age 4, 5, 6, or 7. For the first time, with the use of the computer, I had a shot at being an equal in the world of writing. I am severely dysgraphic. When I am typing just on a keyboard, I still do a tremendous amount of reversals, so with the normal electric typewriter I would end up using more correction fluid than regular ink because I was constantly letter-reversing, the words were out of sequence, and all that kind of stuff. But with the computer you have it all in front of you—you can have spell-check, you can even have toggle switches that reverse letters [back] when you reverse them. You can have all kinds of support, and then you don't print it until you're ready. You can get your thought out in some fashion and go back and revise it through the use of a computer.

Laptop computers and AlphaSmart keyboards can be very helpful for completing in-class notetaking, assignments, or tests. There are a great number of software programs that are available to assist students with LD/ADHD. For example, those who have difficulty organizing their thoughts can access one of several available brainstorming and outlining programs. The writer "dumps" information; then the software takes the unstructured information and helps the writer organize it and work through the process of revision.

Additional assistive technology for the computer is available as well. For example, those with a visual processing disorder may benefit from enlarged cursor control panels or talking large-print browsers that help navigate the Internet.

### Study Techniques

There are several study techniques that students with LD/ADHD may find useful.

*Attending Classes*   It may seem obvious but it is particularly important for students with LD to attend classes so that they can benefit from visual aids and participate in discussions. Many find that by attending all classes and sitting in front, they communicate their seriousness about learning to the professor. In addition, professors tend to be more accommodating when they are familiar with a student (Vogel, 1997).

*Incorporating Structure*   Students should incorporate structure whenever possible. Rich attended a seminary, the ultimate structured academic setting. Even after leaving, its structure helped him move forward in his academic pursuits:

> From an academic perspective, the thing that really helped me was being in the structure that I was in. It was the same routine on a daily basis—set times for study hall, etc. Everybody was doing the same thing at the same time, small classes. Academically, all of those things helped. I was there about 6 months, and I left. We were under the vows of poverty, chastity, and obedience. Poverty and obedience I was used to, but chastity was killing me. I grew out of needing that type of system. By that time, I had my own schedule for when I was studying and things like that. I just fell into the format that I had been in while I was in the structure.

Many students find that they benefit from establishing regimens that facilitate learning. Some establish a study plan for each course they take. Others find general structure around studying to be helpful. For example, one person reports:

> I've learned to always leave my desk set up. I clean up my things from one study session so the desk will be ready for my next go-around with the books. That way I don't get aggravated at having to search for pens or calculators when I sit down to do my assignments.

Students who become overwhelmed by complex, long-term assignments often find it helpful to restructure by breaking them down into a series of less daunting goals, working backward from the due date, developing a series of short-term goals and deadlines. Some professors allow students to write and pass in papers in stages (Quinn, 1994).

*Planning Set Study Periods*    Some find it helpful to study in 1- to 2-hour increments with breaks and rewards for progress made. One student explains her strategy:

> I like to study for chunks of time. So I'll tell myself, "Okay, it's 6:30. At 8:30 I'll break to watch a certain TV show for a half hour." Or I'll plan it by the task and think, "I've got 50 pages I have to read. When I'm done, I can call my boyfriend."

*Minimizing Distractions*    It is critical that students establish a good study environment, beginning with a distraction-free workspace. Some students find it impossible to achieve this in a dormitory setting but find campus hideaways that provide the quiet they need. Dale Brown (1981), for example, found that empty classrooms offered the quietest place on campus after hours, and she would often study there well into the night. Many campuses now offer "quiet dorms," which may be the best option for students who are distractible.

*Taking Medication When Appropriate*    Students with ADHD may wish to consider taking medications if attentional deficits interfere with their studying. Betty recalls that back in the 1960s:

> Once my doctor had diagnosed me with a neurological dysfunction, she put me on a heavy-duty tranquilizer. I would take it 2 hours before a major exam. I would take it to kind of work with [what I later learned to be] the ADHD and the LD symptoms. I found that it would help lower the stress, and that by lowering the stress I could do a little bit better. I only used it for testing.

Since those early years, doctors have learned a great deal about medications that can help to control symptoms of ADHD (see Chapter 2).

*Focusing on One Course at a Time*    Many students find that they are able to focus particularly well when they complete the assignments from only one course at a time. This strategy helped Jule handle a very stressful overload during her college years:

> I totally compensate, which was hard when I had to handle four or five classes. Fifteen hours was a natural, normal load in college, and when I was doing real well, one time I took 21 hours. I started out in college with Ds and Cs and then made straight As. Handling all those classes, it was much better to focus on one course, get that taken care of, and go to the next class because [otherwise] things get mixed up.

*Forming Study Groups*    Students often find it helpful to form study groups. They take fewer notes during class but gather shortly after it is over to discuss the material with others in their group. They may be able to study from old tests or practice exams made available by some professors as study tools. Many also benefit from becoming involved in support groups for students with LD/ADHD, where members share not only study strategies, but also information about instructors whose approach to teaching may match their learning style.

*Reading Aloud*    There are a variety of ways students may approach their texts. Some students find reading aloud helps them understand written text; hearing the words that they are reading provides another channel for processing the material at hand. Many find it beneficial to preview reading selections by reviewing the first sentence of each paragraph and the summary sections prior to embarking on the full text. People also find completing reading assignments prior to class helps them focus on the key points in the lecture. Patricia Quinn recommended that students read the chapter summary prior to reading each chapter in a text:

> If you read through all the bold print, all the highlighted information and outlines, then you'll understand what is going on. In addition, read any questions in the back of the book or chapter first, then read just to answer these questions. This will give you a good idea of the basic points. You can then skim through and you will have all the facts that you're going to need. (1994, p. 48)

Even the text on tests can be scanned as a first step when taking exams. Previewing test items can be helpful. Susan Vogel (1997) suggested that students underline key words that describe the task (e.g., "compare," "summarize"), then begin with the easiest questions first, returning to more difficult items with any remaining time.

*Highlighting Text* For many students, color-coded underlining or highlighted notes provide extra visual reinforcement of the material covered. Some find it useful to copy over their class notes, finding the process of writing helps them understand and memorize the material.

*"Stash and Dump"* Some students find that when they are being tested for memorization of a great number of dates, names and other terms, it helps to jot them all down early in the exam so they will be readily available for use when needed. Nancie made efficient use of this and a variety of other strategies to overcome the biggest academic hurdle of her college experience:

> My [graduate] program required an 8-hour written comprehensive examination, which I was petrified over. I don't catch the important details, the ones that will kind of come up and slap you in the face, so I enlisted the aid of a study partner, someone who had already taken the comprehensives. I did some pretty heavy studying. I had enough knowledge about how I learn and enough knowledge about strategies for people with learning disabilities and attention disorders that I did three major things that I think were critical to my success. One was that I wrote everything that I needed out on notecards. I know lots of people do that, but I had never thought about doing that. I took major areas and just focused on them. The second thing was that I constantly reviewed those note cards in an auditory fashion. I just talked to myself about them all the time, out loud. I would be found walking around saying, "Okay, this is the theory, and why does this theory apply, and how can I apply it?" One piece of advice this guy I know gave me was that, no matter what the questions are, just write the answer as if it was in your own shop, so to speak, meaning in your own work. No matter what, even if you think you can't answer the question, put yourself in that scenario and write related to that scenario. So, I did that. The last thing I did was believe that I would not fail. I truly, truly believed that I would not fail, that people don't fail. I really guess I kind of threw away the failure syndrome at that point.

I'll never forget standing around waiting for the doors to be unlocked on that Saturday morning. I hadn't had very much sleep. I watched people wringing their hands, all nervous and everything, but I just knew that, no matter what, I could do this. I knew that doing it on a computer would be better, but I didn't ask for that. I did ask to make sure that they were going to give us lined paper, because I knew I couldn't write if I didn't have lined paper. The strategy when I went in was really funny. I went in and didn't ever open the envelope for the first hour and a half. I dumped everything that I had memorized off the cards onto the scratch paper, and only then did I start to answer the questions. My friend, a studying person, had also told me to make sure that I divided my time equally and that halfway through my time, I look at where I was and what my final points were and then start writing even if I hadn't finished what I really wanted to say.

*Learning from Mistakes*    Students benefit greatly from reviewing all returned work and analyzing errors. Making appointments with faculty to review their comments can help students with this step.

### Asking Friends for Help

Friends can assist in a variety of ways. Terry found it particularly beneficial to turn to classmates to compensate for her difficulty with notetaking:

I used a lot of strategies, which mainly amounted to getting a lot of stuff from other people. I'm wonderful at finding people who are good at doing things, who could help me. I was not and still am really not able to listen and write at the same time. That was always very difficult for me, so I would have to use notes from somebody else. I mean, I just didn't have notes! I kind of integrate stuff into what I already know, and then it's either a part of me or it's not.

Friends and others are often willing to be available to provide important proofreading services. Pat attributes much of her success in her doctoral program to the support of her husband who, "bless his heart, read every paper that I wrote for my doctorate and helped me correct all those things that spell-check won't correct. He is half of my doctorate."

Sensitive to the burden she might be placing on others and "so no one would get impatient with me," Dale Brown (1981, p. 2) considered it wise to approach many different people for bits of help instead of leaning too heavily on a single individual.

### Using a Private Tutor

Some students with LD/ADHD may wish to consider hiring a tutor. If DSS is unable to provide adequate support, and informal supports are too limited, students may wish to turn to private tutoring. It is crucial, however, to find a tutor who is committed to assessing each individual student's needs and who has the skills to meet them. Without these prerequisites, as Terry notes, one-to-one assistance is not always effective:

> I came home from college one summer and said, "You know, this is really bad. I'm going to be a school teacher, and I can't spell." So, I actually got a tutor to help me with the spelling, but all he did was have me write lists of words over and over again. It was stupid, really ridiculous, so I didn't continue.

### Perseverance

Perhaps the most important tip is to persevere. Determination carries students a long way in higher education. The many frustrations that arise in day-to-day learning are less likely to result in burnout if the student is resolute. Betty recalls that her own tenacity was nourished by her spirituality, "I had the tenacity to hang in. I'm a Catholic and went to Mass daily praying I would get through the next day. I think I prayed my way through 4 years of undergraduate school."

Pat attended college more than 40 years ago, at a time when there were no diagnostic tests and no acknowledgment of LD/ADHD. She recalls the encouragement of one professor who applauded her tenacity and urged her to continue determinedly moving ahead:

> I remember the person who made me feel like I was smart. He was a psychologist at the University of Arkansas. He would say, "You are here because you are smart. You figured out a way to get

here—you can figure out a way to learn. I don't know what is wrong with you, but you can figure out how to do it."

Most students who do persevere and stick with their studies despite the many challenges eventually reap the reward of graduation and experience tremendous satisfaction in this achievement. Allyssa describes how she felt when she completed her Learn and Earn Rehabilitation Program:

Graduation from Learn and Earn made me realize that I really want to go back to school. I'm in a space now that's so much better and healthier than when I was 18, and I really think that going back to school will be awesome for me. My mom's been saying that to me for years, "Any class you want to go to, I'll pay for it." That's awesome. I'm going to be getting out of my new job at 3:30 every day. I'll have enough money to pay the bills because I'm going to get a roommate. And I'm going to go back to school. I don't care if it's one class to start. I'm gonna take that one class, and I can't wait. I might need some help in comprehending things, 'cause that's sometimes where I get a little baffled. I have to really pray about that because as soon as I get stuck on a word or get frustrated, I quit. You know, "I missed a word? All right, the book is closed. Good-bye." I'm really working through that and saying, "You know what? It's okay that I don't understand the word. I'm going to ask for help. I'm not going to put the book down. I'm not going to give up on myself."

After regularly cutting classes and otherwise avoiding work in high school, which he considered "a prison," Glenn relished the validation of his ability when he succeeded in college:

College was a very good testing ground; I was in an environment that accepted and acknowledged my disabilities and would be willing to support me based on those disabilities. It allowed me to perform to the level I was really capable of by providing me the accommodations that allowed me to perform. It definitely allowed me to function and to shine. I ended up getting awards for the best research paper in the university—and I mean me, writing! Five years before I was misspelling my own name, and now I was getting academic awards for writing!

Dale Brown (1982) attributes far more than academic growth to her experience at Antioch College and appreciates that she made a wise match to an institution that was able to offer a full range of learning experiences both in and out of the classroom. She credits Antioch with teaching her how to work, how to learn, and how to be part of a community and reports that receiving her diploma was one of the proudest moments of her life.

Nonnie also was deeply moved by graduation, which she felt was the achievement of a lifetime. The benefit to her self-concept was immeasurable:

> The degree of master of social work was the most important thing of my life. Even though I was married and had a family, I felt that if I could get that piece of paper, I was worth something. The price was high because you are giving up being a better mother and a better wife. I only did about two or three courses a year, because you can't skip a page in a book, so I had to write down every single word, and it took me 5 years to go through the program. I think the greatest moment of my life (I really should say when I got married) was when I graduated.

## SUMMARY

For individuals with LD/ADHD who wish to continue learning during their adult years, there are a variety of options, ranging from literacy programs to vocational schools, from independent living training to both nondegree and degree-granting postsecondary offerings. Within any of these programs that receive federal financial assistance, students are protected from discrimination on the basis of their disability by two pivotal pieces of legislation, Section 504 of the Rehabilitation Act of 1973 and the Americans with Disabilities Act.

Although many students are successful in their pursuit of continued education, many find their learning is affected by the characteristics of LD/ADHD as well as by emotional issues, such as shame and fear of failure. In order to maximize their potential for success in college settings, students are urged to give careful consideration to school selection, taking into account the academic model, services offered, and policies. It is critical that students become informed of their rights and responsibilities under Section 504 and the ADA and familiarize themselves with the accommodations for which they may qualify. Students with LD/ADHD must also carefully consider whether they wish to disclose their disability to their professors, keeping in mind that they will not benefit from their civil rights protection unless they do disclose.

The potential for success is enhanced when students carefully select and plan ahead for courses, take advantage of special registration opportunities, keep organized through the use of a master calendar, use books on tape if necessary, use good study skills, call upon their resources for support, and remain determined.

# Work

Adults with LD/ADHD meet with varied levels of success in the work world, in fields ranging from law and politics to science and education to business and the trades. Several have won prestigious awards, such as the Nobel Prize. Nonetheless, many adults with LD/ADHD have experienced considerable stress in their work lives. Because they grew up at a time when LD was neither understood nor widely acknowledged, most went undiagnosed for decades and struggled without the accommodations that could have made success on the job more readily achievable.

Even with the passage of the Americans with Disabilities Act (ADA) in 1990, many individuals with LD/ADHD continued to suffer from being misunderstood and unappreciated. Betty Pike was one of those people. At the age of 25, Betty became actively involved in the women's movement and quickly emerged as a leader. After being appointed by her state governor to the Maryland Commission for Women and starting a coalition of 15 crisis shelters for battered women, she earned a master's degree in social work and was hired for a position at the State of Maryland Child Protective Services. Her story provides a poignant example of job discrimination, grievance, and vindication in the 1990s:

> [It] was 1990, the year the American with Disabilities Act went into effect, when I originally started working with the State of Maryland. I told them I had a learning disability and that I needed to have at least a typewriter, access to a computer, and for people

to understand that I get wired—they should just kind of wait it out—and that I needed accommodations in order to succeed. I pretty well got the accommodations when I worked at my first job, and I was doing well. A lot of people were coming to me for help.

Then I transferred to Charles County and, again, I included in my application that I had a learning disability, though it was undiagnosed. They never asked for the diagnosis—I'd just explained it in the initial interview. I had started [a] shelter . . . in that county, and the administration in social services had known me for 20 years. I said, "Look, I have a significant reading problem. How much reading is involved in this?" They said most of it was verbal, and I said, "Okay, and I have a memory problem, and you're going to have to understand that it takes a long time for me to remember things." I explained the learning disability very efficiently. "I know exactly how I learn and where my quirks are." And they said, "Well, there's no problem with accommodating. We accommodate anyway."

Well, there I was, [working] in a room of 10–15 people, and the hyper-stimulation! Getting used to a computer system for a lot of clerical-type intake done with protective services, doing the intricacies of the law and the intricacies of the legal system—it's a lot of detail work, and folks with LD and ADHD cannot do real well with details, especially right off the bat. It takes a long time to repattern. The supervisor said, "You're not doing well," and I said, "This is directly related to my learning disability. I'm asking for accommodations under [the] ADA." And she said, "Well, you know you're too old to be learning disabled. I've talked to a special education teacher, and you should have outgrown it. By your age you no longer have it, you've been cured of it. You're too intelligent to be learning disabled. You know you can do it if you try harder."

You know, these wonderful red blankets that you can wave in front of a bull? "You can do it if you try harder" is the classic one for learning disabilities and ADHD. I always tell people that it takes twice as much effort [for us] to do half as much work. She said, "You know, there's no reason you can't spell. Why are you taking so much time on the computer, and why do we have to give you editors? You're not really learning disabled—you're just using it as an excuse." And she tried to fire me. She gave me a performance evaluation that looked like a checklist for LD. It got very nasty, very, very unpleasant. I had joined the union, so every time she did something that was not very pleasant I said, "We need an impartial third party to evaluate the situation." Well, she didn't know [it, but] I was saying, "Hi, lady, I'm taking you to court."

She called my boss, who said, "I want to see your diagnosis." [The] ADA states that you do not have to have a diagnosis—it's [in force when you're even] presumed to have a disability. I said, "My case history clearly demonstrates it, but if you want a diagnosis, I'll go get a diagnosis. Within the 2 weeks, I'd gotten the diagnosis. In the meanwhile, I had submitted nine grievances and a request for transfer to another job. I interviewed with two people who knew me, who said, "Look, you're in trouble. We're going to bail you out. You're too gifted a social worker to lose."

I was in a position of being fired from my current position, and there were some problems about me being transferred. Charles County had to release me, so the Director of Personnel from my new position pulled some strings, and I got the transfer in May. My problems ended in December.

Meanwhile, I kept the nine grievances pending, because I wanted to expunge my record and exonerate myself. I had been suspended. So I kept my legal case pending with the support of my present employer. I did very, very well on the new position. I was away from details. The job was a much better fit. I was doing much more case management and social work. I was in a very supportive atmosphere with people who understood my learning disability and accommodated for it and were very supportive of the law case.

I went to court in October of 1993. It was an administrative law hearing. I called the union and asked for an attorney. They said, "Your legal skills are so good, you don't need an attorney—this is an administrative law hearing. If you lose in this, you can appeal and we'll give you an attorney at that time." Meanwhile, the psychologist finally had given me the diagnosis in writing, a psychological evaluation that supported what I had been saying, that I had been discriminated against for failure to provide accommodations to my handicapping condition, [my LD] . . . The psychologist had [also] diagnosed me with attention deficit disorder. I didn't know much about it at that point.

I went one-on-one with the judge, and I won all my grievances. My record was expunged; I was exonerated. I had been suspended without pay for 3 weeks—I got 3 weeks' back pay. I got an acknowledgment that I had, in fact, been discriminated against under the Americans with Disabilities Act. If you're suspended, it can adversely impact your social work license—when that record was expunged and my license came up for renewal, I could say effectively and honestly that I had never been suspended.

I had proven to the judge that my performance evaluation was very good with accommodations. On my first job, the job without accommodations, the performance evaluations were very poor. I convinced the judge that I had had difficulty in the interim because I had not had accommodations and that the supervisor had failed to comply under [the] ADA. I won.

It is not always apparent to an employer or to co-workers that an adult with LD/ADHD has any disability at all. This is true not only because LD is an invisible disability, but also because there is often considerable "scatter," or imbalance, in the abilities of any single individual with LD/ADHD. This variability can cause issues. For example, an all-too-common scenario occurs when an employee who has not chosen to disclose his or her LD/ADHD is assigned work tasks that call upon his or her strengths, making weaknesses less conspicuous. The supervisor then assigns responsibilities that extend beyond the employee's areas of strength, forcing him or her to struggle with higher expectations than can be met and leading to frustration, disappointment, and, sometimes, even job loss. This scenario reflects the conflict inherent in the wish to hide the disability and yet still be eligible for job advancement. More on this conflict will be discussed later in this chapter.

Jo Ann's story compellingly illustrates the enormous impact LD can have on an individual work history. As she reports, when she graduated from high school, "They said I wouldn't amount to a hill of beans." She lived at home, held entry-level jobs, such as baby-sitting and pet grooming. She did teach nursery school for 3 years, but reports "that turned out to be a fiasco for me because the classroom is a three-ringed circus" and it was too challenging for her to monitor several groups of children at once. She recalls that for a few years:

I wandered around from job to job to job. Finally I found a work-training job with the government that required no written test. That was my ticket into employment. I bounced from field to field. I was basically a mail clerk—didn't do too much typing, because I didn't have very good dexterity. I was slow, and I got cuts and rips all the time. All this time I was never getting promotions or making enough money to be able to live on my own, and so I was still at home.

She worked for a time at an Air Force base. After a long period without promotion, she mustered the courage to apply for a higher position. She recalls:

The job required three things: One, standing at the counter and they'd say, "I'd like such-and-such forms, and where do I take the test?" Well, that's a piece of cake for me. Once you know where the stockroom is and where the things are on the shelf, you just go back and get them. The second part was answering mail. Somebody says, "Send me such-and-such forms." No problem—pull them off the shelves and then address an envelope. I could type an envelope. I wasn't quick, but I could do it fairly accurate. But the third one was a killer. It was the telephones, and I didn't have the courage to ask people how to spell names. I thought you were supposed to be able to spell everything.

She decided that she really wanted to try this job and asked for accommodations:

There was a gal in a wheelchair, and I said, "Why can't she have two blocks of time at answering the phones? She has a headset; she could write. Why can't she do that and—I have good feet, a strong body—I could stand and do it on the floor." That just wasn't an option.

Jo Ann next decided to try the Air Force as a reservist. She took the test and passed by one point. Although she would have loved to stay in the Air Force Reserves, she was again plagued by her LD in poor job matches. Her superiors were unhappy that she was unable to take notes, and her poor coordination caused difficulties. She recalls, "I don't have any sense of marching."

For the next 20 years or so, Jo Ann found her niche, establishing and running Puzzle People, a program for adults with LD. Unfortunately, funding fell through shortly after Jo Ann interviewed for this book, and the organization was closed late in 1997. As of this writing, she is struggling to make ends meet and earns less than

$15,000 per year in a combination of part-time jobs caring for children, older adults, and dogs.

## CHALLENGES ASSOCIATED WITH LD/ADHD AT WORK

Each of the various characteristics of LD/ADHD adds potentially significant challenges to a work life.

### PERCEPTUAL IMPAIRMENTS

People with **poor auditory memory** often have trouble remembering more than one step at a time of complex instructions, and their subsequent lack of follow-through is often misinterpreted as disinterest or laziness. This is of particular concern, because "problems following directions" is the number one problem identified by employers in getting and keeping a job (Hoffman et al., 1987).

Workers with **auditory figure–ground problems** function poorly in open, cubicle-type offices where noise filters in from many directions. Difficulty arises as well in open factory environments, where the sounds of machinery and conversations compete. Individuals who struggle in this area often find it challenging in meetings to filter out superfluous noises in order to devote full attention to presenters; they have difficulty tuning in to one voice while other people are conferring with each other, circulating, or getting coffee.

Individuals who struggle with **visual memory** often get lost, sometimes even in familiar surroundings. They tend to forget where they left their belongings or where they filed their memos and may not remember the face of a customer whom they recently served.

Most people seeking a job use classified ads in newspapers or on-line resources; **difficulties with visual figure–ground perception** make it hard to access this information and, further, make it challenging to complete detailed job applications without inadvertently skipping sections.

### TACTILE DIFFERENTIAL PROBLEMS

Tactile issues affect work life as well, surfacing, for example, when an individual fails to gauge the appropriate firmness of a handshake and uses too limp or too firm a grasp. As Glenn indicates, this can directly interfere with work performance:

> I failed at such jobs as apple picking. The tactile differential issues meant I didn't know how firmly I was grasping the fruit, and I was making applesauce on the trees, bruising the fruit and making them useless, and so I got fired. When you fail as a migratory fruit picker in this country, you know you are in deep trouble.

Another example was offered by a woman with tactile sensitivity. She reported acute embarrassment over an incident with a male co-worker, who had caught her off guard one day when he came from behind while she was working and tapped her on the shoulder to get her attention. Recalling that she had jumped and shrieked and dramatically recoiled from his touch, she shook her head self-disparagingly and acknowledged that her reaction was way out of proportion to what he had done. She was mortified when he looked at her, she reported, "as if I were emotionally unstable."

## SKILLS DEFICITS

Skills deficits have a great impact on the job performance of adults with LD/ADHD. **Reading disorders** limit the ability to read a wide variety of work-related documents, including invoices and the many notices and memos sent via e-mail. Moreover, with more and more professions requiring credentials that involve test-taking, employees with reading disorders are at a considerable disadvantage if they have chosen not to disclose their LD/ADHD and find they need testing accommodations.

Glenn has found that his literacy issues have limited not only his employment options, but his social life as well:

> I got a job in some real remote little upstate New York town loading trucks—two bucks an hour. That was the kind of job I could handle as an illiterate worker. I was getting into fights with fellow workers. It was a very isolating, limiting sort of thing. You couldn't read or write very well, if at all. You couldn't even discuss books with people 'cause you were not reading the books.

Most positions require some degree of **writing**; even the process of applying for a job calls for the ability to fill out an application or to compose a résumé and cover letter. Lilia describes the struggles she had with job applications when she applied for factory work after she dropped out of high school:

> My God, I remember taking my younger sister with me and I'd say, "Could I please take this in the car? I'd feel more comfortable." They'd say, "Oh, sure," because back then, in the seventies, it was okay for you to take the application out of the office and go fill it out and bring it back or whatever. My sister would fill it out, and then I'd bring it back.
>
> She filled it out because I was unable to. I can still see looking at the street names and memorizing how to spell Transit Street because that's where we lived in Providence. I would say it, "T-R-A", and I would repeat it. I couldn't even spell Providence. I would spell Transit, I knew how to spell my name, and I knew how to sign my name, but as far as putting the day, the month, and stuff like that, I didn't know. I knew where to put my social security number, but other things—what I was good at, what my qualifications were—I couldn't read the application in order to fill it out. I couldn't read it or fill it out, so my sister would help me with that.

The challenge persists, of course, after a position has been secured; day-to-day writing requirements on the job can provoke anxiety for those with handwriting or spelling difficulties. Even for those who usually compensate with a computer, writing problems frequently crop up at work. Terry recalls a difficult moment when she was asked to share handwritten notes, a request that she granted but that she had in the past been reluctant to honor:

> I find myself more willing to share what I cannot do well these days. An example of that is I was meeting with a colleague, and we were having a three-way discussion with a student, and then she wanted my notes. I said to her, "Let me take them home. I want to show them to my husband. I want to rewrite them. I'll give them to you tomorrow." But he had meetings late that night [and didn't get to them]. The next day we were meeting with another student, and she was trying to see my notes, and I again was not letting

her. Finally, she asked me to just let her have them. I mean, if you could see what they looked like! It's just shocking the way that I write, especially when I don't care, especially when I'm listening. The listening and writing together is very difficult for me to do, so I won't even be concentrating on trying to get it right because I can't really put my energy into that. I finally said, "Take them. I don't care, just take them." So I guess in my current job setting, because I think that I'm beginning to be seen for my strengths, I'm willing to show the other side of the coin, too. It's just a question of feeling secure that I won't be judged harshly for what I cannot do well.

Job options may be limited by writing difficulties. This has been the case for Lilia, who recognizes that, were it not for her LD, she could be a part-time Portuguese interpreter for the International Institute. Although she is fully fluent and capable of interpreting, such services are needed in ever-varying locations throughout the greater Providence area. As she explains, "I have a hard time when they call me and they give me directions, because I've got to write the street down, I've got to write the directions down, and that's one of my learning disabilities."

Writing difficulties can also limit job advancement, as Harry discovered early in his work life. Raised and educated in Maine, he became a mechanical engineer in a paper mill, where he was surrounded by machinery in a position he loved:

> I was in seventh heaven the minute I walked in there. However, I hadn't solved my language problems, and I had to do something about reports. I had to scheme a way around it. I teamed up with another engineer. He was very happy to sit at his desk and write the reports and the letters and let me be out in the snowstorm with the transit, which I didn't mind—I didn't want to write the letters anyway. After a couple of years, I discovered he was doing a fantastic job and was getting promoted all over the place, and I was not getting raises. I could see that I wouldn't have a career if I stayed there.

Lilia keenly felt the effects of her illiteracy as she struggled to cope day after day with the reading and writing requirements at her job. She regretfully reports:

Unfortunately, I was unable to write checks, write out payroll, make out the slips and the order forms. When I spoke on the phone, I had no problem because I wasn't face to face with the person. But when it was time to take an order down, I'd have to call my sister or my husband so they could write it down. I'd say, "Please hold on." If it was a person who was coming in or even someone who called to see if his order was ready, I'd have to look it up. That I could do because it would be a number on top of the slip, but the name of the company, I would have a hard time with.

Anything related to writing and reading, I would freeze. One of the people there said, "Anything that has to be repaired, I want you to write on the envelope 'repair'." And I froze. I thought, "Oh, my God, they're going to know that I can't read." I felt comfortable with one of the daughters there and said, "I can't write," and her eyes filled with water and she said, "I didn't know, honey." She gave me a children's dictionary and said, "I want you to take this home. This is really helpful." I still have it, and she gave me this in 1972. She taught me how to spell "repair," R-E-P-A-I-R. She would make a list for me and I had it in front—if it needed a stone, if it needed repair, if it needed to be soldered—so I could look up the word and just copy it.

Glenn's difficulties with writing were no less severe than Lilia's or Harry's, but he found it interesting that they were more socially acceptable in certain contexts:

I was doing community organizing and street-level rabble-rousing in a very, very poor neighborhood in Seattle. I was their front guy and mouthpiece, fighting city hall and trying to keep low-income housing from being demolished. I was helping to run a community center, developing food co-ops and health clinics. But this was all done verbally. If anyone asked me to write anything, it was tantamount to an argument. I could sit down and tell them precisely what needed to be said; I just couldn't write it at all. I told people I couldn't write—in a very, very poor neighborhood that was socially acceptable.

**Weak math skills**, too, can create performance issues on the job, particularly for those who handle cash and are accountable for surpluses and shortages. Allyssa describes how she coped in her position at Fotomat:

> I took on a job not too long ago where there was a lot of math involved. It was a little bit scary at first to work in a Fotomat. You're dealing with numbers on the back of the pictures and with money and all kinds of things like that. At first I was not going to stay because I was afraid of that stuff. The boss is a good friend of mine—I let him know that I have a learning disability, although not at first. He sat down and really helped me a lot with my math, and I've kind of overcome that feeling like I can't do things. I take a deep breath, and I ask God to just let me see the words or the numbers or whatever it is. I used to get so frustrated. If I couldn't understand something, I'd get so upset that I'd just feel like closing the book and walking away.

Indeed, some job options, such as cashiering, are inappropriate for people with weak math skills. Betty describes the difficulties she had in her work for a telephone company:

> Everybody knew everybody [in the little town where I lived], and they wanted to help me, so the local phone company offered me a job as a cashier. That's one thing that learning disabled and ADHD people normally are not good at—I couldn't subtract from a checking account, and suddenly I was a cashier with the phone company. Well, that lasted about 3 months before they decided they either should fire me or promote me to get me away from the money. They didn't have the heart to fire me, so they promoted me, and I was a service representative for what is now Bell Atlantic for 16 years.

### DISORGANIZATION

Many individuals with LD/ADHD have serious difficulties with organization and planning. They may have trouble prioritizing work responsibilities, or they may find it challenging to anticipate the effects of their actions. Some have difficulty getting themselves to interviews on time, dressed appropriately and equipped with résumés and other necessary documents. One fellow demonstrated such difficulty when he came to me for a job interview several years ago. He arrived well prepared with a leather portfolio containing his résumé and references and looked quite sophisticated in a navy three-piece suit. Discussing his qualifications, he disclosed his LD and candidly described his strengths and weaknesses. As he became more comfortable, he settled into his chair and crossed his legs, revealing a strikingly large hole spanning the entire top of his sock. Clearly, he had not gone quite far enough in organizing himself for our interview.

Disorganization often results not only in general inefficiency, but also in late arrivals at meetings and in stacks of unrelated papers littering a chaotic workspace. This has been an issue for Nonnie, who has been trying to organize her office for the last 25 years. It is only relatively recently that she has acknowledged that she should control her tendency to accumulate papers, books, and correspondence and regularly discard unneeded items: "What I've done is accumulate too many papers that I don't need. Now I'm throwing things out if they're not going to be useful this year. It's the saving thing that gets me in trouble."

Disorganization is linked to inaccuracy and inefficiency, causing workers to require longer periods of time to complete assigned tasks. Employees who have disorderly desks are more likely to misplace important documents or objects at work; lacking ready access to such items compromises their credibility with supervisors or with clientele who expect them to be able to put their hands on anything they need in a timely fashion. Jule laughs but recognizes the professional drawback when she describes an all-too-frequent scenario in her psychology practice; as she reports, "I'll say to a kid I'm testing, 'Where did I put my glasses?' and he'll look at me and say, 'On your head.' "

## HYPERACTIVITY

Frequently manifested in adults as restlessness, hyperactivity often results in performance inconsistencies. A hyperactive worker may demonstrate wide fluctuations in his or her ability to perform basic duties or to learn new skills at work. Andre discloses that this has been an issue in his own career:

My most memorable and most enjoyable job was being a police officer. I did that for almost 5 years. Once they found out I was ADHD [and taking Ritalin], I was subsequently terminated, and the case is still in court now. In policing, ADHD was actually a great asset, but it was also a hindrance. The hindrance was that I couldn't get court things organized sometimes, so I would get in trouble. Sometimes I didn't get to work on time, and I would get in trouble. I punched one of the other officers one time and got in trouble then, too. I guess that's the short temper.

Glenn found that his hyperactivity had unexpected implications on the job. Because of his high energy level, he welcomed responsibilities that daunted others and managed to get the work done in record time; however, as a result, he tended to alienate co-workers:

[Getting the work done fast] appears to be a major strength, but, in fact, it's also a major deficit. As we all know, keeping the job is about 80% relationships and fitting in and is only about 20% technical. If one focuses on and takes on so much of the technical and can do so much more and get so much out of it, it ends up alienating one's fellow workers. So you're pissing each other off—they don't support you, and you don't support them—it becomes a bad situation. I actually recall being in a work situation where I was literally doing the work of five different people and being the bad guy.

Hyperactivity can also become an issue when a worker with LD/ADHD moves up the ladder to middle management and is suddenly expected to sit for long periods of time at meetings or to accomplish one sedentary managerial task after another.

### DISTRACTIBILITY

Many adults with LD/ADHD have difficulty completing assigned tasks due to distractibility. They begin to write a memo but lose momentum when the telephone rings, or they sit down to make some telephone calls and become sidetracked when they notice that they have e-mail. Dale Brown (1988) recalled with some regret that a promotion at one of her early jobs was delayed for a full year because she was continually distracted from writing a job description that she had been asked to prepare.

### IMPULSIVITY

Impulsive employees are at risk of making snap decisions or impatient comments, both of which may be regretted later. Nancie candidly discusses her own difficulty in this area:

I was just basically the kind of person who was really abrupt with my work-related comments. I'd say what was going on. I'd be real direct about it. I had a real tone of voice and still do to this day. I've gotten into trouble even as a consultant with my tone of voice. I don't understand why people personalize things.

## EGOCENTRICITY AND CONTROL

Egocentrism leads many adults to bring conversations back to themselves, to their accomplishments and to their concerns, with little interest expressed in others' issues or points of view. It also causes many workers to be impetuous, rigid, and in need of control. Jule describes the impatience she often feels at work:

I have very little tolerance for incompetencies in people who are supposed to be in a position of responsibility. I'm very difficult to work with; I demand a lot from myself, and I demand a lot from the people that I work with. As a result, I have trouble finding and keeping office staff—right now I'm on my ninth or tenth semi-permanent secretary.

With her strong opinions, Jule has always felt she should have a say in management on her various jobs. She acknowledges that she has experienced difficulty when her suggestions have been disregarded by superiors, noting that she has an attitude of "I can do it better," or "I'm the only one who can do it." For this reason, she started her own business, ensuring her own control over personnel, policies, and the work environment:

For me with my intensity, with my not being able to tolerate incompetence in people with responsibility, it's very difficult to work for someone. I had to set up my own business. I had to be in charge of an environment that was comfortable. There's no pettiness where I work. I could not take being in a situation where, if I were uncomfortable with someone, they got to stay.

Nina, too, has a need to maintain control. Flexibility in her positions over the years has been helpful:

Many of my jobs have had flexibility. The interesting part, too, is that I've also been in charge at most of my jobs. I think because of my talent and my intelligence that that's worked for me, because then I don't have to answer to anyone. A rigid schedule has never worked for me. I do need a schedule, but make it a rigid one, and I'd feel handcuffed.

## SOCIAL SKILLS DEFICITS

Among reasons for job termination, social skills problems rank second only to incompetence (White, 1992). Adults who struggle with social skills often have difficulty reading the nonverbal signals of others and adjusting their own body language. Nancie describes her difficulties with controlling her own voice tone:

> I don't hear the tone of voice. I don't hear it when it comes out—people have to tell me. I can recognize it in other people, but I can't recognize it in my own tone of voice. Sometimes I think I've been screaming. I'll say to somebody, "Was I kind of loud in that last section?" because I was really animated or something. I'll make some kind of excuse and people will say, "No, I don't think so at all," but at that point it sounds like screaming in my head.

Issues of modulation interfered with the job performance of a child care worker I once knew, who was reprimanded for walking too heavily and talking too loudly during the children's nap time. Neither whispering nor tiptoeing came naturally to her.

A person came to me complaining that she had been terminated from several jobs. She lacked insight regarding the reasons. It soon became evident that she, too, struggled with modulation; her difficulty became evident during our first role play of a job interview when she asked me, in my role as the employer, no fewer that 25 questions, most of which were far too detail-oriented for a first interview.

Trouble making "small talk" at the water cooler or in the lunchroom is another significant issue on the job, causing discomfort not only for the employee, but very often for his or her co-workers and clients as well. The ensuing awkwardness can become the focus of negative performance evaluations and often results in social isolation in the workplace. This was the case for Jo Ann when she was working for the U.S. Army more than 2 decades ago. As she recalls: "In my work situation, I was a total wallflower. I talked very little, was not very outgoing, and felt worthless. Everybody seemed like they were so much above me. I didn't have lunch with anybody or socialize particularly."

When an individual is oblivious to office culture and politics, difficulties with social judgment often develop. One individual came to me struggling to determine whether to address people at her job by their first or last names. Rather than observing how others handled this issue, she decided it was easier to make a blanket policy of simply referring to all her colleagues by their surnames; this proved to be a stilted solution, however, as the majority of personnel commonly referred to one another by their first names. Thus, her solution was inappropriate to the culture of her particular work environment and served to set her further apart from her co-workers. Further difficulties related to social judgement are when workers are unaware of how much personal information to share with co-workers, ignore boundaries, and offer unsolicited advice.

Nonassertiveness is a further impediment to success on the job. Many adults have difficulty asking for help, saying no, and with other issues of assertiveness, often resulting in their becoming involved in tasks that they never meant to assume, are unable to perform well, or cannot complete within the allotted time frame.

## EMOTIONAL OVERLAY

As discussed in Chapter 2, living with LD/ADHD has emotional consequences that affect the work place.

### Embarrassment

Workers with LD/ADHD often experience a deep level of embarrassment that limits their employability in significant ways. One woman reported feelings of shame about never having completed her master's degree:

> I've been told by four different people that I should work for a particular organization that does a lot of what I've done in the last 10 years. People have said, "You should really work there because there are a lot of people like you who work there, blah, blah, blah, blah." I'm afraid to go there and tell them I've done all this great work but I don't have my degree or that I'm in this master's program, but I'm not attending. There's a sense of shame there about that, and a lot of this is because I have attention deficit

disorder. They actually called me to do consulting last summer, and I was too afraid to do it. I thought that I would be found out again.

## Anger

Those who have lived with LD/ADHD for decades often simmer in a variety of negative emotions that influence their work performance. Anger, for example, reflects the wounds experienced by the individual, who is like "a simmering pot. All the frustrations and shattered dreams, missed assignments, and failed attempts have been thrown into that pot, and often it boils over" (Whiteman & Novotni, 1995, p. 239). Nancie describes inadequate control over the anger that surfaces too frequently in her professional interactions:

> [The anger] affects me when I work. Sometimes, when people have asked me questions, unbeknownst to me, the tone of voice or the snappiness comes out, and they're offended. If it comes out, and I realize it—I'm pretty good at reading nonverbals—I'm concerned and remorseful, but it's one of the things that you can just keep living with until you figure it out.

### Self-Esteem Problems

Low self-esteem can cause an individual to make a variety of self-denigrating remarks and provide the foundation of a self-defeating "failure mentality." A negative cycle is created when, questioning whether he or she will be able to meet expectations and fulfill the requirements of his position, the worker becomes too insecure to ask the questions that would, in fact, enhance his or her performance (Whiteman & Novotni, 1995).

### Impatience

A further aspect of emotional overlay can be difficulty tolerating delayed gratification. Jule describes how this has created personnel issues within her own office:

> I've been held back by my ADHD in that it's meant I don't keep secretaries for long. My longest secretary lasted about 2 1/2 years. They have to tolerate the fact that when I need something done, it needs to be done then. [My need for] immediacy is incredible. The thing also has to be done well. Plus—and, again, I think this may

be pretty characteristic of ADHD but I know it is with me—I'm involved with many different things at the same time, and that can drive people crazy because that means they have to shift along with me. Not everybody can shift.

## INCONSISTENCIES IN INTEREST

Intense interest can quickly turn to oppressive boredom in workers who have ADHD along with their LD. Such rapid shifts in levels of interest can generate a variety of work-related issues. Andre describes his employment history as "somewhat like a seesaw" due to this issue. Rich details how this affects his work life:

> The disadvantage of ADHD is that in the same way that you can be involved and untiring and totally focused, you can go along and, all of a sudden, overnight it's no longer motivating to you. Once that happens, you don't want to do it anymore, and then you have to look for another job, and you can get real impatient with the process of looking for something else. It can be almost painful to be in a situation once you're not motivated in it and you're wanting to find an alternative. It's real difficult staying in that situation until you find the alternative.

## CONCEPTUAL DIFFICULTIES

For individuals who struggle with new terminology and concepts, a variety of work-related issues come up. One young woman I know was clearly struggling conceptually when she was advised by a vocational counselor to ask for a raise, and she shook her head no. When the counselor reiterated the suggestion and explained that she had been working well on her job for several months and that her job performance warranted an increase in salary, the young woman shook her head once again and explained she was not allowed to negotiate a raise. With some delving by the vocational counselor, the conceptual misunderstanding became evident. The counselor learned that this young woman had signed up for direct deposit of her paychecks into her bank account. Thorough and observant, she had carefully examined the paperwork she received each payday, and it was a misinterpretation associated with that observation that had led to her reluctance. "I can't ask for a raise," she sighed in disappointment, "because across my paycheck in big letters it says, 'NON-NEGOTIABLE!' "

I heard another story about a young man who, similarly struggling with new concepts, kept arriving at work rather late. After having been advised repeatedly that he should plan to get up earlier in the morning, he continued to be tardy. When he persisted in being late, his supervisor had a stern talk with him and discovered that, although this worker had indeed been setting his alarm and rising earlier and earlier each day, no one had thought to advise him to leave the house earlier. Thus, he had failed to grasp the concept behind the suggested plan for resolving his tardiness.

### FATIGUE

The process of continually compensating can be deeply tiring. Betty notes that she is often exhausted as a direct result of the enormous effort that she expends building on her strengths and working around her weaknesses. She notes, "You're always compensating, and you're always tired a lot."

### STRENGTHS ASSOCIATED WITH LD/ADHD AT WORK

Despite the challenges described above, workers with LD/ADHD bring a number of critical strengths to their jobs as well, including qualities such as "creativity, self-discipline, overcompensation, and inner-directedness" (Brown, 1994, p. 287).

Employers appreciate the unique solutions generated out of creative problem solving, the self-discipline developed out of necessity, and the determination to find ways to compensate for weaknesses. One woman describes the latter:

> I am an incredibly slow worker. I can't help it—I read slow; I write slow; I am not the most organized person. But I am determined to get the job done, so I go in early every day and stay late when it's necessary. So far this has worked for me.

A child care worker I knew, who was expected to read to the 3-year-olds in her charge on a daily basis, was similarly determined. A very weak reader, she managed to meet this challenging job requirement by preselecting the books each week and practicing reading them aloud at home during her free time.

Employees with LD have also been found to be punctual, to have good attendance records, to have a positive attitude, to accept criticism well, and to be dependable over time (Reisman & Reisman, 1993). These are highly valued qualities.

Betty describes the up side of her difficulties with reading and writing. When she was working on development of a new model of services for battered women, she would never take notes in planning meetings but would produce minutes that were widely appreciated for their brevity and conciseness:

> I published minutes from these meetings. I didn't take any notes. I just kind of remembered what was said and typed it up 2 weeks later and sent it off to the commissions office to edit it and send it out to the legislators and everybody on their mailing list. Well, the legislators began to use my minutes of the meetings because they were only two pages.

Employers also appreciate the ability of many workers with LD/ADHD to positively channel their excess energy. Just as Glenn reported being able to complete the work of five people on one job, Andre, too, found that his symptoms could have positive implications at work. During the period when he was police officer, he directed his excess energy well and was recognized for his contributions: "On the flip side of the coin, I have a big stack of awards. I have two department commendations. Most officers don't receive one in 20 years; I had only been there 3 years, and I had two!"

## DISCLOSURE

Whether to self-disclose on the job is a controversial topic. Employees with LD/ADHD should carefully and thoroughly consider this issue, as the protections afforded by the ADA are not triggered until an employer has been informed that an individual has a disabling condition and may need accommodations in order to perform the essential functions of his or her job. Although the law does not require individuals to disclose their disabilities, "employers are not required to accommodate an undisclosed disability" (Latham & Latham, 1997, p. 54).

Because disclosure is required in order for an individual to be guaranteed the civil rights protections of the ADA, each worker with LD/ADHD must carefully consider whether, when, and how to take this step. It should be noted that there are no right and wrong answers when it comes to this issue; decisions should be based upon an individual's specific circumstances and the nature of the position being sought. A number of opinions about the pros and cons of disclosure are offered on the following pages.

### ARGUMENTS AGAINST DISCLOSURE

There are a number of common arguments that many people give for not disclosing.

#### "It Is Better to Work Around the Label"

Many adults with LD/ADHD feel they should not disclose unless it is absolutely necessary. They prefer to work around the issue, communicating their strong motivation to compensate for any weakness they might mention and simply stating what they need (e.g., "I can be more productive if I have a quiet place where I can do my work without distractions") rather than by labeling themselves. Rich advocates this approach:

> If you don't need to self-disclose to an employer, why should you? If you're empowered, if you're in control, if you're doing what you need to do to be successful, then there's very little for anybody else to do. We teach our kids going on to college how to understand their strengths, talk about what their strengths are. That should be the focus when you're talking with an employer or a professor at a university. Talk about what you do to be successful, what type of strategies you're working on in order for you to be successful, and how you are empowered and how you're taking control of a situation. You're really only asking about one or two things from anybody else, and it should not be a big deal. Unless you need to, why bring it up? I don't use it as a red badge of courage or anything like that.

Like Rich, Terry has successfully avoided the need for disclosure by working her way around her areas of difficulty: "I've always just negotiated away the things that I couldn't do well and took that stress level away from myself because of it. I don't see myself ever disclosing to someone that hired me that I have certain limitations."

### "Accommodations Represent a Favor to Be Repaid"

Reluctant to ask for accommodations on the job, some adults with LD/ADHD worry that if they take advantage of their civil rights by asking for accommodations, they will somehow be indebted to their employer.

### "People Who Disclose Are More Vulnerable to Being Accused of Making Excuses"

Many people choose not to disclose because they fear being misunderstood. Nina explains:

> I don't know what to do about self-disclosure. Tied into the issue for me still is a big part of my growing-up message, "Oh, stop it, you're making excuses for yourself." I come from that kind of family, blue collar and very much "pull yourself up by your bootstraps." My father was a steel worker who went to Columbia. That's the kind of guy he was. So, there's a sense of not wanting to self-disclose because of that.

### "People Who Disclose Are More Vulnerable to Being Pitied by Others"

Nina also fears being pitied, a reaction she finds intolerable:

> There's the thing about acceptance—if I could just say I have LD and ADHD and not have anyone either say—which would drive me crazy—"Oh, I'm so sorry." I hate people feeling sorry for me. And I hate feeling sorry for myself, because then I go to a place of feeling ashamed. I feel like it's an unproductive thing, the feeling sorry business. I haven't been in a work situation or a school situation where I felt like I could say, "This has affected my whole life," that I want it to change. And that's what that disclosure means. Part of it is because I can't do it without crying.

### "Folks with LD/ADHD Are More Vulnerable to Being Treated Differently When They Disclose"

Some people are concerned that once they identify themselves as LD, others will fail to understand and will respond negatively to them. They worry that they will be treated differently, that they will be perceived as less capable, that expectations will be lowered, and that they will have fewer opportunities for job advancement.

### *"People Who Disclose Are More Vulnerable to Job Discrimination"*

Research (Minskoff, Sautter, Hoffman, & Hawks, 1987) has suggested that this is a valid concern. Despite their positive views about hiring individuals with disabilities as a general category, only half of 326 employers surveyed said they would hire employees with LD. Jule expresses her concern about self-disclosure:

> I don't care what people say—the law may say that they can't discriminate, but if they've got two people with equal talent and one goes in and says, "I have a reading disability" and the other one doesn't, they're going to figure out a reason not to hire the LD one.

She recalls helping a patient at her clinic who told her that he had never had to disclose his reading disability on his job before because he had always successfully solicited the help of his co-workers. When there was a sudden change in management, however, he found himself in big trouble with a new boss. Jule helped him secure the services of a lawyer. She describes another patient:

> We had a cameraman who could not read. This cameraman was scared to death to say anything. And he was right. What he did to compensate was when the phone rang, instead of taking a message, he'd say to a co-worker, "Do me a favor—I don't have a pen." He made sure he never had one. We gave him different ways of setting it up until he was secure in his job. Also, he would get lost because he couldn't read a map, so we taught him where all the gas stations were. We waited until he reached a point in that job where they couldn't fire him without making a discrimination issue. I'm very concerned about this. I would *not* self-disclose.

#### Arguments for Disclosure

It seems for every argument against disclosure, there is a counter argument in favor.

## "Without Disclosure, There Is
## No Guaranteed Protection Under the ADA"

Many people adamantly advocate for disclosure, noting that it is a necessary step toward taking advantage of the civil rights protections under the ADA. It should be noted that individuals who do choose to disclose may be asked to document their disability. "Documentation is provided by a qualified professional and involves diagnosis, evaluation of how the impairment impacts upon the individual in learning or working, and specific recommendations" (Latham & Latham, 1997, p. 54).

Many people choose to disclose only after a position has been offered. In fact, many employees with LD/ADHD are on a job for long periods of time and only disclose if there is restructuring or if new technology is introduced into their work life and they need accommodations in order to learn new skills. Disclosure should begin with a meeting between the employee and a staff person from the personnel department who can help the individual identify specific accommodations and a plan of action (Payne, 1997).

## "Without Disclosure, There Are No Guarantees of
## Receiving Accommodations that Are Needed to Perform the Job"

Reasonable accommodations are meant to make it possible for an employee to take advantage of his or her skills, knowledge, and abilities to do the job as well as he or she might have without the disability. Provision of accommodations serves to improve the quality of work and lower the stress level in employees with a disability.

Those who feel they need accommodations may seek the assistance of the Job Accommodation Network (JAN), an agency that provides information to all individuals with disabilities. JAN can help a worker with LD/ADHD determine helpful accommodations for his or her specific position. Most accommodations are easily arranged and cost under $500. An example of a free accommodation that can be highly beneficial is establishing a set period per day when a worker with hyperactivity or distractibility has no other distractions and is able to focus solely on paperwork (Payne, 1997).

## "Disclosure Is the Best Route If
## Accommodations Cannot Be Obtained Informally"

Nancie Payne (1997) recommended that employees with LD/ADHD ask themselves whether accommodations will be critical to maintaining an acceptable performance on the particular job being considered and whether they could initiate their own accommodations without disclosure. Disclosure is the path individuals should follow if they need accommodations and are unable to attain them through informal means. Allyssa found herself in such a position and had to disclose her difficulties when she was expected to be proficient in math at her Fotomat job:

> I never really did ask for accommodations except for one job, which was the Fotomat, cause I really had no choice. I was working there for a week, and the boss was leaving and he was like, "You're gonna run the store." I was like, "Wait a minute. You got to leave a times table because I need help here!" I think that if somebody has a learning disability and they feel they need accommodations, just go to that boss as you would go to any human being. They're just another person like you.

### "Although There Is No Need to Flaunt a Disability, There Is No Reason to Hide It Either"

Many who advocate disclosure feel they need not be on the defensive about their disability. Andre comments:

> I'm having my third interview for a job, so probably they're going to hire me. I may disclose. I really don't need accommodations or anything so that's the reason I'm kind of iffy about it. But I wouldn't have any problems if I felt like I needed something. I'm not ashamed of it.

### "Disclosure in a Disability-Friendly Environment Has Fewer Potentially Adverse Consequences"

Glenn notes that an adult with LD/ADHD could be fired because he did not disclose and failed to pick up cues that his supervisor was dissatisfied. He advocates disclosure, but recommends doing so in a disability-friendly environment:

> Disclosure for me was a strong benefit. I have worked in disability-friendly environments, in nonprofits that focus on disability or for city, or state or federal government, which had very strong restrictions. So I wasn't in the private sector. I wasn't in the traditional work environment. I chose where I worked. What I did was find programs that were disability friendly.

However, he does note that there can be a down side to disclosing and benefiting from accommodations:

> If anything, the interpersonal things in the workplace have always been problematic. I was always getting these promotions and perks and was skyrocketing because I brought in this new field and concept and endeavor, and my bosses were supporting me, allowing me to set up conferences and doing way above my grade level, which allowed me to get promoted. Other people in the office were saying, "Why is he getting all this crap?" Again, this goes back to my performing at a higher level, which leads to the social tension.

### "An Employee with LD/ADHD Optimizes His or Her Chances of Success on the Job by Disclosing"

Many people perceive disclosure as the best route to survival on the job and believe it is critical to articulate what is needed if one is to succeed in an employment environment. Betty offers an example of an incident where this strategy was effective:

> My work has always been social work, where I could talk and I wasn't dealing with a lot of details and a lot of clerical requirements. As soon as they informed us that a new computer system was coming in, I informed them that they're going to have to be very aware that I don't do real well with details, they're going to have to expect mistakes, and I will expect accommodations. I'm very knowledgeable and articulate about what I need.

## STRATEGIES TO FACILITATE SUCCESS ON THE JOB

There are several strategies available for adults with LD/ADHD who want to be more successful on the job.

### BEING SYSTEMATIC IN THE JOB SEARCH

A good beginning is to be systematic when looking for a job. Young adults who are making the transition from school to employment often need help focusing on realistic career goals. A comprehensive assessment of career awareness, vocational interests and aptitudes, learning styles, values, attitudes toward work, and self-concept helps them begin the process of narrowing down the choices. They will also find it helpful to attend career fairs, where they can hear about a range of employment options and meet with employers. Gaining actual work experience is a crucial step in the transition process; this can be accomplished through volunteering, working part-time in internships, or "job shadowing," which entails following a worker through his or her day to achieve a full understanding of the scope of that person's position. In addition, many teenagers and young adults find it beneficial to form job clubs, where they can learn goal setting and other self-determination skills, where they can establish peer support networks, and where they can practice using the inter-personal skills needed for work and community life (Roffman, 1997).

Much of the above can be arranged through the Office of Vocational Rehabilitation (OVR), which provides evaluation, counseling, job training, placement, and follow-up. Individuals with LD/ADHD should check with their local branch of this federal agency to determine whether they are eligible to receive these services.

To qualify for vocational rehabilitation services, it must be shown that the disorder results in a substantial handicap to employment and that there is a reasonable expectation that vocational rehabilitation services will improve the individual's employability (Minskoff, 1994). For those who are eligible, OVR develops an individualized written rehabilitation program (IWRP) to help with finding and keeping a job.

## Learning About Relevant Legislation

It is critical that employees with LD/ADHD familiarize themselves with the provisions of both the Rehabilitation Act of 1973 and the Americans with Disabilities Act (ADA) of 1990. These laws protect them from discrimination based on their disability in all aspects of employment, including recruitment, application, hiring, promotion, transfer, layoff, termination, and leaves. LD does qualify as a disability under the ADA, but both the Rehabilitation Act and the ADA stipulate that individuals must be "otherwise qualified," that they would be eligible for the particular job were it not for their disability.

Individuals with LD/ADHD should be aware that they may be entitled to reasonable accommodations on the job. "A reasonable accommodation is one that does not alter the essential nature of the job and does not result in significant difficulty or expense to the employer" (Latham & Latham, 1997, p. 54). Accommodations ensure equal opportunity in the job application process, enable individuals with a disability to perform the essential features of their particular position, and enable them to enjoy the same benefits and privileges as those available to others without disabilities (Latham & Latham, 1997). Types of accommodations include (Latham & Latham, 1997):

- Modification of the workspace, such as a distraction-free environment—optimally, a private office but, at a minimum, provision of earplugs or soundscreens
- Modification of instructions, such as instructions in writing, checklists, and oral directions said slowly
- Modification of supervision, through more frequent reviews and performance appraisals
- Modification of work schedules, such as flextime
- Reassignment and retraining for a position that better matches the employee's strengths
- Modified equipment, such as low- and high-tech devices, ranging from day planners to voice synthesizers and scanners

Glenn describes the set of accommodations that allow him to perform well at his job:

I have a whole list of accommodations that are agreed to and signed off on. I am recognized as a person with a disability, and I am provided with the accommodations. My favorite is that under no circumstance will the condition of my desk be taken into consideration in my performance appraisal. That is written down, signed off, agreed to, all the way up the line to the assistant secretary level. This is the agreed accommodation—also that I will never have to handwrite in public. I will never have to provide anything in a handwritten way. Even though my job grade level is not such that I am entitled to secretarial support, for key documents that have to go out, I will have secretarial support to review, check for spelling, etc. Even though I am in a cubicle, if I need to, I can take over an office and use it in isolation. These things allow me to be functional in the workplace.

Andre reports with regret that his career was significantly affected by his earlier lack of knowledge about the ADA and his right to accommodations on the job:

> I was ignorant of [the] ADA when I was terminated. Had I known, I would still be a police officer to this day. This is one of the reasons I'm trying to help people as much as I can and get the information out there. I just did not know where to go, what to do, how to do it, and I didn't have a time frame to do it.

### TAKING ADVANTAGE OF CONTACTS

Individuals should make use of contacts when seeking employment. Many jobs are never advertised; it is only through word-of-mouth that they are filled. Thus, it is important to make use of contacts and incorporate networking in the job-search process. Support groups and job clubs can be beneficial in this regard.

### MAKING A GOOD JOB MATCH

To be content and comfortable with a job, adults with LD/ADHD must choose the right job match. As they foray into the work world in search of an appropriate job match, people with LD/ADHD should make every effort to capitalize on their strengths, work around their weaknesses, and seek what Gerber, Ginsberg, and Reiff (1992) referred to as "goodness of fit" between their abilities and their work environments. Prior to considering positions that might constitute an appropriate match, it is essential that they first develop an understanding of their learning and working style. As Jule notes:

> I think you have to figure out what you need to do to be accommodated. It may mean you take a walk when you get intense. It may mean if you've got a boss you don't like working with, you either deal with it through counseling or something else or you change jobs or you go out and be a forest ranger. You've got to be very careful what you pick to do for work. If you have a hard time working in a military-type set-up, then you don't go to a military-type set-up.

The individual who becomes easily overloaded should recognize that he is probably not well suited for work in a fast-food restaurant. The person who is hyperactive may want to consider taking a position in sales or in another field that incorporates physical movement into each work day. Betty learned through experience that teaching was a bad job match to her particular configuration of strengths and weaknesses:

> I had a degree in education, so I decided to go ahead and try to teach social studies in high school. I got a teaching job, but that's where the learning disability and attention-deficit disorder began to play a part because of my organizational difficulties. Teaching requires a lot of discipline, a lot of consistency, a lot of knowing how to keep kids quiet, and I was terrible at it. I'd gotten a degree in education just to get a degree, and I don't think I was really cut out for teaching. I was fired after 2 years.

Pat, too, learned through experience. After a number of years in educational administration, she has now found a better job match:

> For 5 years I was director of special education for a school system in a little town in Missouri. My job in this federally funded project was designing and operating the program—I didn't want the part of the position that involved sitting behind a desk and going to board meetings and keeping the budgets and all those kinds of things. When I moved to Arkansas, I stepped down one layer, and I am now a coordinator. There is a boss above me who does those kinds of things and understands what I do best. I am right where I should be.

As a mechanical engineer with language difficulties, Harry was unable to handle writing reports; however, he did ultimately find a niche where he was able to achieve success:

> I went off on my own. I had been involved in small businesses all my working life, and I had found that I could handle that very nicely. What I have been doing for the last 20-odd years is designing and building classic sailboats, and I have been relatively successful.

## Seeking Disability-Friendly Environments

People should seek work environments in which supportive staff accept and understand their disability and recognize and respect their talents as well as their LD symptoms. Glenn advises adults with LD/ADHD to become informed consumers and to actively seek places that are disability friendly by speaking to personnel representatives and to the people who work in the companies where they are seeking employment. They should also check with the Equal Employment Opportunity Commission to see if there have been any complaints against the company about noncompliance with the ADA. Glenn describes his own work environment, within which he can not only acknowledge but also embrace his disability:

> [Where I work] the fact that I know I am LD, I am overt about LD, I talk about being LD, and I am working in the field of LD has been a dramatic vehicle for my success. I was able to create a whole field of LD in welfare programs. Nobody was doing that before I came in. They kept on promoting me in the government and giving me more responsibilities and special assignments and actually created a new job description just for me. By actually embracing it and not denying it, by focusing on it and not rejecting it, by saying this is what it is, I have actually become highly successful in my work world. I actually ended up being an advocate and talking about it in progressive ways and becoming a national figure around it. I didn't hide from it; I didn't shrink from it. In choosing an employer, I chose somebody who is disability friendly. I got into the jobs because people who had LD in the family and had failed their own children were saying, "Maybe I could help this guy along."

Betty has benefited from this kind of environment as well:

> I have an incredibly supportive staff who are grateful for the great gifts that I bring to the profession, the instincts and knowledge. We all have weaknesses, and when I'm having a rough day, they say, "Oh, Betty's having a rough and ready day. Okay, that's cool. We'll just give her some space."

Flexibility that enables an individual to use coping skills can make an environment disability friendly. For example, Rich, who is only able to sit still for 45 minutes at a time, has built movement into his administrative routine as a school headmaster. Getting up from his desk and making the rounds of all the classrooms proves advantageous to the school as well as to himself:

> From my perspective, you've got to be proactive about it, and if you understand what your strengths are, then capitalize on the strengths. If you understand what your weaknesses are, then develop a strategy whereby you cope. My coping skill is to get up, take a walk around, come back, and then I can be more productive. If I pop my head in the classrooms for 30 seconds, because of my ADHD issues, I pick up on all sorts of stuff that most people would only pick up in 10–15 minutes of sit-down. It allows me to get a feel for what's happening any period of the day. If I tried sitting at my desk, I'd be unproductive. I also wouldn't be able to have a good understanding of what's happening in the school.

## DEVELOPING SELF-ADVOCACY

Self-advocacy is critical to success both on the job and off. It is crucial that individuals create a strong foundation for self-advocacy by developing both an understanding of their own LD/ADHD and the ability to explain their strengths and weaknesses to others.

Individuals with LD/ADHD often benefit from writing out, memorizing, and extensively role playing the process of explaining their strengths and needs aloud. In *Guidelines for Supervising Employees with Learning Disabilities*, Reisman (1993) provided a number of examples of specific job-related requests for which an employee may choose to self-advocate:

- A clear explanation of his or her own responsibilities and expectations and those of the supervisor
- A regularly scheduled, distraction-free meeting time with the supervisor for feedback and planning to supplement immediate feedback, whenever possible, to contend with issues as they develop
- A list of other workers with whom the employee will interact and what they do
- A written list of rules of the workplace, such as the protocol for handling absences, tardiness, or personal emergencies

- A calendar of events relevant to the job
- A written schedule and list of routines, and notification when these will change for any reason
- Tasks assigned in small steps or one at a time, if necessary, with oral directions supplemented by written directions
- The opportunity to repeat directions back to the supervisor to ensure that they have been understood

Many adults also find it helpful to have a book or pamphlet about LD/ADHD on hand as a tool in self-advocacy to help the employers, supervisors, and co-workers to whom they are disclosing become more fully informed.

## USING TECHNOLOGY

People with LD/ADHD can take advantage of recent technological advances in numerous ways. For example, it is now possible to divert a telephone when necessary to ensure an uninterrupted stretch of time for concentration on work; to plug a tape recorder into the telephone during conversations to capture important information; to record telephone numbers, facts, and appointments via voice organizers; and to set a watch as a timer for reminders of meetings. Further, calculators and spell-checkers are now commonly used as auxiliary aids. Terry explains how a computer has eased her workload:

> When I first started working at my current job, I hand-wrote reports. My husband would edit each for me, correct it all, and then I would rewrite it again because I wasn't comfortable with the computer. I am now at a point where I could get the work that I do 90% perfect, maybe 95% sometimes, and it's basically because of the computer.

Terry is using her computer as a teaching tool as she tries to learn how to spell better. She explains that one of her issues is that she proofreads her work the way that she thinks it, and because she hears words incorrectly, she leaves endings out and misspells the same words over and over again:

> One of the things that I've been trying to do lately as sort of a little self-improvement thing is to pay attention when spell-check

comes up on the computer. It always comes up the first word, since I spell things in a very sort of make-sense way, like they sound to me. What I've been trying to do is when I look at that word and it says, "Change to" I look at what I actually wrote and what it says to change to, and I say, "Okay, there isn't a P in that" or "there isn't an A in that—try to remember that." But somehow, unfortunately, I don't.

In *The Road Ahead*, Bill Gates quoted a letter written to him in praise of the computer:

Mr. Gates, I am a poet who has dyslexia, which basically means I cannot spell worth a damn, and I would never have any hope of getting my poetry or my novels published if not for this computer spell-check. I may fail as a writer, but thanks to you, I will succeed or fail because of my talent or lack of talent and not because of my disability. (1995, p. 273)

## DELEGATING WHEN POSSIBLE

Creatively seeking and obtaining assistance from others can be advantageous within the work world. Terry delegates extensively. For example, when she started a child care center at Framingham State College and had to produce a parent handbook, she made writing it a project for people who were in the English department. Within the classes she currently teaches at the Threshold Program, she asks certain students to monitor her spelling:

I hate spelling on the blackboard. I student-taught first grade—I didn't want to go above that because I was afraid. Even now I don't write very much on the blackboard. I hate it so much, I can't tell you! When a few of my [young adult] students said they really wanted me to write on the blackboard, I thought, "Well, I have to." But there's always at least one, if not two or three students in this program of kids that have below-average IQs that are much better spellers than I am. And, so, they're my checkers. Basically, I'm saying to them, "This is something that I cannot do, and I'm really bad with it, so if something's not right, I'm just going to ask who knows how to spell it." Basically, I am not going to allow my insecurities to not let me do a good job.

Terry has often offered creative deals to co-workers to contend with responsibilities that would be difficult for her due to her LD. For example, when she was a preschool teacher, she was required to write and post a daily letter to the parents explaining everything that had been done that day, with each child mentioned at least once. She shares her solution:

> I remember saying to the co-teacher, "I cannot do this. It's so stressful for me thinking that this is what I have to accomplish at the end of the day, even if we're sharing it. What's the thing that you hate to do the most in this class?" She said, "I hate when they have diarrhea and it's a big mess." I said, "I will clean up every diarrhea mess and big disgusting mess in this entire classroom whenever it happens if I never have to write that letter." And that's what happened.

The same delegation skills also serve her well in her volunteer activities. She recalls:

> I was asked to be a PTA president, and I wanted to do it, but there was one segment that I wasn't interested in, and that was writing a page for the weekly newsletter, which was an ongoing sort of requirement. I said, "This is what I will do. I will call you on Tuesday, because it's due Wednesday morning, and we will chat. But you have to write it. Other than that, I can do all of this, but I'm not going to do this part because it's stressing me out too much." The person that was trying to talk me into it said that was fine.

## USING LISTS AND CUES

Many adults with LD/ADHD find it helpful to carry a pad of paper and write down anything that must be remembered and might be forgotten. With a pad on hand, they can spontaneously write their own notes at meetings, or they can write down each individual step in complicated oral directions. Such lists and other visual cues can be invaluable, as Allyssa recalls from her days at Fotomat:

> We made little charts all over the place that were awesome—like times tables and a little chart of how to add tax on, little stuff like that. My boss left little reminders all over the place for me,

which was great because that's exactly what I need. I could do things great if I had little reminders.

## USING RELAXATION TECHNIQUES

Relaxation techniques can be highly effective in deflecting anger or anxiety in work-related and other settings. Some individuals use positive self-talk messages, such as, "I can handle this," or, "I'm not going to let this get to me," to cope with their feelings. Nancie finds that deep breathing is effective as well:

> I have a really good relationship with the people who I work with now. I work overtime in making sure that I'm taking big breaths before I say anything, looking at the work and not anything related to the staff. I really work very, very hard at that. It takes a lot of stamina.

## ROLE PLAYING

Many adults with LD/ADHD find it helpful to rehearse solutions to difficult interpersonal situations that arise at work. For example, when Dale Brown was anticipating a difficult interaction with a co-worker or supervisor at work, she found it helpful to write down what she wanted to say and role play the scene with her father, who would act out different reactions.

## COMPENSATING FOR SPECIFIC SYMPTOMS OF LD/ADHD

Each individual should plan to make use of specific workplace strategies to compensate for his or her specific symptoms of LD/ADHD. Nadeau (1995) suggested several such strategies:

- Hyperactive workers should plan to do something active, such as take a walk, during coffee breaks and lunchtime.
- Distractible workers should clear their workspace of all but materials on which they are currently working. They should also carry a notepad to jot down notes of off-task thoughts that can be pursued at an appropriate time.
- Disorganized people should team up with more organized co-workers who can help with organization and follow-through. They should also set aside a 15-minute period each morning to

plan the day on paper, setting priorities and making sure not to overschedule.

- Employees who have difficulty with time management should build in a "catch-up" period or an extra cushion of time to meet deadlines. They will often benefit from setting a timer to go off when a task or conversation should be ending.
- Those who procrastinate should set deadlines and reward themselves for those goals that are met (e.g., "I'll take a break when I finish this memo").
- Workers with memory impairments should take notes and tape record important meetings, marking the reference point on the tape recorder's counter of points to which they may wish to return.

### BEING TENACIOUS

Most adults with LD/ADHD find that hard work pays off and that tenacity is an invaluable characteristic. John Corcoran, an illiterate teacher who managed to succeed through pure tenacity, wisely noted:

> The key to success is hard work. Tenacity is more valuable than knowledge and skills. The difference between success and failure is that when you fall down a million times you fail, and when you get up a million and one times, you succeed. That's all you need is one. (as cited in Reiff, Gerber, & Ginsberg, 1994, p. 33)

### SUMMARY

The characteristics of LD/ADHD tend to have a broad impact within employment environments; thus, many of the adults interviewed for this book have experienced considerable challenges and stress on various jobs throughout their lives. However, along with other employees with LD/ADHD, they also bring strengths to the workplace, including creativity, self-discipline, a positive attitude, and dependability.

Employees with LD/ADHD are urged to become familiar with their rights and protections under the ADA and the Rehabilitation

Act of 1973, both designed to protect them from discrimination based on their disability. Further, they should become aware of reasonable accommodations to which they may be entitled on the job, including modifications of space, equipment, instructions, supervision, and schedules. Because disclosure is necessary in order to access these accommodations, they must carefully consider the pros and cons of disclosing their disability to their employers.

In order to maximize their potential for success on the job, individuals with LD/ADHD are urged to seek the best possible job match, including a disability-friendly work environment; develop strong self-advocacy skills; make use of technology; learn to delegate; use lists and cues; prepare for difficult interpersonal interactions through role playing; and be tenacious.

# 10

## Quality of Life

How do adults with LD/ADHD feel about themselves and their current lives? What are the various factors that influence their quality of life? I asked these questions to the people whom I interviewed; their responses offer a glimpse into this much understudied area. This chapter will explore many of the influences that surfaced and will offer suggestions for adults with LD/ADHD who wish to enhance their quality of life.

### INFLUENCES ON QUALITY OF LIFE AMONG ADULTS WITH LD/ADHD

The variety of factors influencing quality of life include characteristics of LD/ADHD, employment status, financial status, personal relationships, and mental and physical health.

#### CHARACTERISTICS OF LD/ADHD

As has been discussed throughout this book, specific characteristics of LD/ADHD affect postsecondary experiences, work performance and day-to-day life within the community and, thus, have a direct effect on the overall quality of life of individuals within this population. The impact becomes apparent when **tactile defensiveness** makes people uncomfortable with getting a basic haircut; when **hyperactivity** makes it difficult for them to sit through a 2-hour staff meeting at work; when **directionality problems** lead them to lose their way again and again on their college campus. The effects of LD/ADHD are painfully apparent to Rich, who notes that distractibility affects the quality of his life on the job, within relationships, and even in leisure time pursuits, such as carpentry:

> Every once in a while, [when I'm building stuff] I measure things wrong due to lack of attention to that type of detail, or if I'm not totally concentrating, I'll reverse an angle cut on a molding or something, and then I kick myself that I just wasted $15 on the board.

Rich's quality of life is further affected by his **auditory figure-ground problem** when he plans social outings:

> I would prefer to go to a movie than to sit down and try to have a conversation with six or seven different people at the same time in a noisy place. If I'm in a quiet place, it would be fine, but if I'm in a noisy place like in a bar or something, it's almost painful to me because there's too many distractions going on between the noise and all the visuals.

Because no two people have the same set of symptoms of LD, the effect on quality of life differs from person to person. Thus, although Rich struggles in noisy environments and prefers going to the movies, Glenn's difficulty with **visual figure–ground perception** makes him uncomfortable in theaters where, unless he sits in the front row, he finds he is very distracted by the bobbing of heads between him and the screen.

**Disorganization** is another of the LD/ADHD characteristics that can significantly affect quality of life. Betty reports that she is chronically frustrated by never being quite on top of the little tasks that add up to a sense of order:

> In terms of quality of life, there are upkeep projects that I would like to see done. A lot of times my apartment looks like chaos unless somebody's visiting. The ADHD issues around getting things done are always there and always need to be compensated for. I'm always aware that I have a learning disability.

The impact of organizational issues on quality of life is further evident when Nina's son refuses to invite friends over because of the piles and piles of paper on the dining room table or when Glenn's friends refuse to ride in his garbage-strewn car.

## PRESSURE AND OVERLOAD

Several individuals interviewed for this book admitted to placing an inordinate amount of pressure on themselves to prove their worth, their intelligence, or their determination. With a tendency to push themselves too hard, they regretfully find that they have few opportunities to relax and enjoy life. Some admitted to comparing themselves to others, suffering in the process. One woman sighed, "I wish I liked myself better."

Many adults with LD/ADHD find that a chronic sense of overload undermines their quality of life. Nancie talks about anger that surfaces in outbursts when she feels pressured. Rich describes brief periods of depression when he has taken on too much.

## EMPLOYMENT ISSUES

Several of the people whom I interviewed spoke of job-related difficulties that had a negative impact on their life as a whole. Jule reports that her quality of life was affected when she tried to work under the supervision of anyone else. Glenn describes years of employment-related frustration and reports that the low social status associated with his dead-end beer-selling job was a distinct impediment to his quality of life. Jo Ann speaks of feeling disheartened by barriers to success and an ongoing lack of professional opportunities:

> I just think there should be more opportunities for some of us. I wish people would open a few more doors for me [in my professional life]. I feel like I'm constantly knocking at very heavy metal doors. I get maybe a little crack here and then I might get through, and then [I find myself facing yet] another iron door.

## FINANCIAL DIFFICULTIES

An individual's financial status has distinct impact on quality of life. Jo Ann speaks of her ongoing financial difficulties:

I was never able to set up any kind of full-time salary [with Puzzle People] or any amount of money with a retirement system, and I haven't been able to save. My trouble now is trying to still survive with what little money I earn. I don't want to touch the monies my parents left because that's what I'm going to retire on. I earn [about] $14,000 cleaning houses, baby-sitting and little piece-mealing with dog walks and elder care. Some months I do pretty well, but sometimes I have practically nothing, and there are days [when] I don't eat.

Nina, too, has struggled with a tight budget. She reports:

My big concern is around money. I've typically been in somewhat low-paying jobs—the arts and working with children don't pay very well—though I have a great deal of satisfaction in the work that I do. In terms of quality of life, it depends what you are talking about. Do I live in a house? I'll never own a house. I only buy cars that cost $1,000. I don't make enough money, and that's an issue that concerns me because I'm single and have a 13-year-old son, and how is he going to go to college? Over the years I've said that I'm not a materialistic person, and materialistic things are not important to me, but I've almost had to make them not be important to me because I'm not there, I'm not achieving that kind of financial security.

## PERSONAL RELATIONSHIPS

Connectedness to others has a direct effect on quality of life. Those who have healthy relationships—whether with friends, lovers, or family—enjoy a fuller life than those who do not. Rich reports, "Quality of life for me at this point is my family, my wife, my kids, helping them through their struggles—[after all,] the apple doesn't fall far from the tree—and hoping that they're happy." Nina speaks appreciatively of her circle of supportive friends who figuratively take her by the hand in their offers of assistance. Such relationships, she notes, are a source of great pleasure, satisfaction, and comfort.

Just as positive relationships enhance quality of life, negative relationships can be a distinct detriment. Thus, Lilia describes tremendous pain in a verbally abusive relationship with her disrespectful spouse, and Betty talks of having to distance herself defensively from her toxic family. Lack of relationships can be an impediment as well. Jule reflects upon long-felt pressure to find a mate, tension that has only recently settled into a less prominent place in her perspective:

> I think there's a normal trend—wanting to be married and then not being married and immediately wanting to have another relationship because quality of life meant a twosome. Then reaching a point where quality of life was doing so well in the area that I picked to work in [and relationships didn't mean quite as much].

As discussed in previous chapters, many adults with LD/ADHD experience ongoing isolation. Glenn struggles with this issue. Despite all of his efforts to cope with the various aspects of his LD/ADHD, he still experiences a stinging loneliness and reports self-disparagingly, "I am getting older, fatter, balder, less attractive. I would say that the major issue around quality of life is a real undermining issue of isolation that exists even when you're with people." He recognizes that, by isolating him, his difficulties with interpersonal skills have influenced his overall quality of life:

> My quality of life has been greatly impacted by my LD and ADHD. They have greatly limited my options as to who would relate and how they would relate to me. I have been pretty isolated. [For example,] I am a chess player who can't find any partners, and I love playing bridge, but I can't find anybody to do it [with].

### Residual Sadness

Most of the individuals whom I interviewed were not diagnosed until relatively late in life. Over the years, many have contended with chronic sadness that has arisen out of repeated failures and misunderstandings. For example, despite all the wonderful work that Nina has done to understand and accept herself, she still weeps as she recalls painful experiences from her past:

> The diagnosis, the therapy, the treatment, all of that coaching, has helped me with the emotional results of my whole life being told, "You're lazy or stupid and somehow worthless." It still hurts, but I'm starting not to believe it.

Jule shares this vulnerability. She notes that self-acceptance, once achieved, still wavers, commenting, "You're catching me on a very good day. And that's the way it is with ADHD—it depends on the day."

## HEALTH ISSUES

For all people, with or without disabilities, quality of life is also tied to health status. As the years pass, health is more apt to change for the worse and, as Jule notes, "Regardless of what your issues are, health becomes a major issue." Many people with LD/ADHD find the process of continually self-advocating and compensating to be exhausting. One person reported with a sigh, "I'm just wiped out by always working and working and working just to deal with my disability."

## STRATEGIES FOR ENHANCING QUALITY OF LIFE

There are a number of ways for individuals with LD/ADHD to enhance their quality of life.

### RECOGNIZING THE DISABILITY

Throughout this book, many quotes suggest that recognition of their LD/ADHD was a first step in changing the lives of the individuals interviewed. Nonnie talks about the relief she felt at finally having a name for what had all her life seemed an odd compilation of symptoms. Nancie speaks of recognizing herself in a book about ADHD and embarking upon exploration that has since helped her understand LD and ADHD and build a career around serving others with these disabilities. Harry and Janet report that recognition of Harry's LD was the first step in turning around a dysfunctional marriage.

Glenn poignantly recollects the moment of recognition, when his daughter was being tested and his own LD came to light, when he was finally able to recognize that he was "not an idiot." That moment of recognition lit a spark that led him on a path from literacy training to mental health counseling to college and, ultimately, to major career changes. Indeed, having moved rather meteorically in the past decade from the state of Washington to Washington, D.C., from peddling beer to promoting policy changes in several important U.S. governmental roles, Glenn feels very positive about the marked improvement in his employment status and, subsequently, in his overall quality of life:

> There is a very sharp upward curve from where I was 10 years ago as a beer vendor in the King Dome in Seattle. There was no real hope of getting out of that environment 14 years ago to where I am today. There has been a sharp, sharp, sharp increase of quality of life on that level. Financially I am better off. My work is better— I am much more established as a professional and much more accepted as a valued member of the community, although many people still see me as a very weird person, and maybe I am because of the ADHD and LD.

## UNDERSTANDING LD/ADHD

Lee wisely noted that recognition of weakness opens the door for recognition of strengths (Lee & Jackson, 1992). It stands to reason that quality of life increases with self-understanding. This is particularly true for adults with LD/ADHD, who are able to use this understanding to develop compensatory strategies that offset the negative influences listed earlier in this chapter. Moreover, comprehension of LD/ADHD in general and of their own disability in particular forms the foundation for development of important self-advocacy skills (Roffman, Herzog, & Wershba, 1994; Yuan, 1994). When people like Nonnie, Nina, Andre, and Jo Ann understand LD/ADHD and how it manifests itself in their lives, they can explain and express their needs to relatives, new partners, bank managers, therapists, employers, teachers, and the many others with whom they regularly interact. In doing so, they are empowered to positively influence their own quality of life.

## ACHIEVING SELF-ACCEPTANCE

Ultimately, quality of life depends upon an individual's relationship with himself or herself. Jule feels comfortable with her accomplishments and her style. She acknowledges that she likes herself and reports that she no longer looks to others for approval:

I'm very comfortable with who I am. I'm past the point of worrying about the kinds of things I would have worried about 5 years ago, even 2 years ago. I like my ethics. I like how I've worked with the people I've been able to work with. Things that once were so carefully guarded aren't such a big deal. I don't need the approval I used to.

Terry feels much the same and, speculating that self-acceptance is a developmental process, wonders aloud whether with age, "You just get more satisfied with who you are, and say, 'This is it.' " She explains that accepting herself for who she is makes it possible for her to be more genuine with others:

[It's] only over the last few years that I'm very comfortable with my LD. If I've had interactions with people, and they know me for what my strengths are, I'm now able to sort of unmask what my disabilities or liabilities are, and it doesn't feel like it's the sum total of what they think of me.

Nina is able at last to cast off a negative self-image and accept the positive regard of others:

I feel good about myself now. It's always been a paradox. I've always had a strong sense of my intelligence and my talent. On the other hand, the nondiagnosis for so long and not figuring out what the ADHD was, that sense that something was wrong kind of undermined the talent and the creativity part. So I [felt] very much like Woody Allen says in Annie Hall, "Any club that would have me as a member isn't worth joining." [My version was,] "I understand why people are drawn to me, but if they really like me, they must be schmucks." I'm kind of getting over that, I think.

Gerber, Reiff, and Ginsberg noted the importance of reframing as a step in the process of self-acceptance. With understanding an essential prerequisite to this process, they define reframing as "the set of decisions related to reinterpreting the learning disabilities experience from something dysfunctional to something functional" (1996, p. 99). As Christopher Lee wrote:

What you see in the mirror is important. If you see a person who cannot spell or cannot read well, you are looking at a handicapped person. If you see a person who is creative and has unique abilities, you are looking at a human being with potential. (Lee & Jackson, 1992, p. 122)

Many of those interviewed have successfully reframed. For example, after decades of defining herself as "dumb" and incapable, Lilia has emerged as an adult who is able to recognize her strengths and see that many of them have developed as a direct result of her day-to-day coping with LD. Although she reports that she felt "dumb" most of her life, she now perceives and values her own unique abilities. Although she wishes she were more educated, she now recognizes, "I might not have a bachelor's degree, but I can go to school, I can go to work, I can take care of six kids, and I can come home, cook dinner, do dishes, and be ready for the next morning."

Allyssa has come to terms with her limitations and has developed more satisfaction with her life:

I have acceptance of exactly who I am today. I accept that I get stuck on a word, and I don't beat myself up. I can accept that I don't know my times tables perfectly today. Twenty-one, and I don't know what four times eight is off-hand. You know what? I don't care, 'cause you know what? If I wanted to figure it out right now, I could. It may take me longer than it would take somebody else, but I don't care—'cause that's me.

She joyfully explains that after a very difficult period during which she was filled with self-loathing and wanted to die, she has discovered her own self-worth:

I used to feel stupid, like there was a dark cloud over me my whole life, and I've been saved from all that. I feel so good about myself that when I look up in the sky and I see those birds, I feel like a bird! It sounds nuts, but I do. I feel so good about myself that I feel like I could fly. I look in the mirror, and I could smile at myself because I love what I've become. People call me up and they want advice and they want help, and I'm always there to help because there were people there for me.

Reframing involves the development of perspective. When the diagnosis starts to become a less important factor in how the individual feels about himself or herself and takes up less space in the person's self-concept, quality of life improves. Terry articulates this well:

> In terms of my relationship with myself, I do think that's it's been better over the last couple of years. One thing that's really been helpful to me is that I've gotten involved in an elementary school's disabilities awareness program. The way this program is set up is that there's a lot of hands-on activities for kids, and the culmination of it is that someone comes and speaks to them who is living the challenge in their life. I've become a guest speaker for the unit on learning disabilities.
>
> [As a speaker] I'm saying, "Hey, you know, this is it. This is who I am, and I'm trying my hardest." I'm trying to ignore the things that aren't easy, and I'm trying to give myself opportunities to achieve in the ways that I know are easy for me. Right now the LD doesn't feel as important as it used to—it used to feel very important. I went from hiding, denying, to basically going out and wearing it on my sleeve. So in a 30-year span, it's a huge change.

## SEEKING AFFILIATION

Many adults with LD/ADHD have found belonging to LD-related organizations (see Resources) to be fulfilling and beneficial; they enjoy not only making new acquaintances, but also being among others with similar issues. Lilia found a whole new world when she became involved in LDA:

> I'm associated with Adults with Learning Disabilities. They're wonderful people. This LDA group taught me that the right way to teach one person is not the right way to teach me. There's different ways of teaching different people, and I just happen to be one of them.
>
> [A while back] Glenn Young called me and said, "Look, we want somebody who has a learning disability from Dorca's [Place], who's outgoing and who has a great personality, who can speak out [at a conference in Colorado] and be an advocate." And they chose me! I was honored. I met wonderful people. I was amazed, too, because here I am thinking, when I was diagnosed with a learning disability, "Oh, God, there goes my GED. I'll never get a good-paying job." And

then I sat around this table with these wonderful people who had learning disabilities, who were scientists, who were book writers, who had their own businesses, who had their own magazines. I was amazed. I was like, "Oh my God, this is wonderful!"

**Betty, who has also been active in LDA, comments on how much better life has gotten for people who have LD over the past 30 years:**

LDA has made the difference for those of us with learning disabilities. Life was a whole lot different in 1968 than it is now. In terms of identifying what the issues are, getting it into the DSM-IV [*Diagnostic and Statistical Manual of Mental Disorders, Fourth Edition*], getting it into legislation. If LD had not been included into the Vocational Rehabilitation Act of 1973 with Article 504, my education would have been certainly as much of a struggle as it had been in the 60's. If LD and ADHD had not gotten into the Americans with Disabilities Act, I probably would be out looking for a job or homeless. So I credit the ADA and the Congress that got it through and also with the Rehabilitation Act in terms of making life less of a struggle. I strongly credit the LDA and probably CHADD [Children and Adults with Attention Deficit Disorder] also. I'm incredibly grateful for the difference between pre-1968 and now.

### Using Technology

Technology has had a significant impact on the quality of life of most of the individuals whom I interviewed. From simple tape recorders to sophisticated scanners and voice synthesizers, adults with LD/ADHD find their lives enriched by the possibilities created through assistive technology. The computer, in particular, has made an enormous difference, for a variety of reasons. For Nina, it is the grammar-check function that has been a great boon:

The computer has helped me so much. About 5 years ago, when I first got one, the computer really helped me see how bad my dyslexia was. I remember in high school being told that I made too many typing errors, but I actually didn't and don't now. When I got Microsoft Word with spell-check and grammar-check, I remember sitting at the computer saying, "Oh, God, this is really wonderful!"

*The thing with the grammar-check is that it has you read your sentence a few times. You go though it for spelling, and then it comes back and says you've used the passive voice—which it always says—and sometimes you need to lose that, but you still have to look at that sentence. When I do go over things again, that's when I see where my mistakes are.*

For Terry, although she appreciates the computer's other functions, it is the delete button that has transformed her attitude about writing:

*The thing that's really changed my quality of life is that I've gotten comfortable with computers, and that's only happened in the last few years. [For example, it was computers] that made me think I could go back to graduate school. [In my] guest speaking in elementary schools, I often say to kids, "Thank God for computers. I love computers. What do you think is my favorite part of the computer?" They always say the spell-check, and I say, "No, it's not, actually. Spell-check actually messes me up, because if it's a real word, it doesn't pick up the mistake. I love delete! Delete is my friend because now I can write what I think, I can do what I want, and I'm not bogged down in any way by the burden of having to be right or almost right. What it does is it frees me up to really think and express myself in a way that I never could before."*

And of course, spell-check is almost universally valued. Betty notes: "Technology and assistive technology have made a huge difference in terms of coping with the learning disability. I wouldn't dare function without my Franklin Spelling Ace, without a calculator or a typewriter with spell-check on it, or without a computer."

### DEVELOPING A SENSE OF PURPOSE

Recognition that they have something to offer others adds a sense of purpose to the lives of many adults with LD/ADHD. Andre conveys enthusiasm for his mission to help others with the disability:

*I'm learning so much [about LD] at a fast rate that I feel I can't reach enough people fast enough to tell them and share the things that I've learned. To me, even though I'm moving 100 miles an hour,* that's too slow. I get very frustrated. But on the whole, I feel satisfied with myself because of what I'm doing to serve and help other people.

In Terry's capacity as guest speaker in the Understanding Disabilities Program, she notes the power of adults with LD/ADHD stepping forward as role models:

Having gone through graduate school and gotten a sense that there's more than one way of being smart, that's what I talk to kids about—"This is the way I'm smart, and this is the way I'm not, and [you should] try and find the way you're smart." I feel that sharing [those feelings] has been very positive. I've had lots of teachers come up to me afterward and say, "You know, you're such a great role model, and that's really wonderful. These are the kinds of things kids really need to hear."

Glenn has found purpose in his advocacy for others with LD. This mission has significantly affected how and with whom he spends his time and, thus, has had a very positive impact on his personal life:

Much of my life now is consumed with this whole issue of trying to develop this movement, so I am on the national board of LDA, and I travel to conferences all over. LD has become an avocation. It has actually been a tremendous vehicle that has increased my job, my prestige, my capacity to do things, and function. I have taken this disability and, by championing it, it has enhanced my personal life.

### ACHIEVING BALANCE

Several people mentioned that quality of life is enhanced when an individual is able to strike a balance between work and the many other elements of life. Jule, a single woman who has been professionally driven throughout her adult years, faces this challenge as she moves into her fifties and contemplates cutting back on her career:

As I've gotten older, to me quality of life is to figure out how do I, as a single woman who has to support herself, get into a position where I can continue to do what I love to do but not have to do so much of it because I get tired? I think [getting] tired is a function of age, but I think it's also a function of enjoying work but not having the kind of drive internally to want to do it all the time. I think the tremendous drive was related to my ADHD. As I grew up, the drive got so strong—you have to be so focused that you don't stop—it almost became a compulsion. Having accomplished so much of what I feel now is important, I'd like to be able to take the time to rest and enjoy. I'm always so invested in what I'm doing and so invested in my work that I haven't been able to spend as much time doing other things that I now want to do. I don't want to look back and say, "Gee, they're going to stand over me at my funeral and say, 'Ah, she worked 20 hours a day.'"

Balance includes taking time for satisfying leisure time pursuits. The adults interviewed describe numerous interests. Glenn, who considers himself an historian, enjoys travel. Rich enjoys carpentry; Nancy loves to sing; and Terry often attends parenting workshops. Nina fills her need for continuous action by sewing between other leisure activities. She reports:

I'm always doing something. Right now at home there's a sewing machine sitting on the table, so when I leave here and go home and wait for someone I'm expecting to come, I'll be sewing while I'm waiting. There's a lot of levels of this. It's not always great for the people around me, but it's kind of who I am.

Many of these individuals manage to maintain balance by exercising on a regular basis. Andre is among them, benching more than 400 pounds and regularly taking 3-hour runs. He reports, "Those things, in addition to the medication, make me feel alive." Andre also loves to read, a pastime that he feels has had a protective influence throughout his life:

Books—I have a thousand or more—I love to read. My biggest hobby is reading because reading literally saved my life. My friends continued to drink in different situations. When I found out I was ADHD, I stopped drinking because I knew that wasn't the answer, so the books would distract me from the pain. It's been a great asset to me, reading all those books.

Lilia takes pleasure in reading to her children, an activity that only became an option quite recently when she finally achieved literacy. When asked about leisure time pursuits and hobbies, she replies:

> I don't know if you'd consider it a hobby, but lately, since the kids started school, I find it so soothing reading them a story just before they go to bed. And it relaxes them. It makes me proud to say, "Look, guys, I'm gonna read you a story. I can do this." I'm not talking big words—there are sometimes a few words in there I have to go back to because the sentence doesn't sound right.

## ADDRESSING MENTAL HEALTH ISSUES

Quality of life is enhanced when people are able to address and resolve their own mental health issues, such as anger and low self-esteem. Nonnie notes that she has calmed down considerably over the years and that the anger and impatience of her earlier days have dissipated:

> My quality of life now is much better than it ever was. I don't think it has to do with age. I was angry a lot of the time because I knew that I was more intelligent than others thought I was. Also, there was so much chaos during my marriage. My life is calmer now. I don't try to do everything in one day. I used to want instant gratification, but now I can wait.

Betty finds that as she has grown older and achieved a deeper understanding of her disabilities, she has been able to relax into more self-accepting thinking and stop "putting herself down": "I think we're always striving to do better and to accept ourselves as we are. Sometimes I'll hit myself and think, 'Oh, God, I'm acting ADHD again.' And then, 'Oh, that's [okay, it's] neurological.' "

Glenn, too, has become less negative. With the passing of years, he has developed perspective about the isolation he has experienced for so long and, in doing so, it has grown less weighty to him:

> I think the underpinning issues of isolation are still there. Whether they mean as much to me now is another question. I have come to

terms a great deal with a lot of the social and emotional baggage, so I am healthier as a person.

As people with LD/ADHD let go of their negativity, they are better able to recognize their achievements and take pride in their accomplishments. Like several of the other individuals interviewed for this book, Lilia feels proud of her growth. Her sense of accomplishment has led her to feel good about herself, which has increased her motivation, resolve, and confidence to strive for further goals. Achieving these, in turn, has led to further boosts in self-concept, rounding out a positive cycle that has the power to propel her indefinitely:

> I am growing every day. I'm only 4'11", but I'm growing with knowledge coming in. Every day I learn a little something, and it feels so good. When it feels good, you get that confidence, and when you have that confidence and somebody pats you on the back and says you did a good job, you stop and say, "I did, didn't I? Well, if I did this today, can you imagine what I can do tomorrow!"

Rich takes pride in his achievements as well. He finds that he has been able to eliminate much of his self-doubt, develop perspective, and embrace his own successes, particularly in writing, which has always been his nemesis:

> Part of [improving] quality of life is working through all of the self-doubt issues, which still are there even though you are very successful at the things you do. For example, I think part of my quality of life is getting to the point where I'm working through some of my anxieties and fears about writing. It's not necessarily that I don't think I have something to say; it's working [to get beyond] all of the red ink that I went through as a kid and that whole validation process—it's getting to where you don't give a damn anymore. I'm [finally] to the point in my life where I'm writing.

## SEEKING SUPPORTIVE RELATIONSHIPS

When possible, adults with LD/ADHD should seek encouraging and supportive relationships, which have the potential to empower them and positively affect their quality of life. Andre recalls that his confidence was initially boosted in his youth when one particular coach in high school not only believed in him, but also urged him to see his potential and doubt himself less:

> [What really has helped in my life has been] people believing in me. If I had just a little bit of success, it boosted me into greater things. I can give you a perfect example from high school. My motor coordination, especially as a freshman, wasn't very good, but when I started playing football, the coach told the guys, "Andre will work to better himself. I admire that." I think that caused a chain reaction because every time I had a little success, it boosted me. I kept going, I kept going, and to this day I haven't stopped. Things like that are very important.

## COMMITTING TO CHANGE WHERE CHANGE IS NEEDED

Several of the adults with whom I spoke made a significant step toward a more satisfying life by committing themselves to change. This was true when Terry vowed that in college she would no longer resort to cheating; this was true when Harry and Janet committed to counseling to better understand the tensions in their marriage; and it was true when Lilia took the courageous walk back into a classroom after having dropped out of school 2 decades earlier. She describes this journey:

> It wasn't easy. Here's a women who's 35, who has four children, and who can just barely read, can't write, and is scared stiff of going to this school of the unknown. To me that was the biggest accomplishment that I made in my life. It took a lot of courage to walk through that door [of a GED prep program] and to be tested, to see what grade I was going into. The first thing came into my mind was, "My God, they have to start me in kindergarten. That's how bad I am." But you know I got in there and they gave me self-confidence and self-esteem. And they said "You can do it." And you know what? I could do it, and I did it. So to me that was a big accomplishment. And then bringing it home to my children—it feels so good to sit down with my kids. Not that I can help with them with algebra, but there's so much more that I can help them with now.

## Exploring Spirituality

Many people with LD/ADHD find it helpful to explore their spirituality, considering it a lifeline, the ultimate support, ever accessible to ease the trials and tribulations of day-to-day living. Spirituality affects a person's world view and has a significant impact on how he or she looks inward. Allyssa describes how her renewed relationship with God has helped her turn around the devastatingly negative self-image of her youth:

> When I was younger, people used to always put me down. They grabbed my dreams from me and just yanked them away. I was a little kid, and I didn't know any better, and I was like, "Yeah, you're right. I can't do that." Now that I'm an adult and I have God, I don't allow that to happen. I don't allow people to tell me that I'm not worth it 'cause I know I am.

She feels it is critical for people to understand that spirituality can expand a person's horizons, offering hope for accomplishing the unattainable. As she articulately explains, this was certainly the case in her own life:

> I want people to know that no matter where you are, there's hope. I've been at the pits of hell—I've had guns put to my head; I've been beat up; I've been a drunk mess; I've been involved in drugs; I've tried to kill myself. I've been there, and I'm not there today. My life is awesome today! And I want everybody that reads this to know that no matter where you are, if you truly believe, you could go places you never imagined and where society taught you you'd never go. You can go anywhere—I want to make that really clear—I do!

With her hopes raised, Allyssa experienced a boost in confidence to persist in her search for a job where she could be helpful to others:

> When I found God, I started to get confidence in myself. I went into big companies, where people with college degrees would go in and be nervous, and I just walked in, and the big boss of the whole company asked, "Do you have a college degree?" I said, "No, I have a high school diploma," and she said to me, "We have absolutely no position

available." I said okay, and I kept going back every month until finally she hired me. She offered me a full-time job at Federation Employment Guidance Services [FEGS]. What we do is we train handicapped adults how to get jobs and train them to take city buses and all that kind of stuff. It's awesome, and it makes me laugh that I have this position, because that's what people did for me not too long ago! Really, and it's like I'm doing that now!

Spirituality can offer a person a sense of direction. Nina clearly feels this as she comments that she thinks of her job as being her pastoral work and that her mission is with children in the arts. Nancie, too, feels her spirituality has guided her to her mission in life:

The most important part of life is my spirituality, and LD affects it from a couple of venues. I can look at it from a real practical sense and then from a higher-thinking sense. Probably 15 years ago, I said to myself, "I don't know what I want to do, where I want to go. I'm not happy in the job I'm in." Through spirituality, I prayed and said, "I'll listen to the answer of whatever I'm supposed to do. I'll work at doing it." I really believe that my private practice and the people that I've been able to meet with and that have benefited from whatever information or whatever service I have offered has been because of that spirituality. I believe that I am guided and that I'm supposed to be in the field, and I'm supposed to be doing what I'm doing. It's a real deep feeling.

Betty shares Nancie's sense of purpose. Deeply religious, she has always felt nurtured by the church and feels that spirituality provides a comforting explanation for the suffering in life, including her own struggles with "feeling broken" and needing to be fixed. She recalls being on a religious retreat and dealing with anger at not being normal, at "being unfixable":

The priest did a wonderful job in terms of saying that we were created this way for a purpose. I see that in the work that I've done and in the lives that have been changed, probably because of my being learning disabled—because of the tremendous creativity that I could see things that others couldn't and because of the energy and the drive to get other people to cooperate, to change things, to really positively impact upon people. Spirituality has played a tremendous role in my dealing with LD and ADHD.

Spirituality can give an individual inner strength. Nina comments, "I think it is because of my spirituality that I've been able to get through this whole LD thing." It can also give a person the strength to ask for the help he or she needs. Allyssa, whose reading difficulties have always been the source of deep embarrassment and shame, finds herself newly emboldened to ask for help from others:

> I go to Bible School every Wednesday. We read the Bible, and we ask questions and stuff like that. Sometimes I get stuck on a word—I do. I'm not ashamed to say, "You know what? I do have trouble reading sometimes. Can you help me out with this word? What does this word mean?" That's awesome for me to ask for help. It's like my wildest dreams, because I was always so embarrassed and ashamed.

Lilia turns to a higher power for help and reports that she finds strength as well as patience through prayer. Raising six children is clearly a challenge to which she has risen; she continues to seek the strength to contend with the tremendous difficulties and pressures she faces as she goes to school to achieve her dream of earning her GED. She explains, "I believe that there is a God, and I've asked him to help me get through school . . . to please give me the patience and strength to stick with this. And so far, God has listened."

Not everyone attends religious services in pursuit of a spiritual life. Jo Ann describes her own brand of spirituality, a connection through nature:

> My mom and I always went for walks in the woods. Just feeling the wind, that's the spirit. The sun is a spirit; the rain's even a spirit. Flowers. I look for things in the different seasons—in the fall the road is all covered with moss, now the road's all covered with the droppings of cassia trees; in the summertime, it'll be all the pine needles coming down off the pine trees. I just connect with nature. I see the deer, and I see all the little animals. There's a crow that

sits up in top of the big tree over my folks' grave area, and it caws real loud and I'll say, "Hi, Mr. Crow," and he caws right back at me.

## EMBRACING THE DISABILITY

Ultimately, quality of life is enhanced when individuals are able to come to terms with their disability and recognize that it is merely a concoction of society, based on guidelines that it has assigned to success. As Lee noted, "We must realize that success cannot be defined by society; it must come from within. . . .We must find our strengths and develop them. Then we will be ready to confront and attack our disabilities" (Lee & Jackson, 1992, pp. 138–139).

Along with nurturing their strengths, individuals with LD/ADHD must stop feeling ashamed and start embracing the diagnosis of LD/ADHD. As Glenn articulates, society paradoxically deepens the shame by trying to sidestep around the label:

> The real overriding issue is the overwhelming sense of shame about having LD, that LD is looked upon as a shame issue. People with LD are supposed to hide it. We are supposed to call it "learning differences," "learning styles"—we are supposed to do everything we can to soften what the reality is so we cannot embrace it. As long as we feel that it is shameful and we hide it or deny it or call it something different, we are perpetuating the myth that LD is shameful. We need to go from there to say, "It is what it is. How do I deal with it in my life? How do I make it a powerful thing? How do I get civil rights protection? How do I accommodate for it? How do I do all these things without being ashamed?"

These critically important questions can lead adults with LD/ADHD to redefine themselves, to recognize that along with their challenges, they bear many strengths and talents and can indeed live very satisfying and productive lives.

## SUMMARY

A number of factors influence quality of life for individuals with LD/ADHD. The characteristics of the disability affect them in venues ranging from the kitchen to the community to the workplace. Job-related issues often color an individual's life, and unemployment and underemployment of individuals with LD/ADHD result in significant financial limitations. Further influences on quality of life include interpersonal connectedness, the persistence of mental health issues, and the existence of other health concerns.

To enhance quality of life, it is suggested that adults with LD/ADHD recognize, understand, and accept their own strengths and weaknesses, resolve psychological issues related to their disability, develop a sense of purpose in both work and leisure time pursuits, achieve balance in their lives, take advantage of technology, explore their spirituality, and embrace rather than fight their diagnosis.

# References

American Psychiatric Association. (1994). *Diagnostic and statistical manual of mental disorders* (4th ed.). Washington, DC: Author.

Americans with Disabilities Act (ADA) of 1990, PL 101–336, 42 U.S.C. §§ 12101 *et seq.*

Andresen, L. (1997). Reasonable accommodations: Just what is reasonable? *Linkages, 4*(2), 10–11.

Barkley, R.A. (1998). *Attention-deficit hyperactivity disorder: A handbook for diagnosis and treatment.* New York: Guilford Press.

Barton, R., & Fuhrmann, B. (1994). Counseling and psychology for adults with learning disabilities. In P. Gerber & H. Reiff (Eds.), *Learning disabilities in adulthood: Persisting problems and evolving issues* (pp. 82–92). Austin, TX: PRO-ED.

Brinckerhoff, L.C., Shaw, S.F., & McGuire, J.M. (1993). *Promoting postsecondary education for students with learning disabilities: A handbook for practitioners.* Austin, TX: PRO-ED.

Brown, D.S. (1979). Learning disability: Unsure social behavior means insecure sexual relationships. *Disabled USA, 3*(2), 1–5.

Brown, D.S. (1981). Overcoming auditory handicaps. *Perceptions, 4*(1), 2–3.

Brown, D.S. (1982). Learning despite learning disabilities. In M.R. Schmidt & H. Sprandel (Eds.), *Helping the learning disabled student* (pp. 13–25). San Francisco: Jossey-Bass.

Brown, D.S. (1983). The learning disabled adult. In R.L. Jones (Ed.), *Reflections on growing up disabled* (pp. 140–157). Reston, VA: Council for Exceptional Children.

Brown, D.S. (1988, Fall). Getting ahead after getting the job. *Careers and the handicapped, 46.*

Brown, D.S. (1992). Empowerment through peer counseling. *Office of Special Education and Rehabilitative Services News in Print, 5*(2), 27–29.

Brown, D.S. (1994). Personal perspective—Problems and promises: Adults with learning disabilities in the past and in the present. In P.J. Gerber & H.B. Reiff (Eds.), *Learning disabilities in adulthood: Persisting problems and evolving issues* (pp. 46–51). Austin, TX: PRO-ED.

Brown, J., Fishco, V., & Hannah, G. (1993). *The Nelson-Denny Reading Test.* Itasca, IL: Riverside Publishing.

Gardner, H. (1993). *Frames of mind.* New York: Basic Books.

Garnett, K., & LaPorta, S. (1991). *College students and learning disabilities.* New York: National Center for Learning Disabilities.

Gates, B. (1995). *The road ahead.* New York: Viking.

Gerber, P.J., Ginsberg, R., & Reiff, H.B. (1992). Identifying alterable patterns in employment success for highly successful adults with learning disabilities. *Journal of Learning Disabilities, 25*(8), 475–487.

Gerber, P.J., Reiff, H.B., & Ginsberg, R. (1996). Reframing the learning disabled experience. *Journal of Learning Disabilities, 29*(1), 98–101.

Hallowell, E., & Ratey, J. (1994). *Driven to distraction.* New York: Bantam.

Hoffman, F.J., Sheldon, K.L., Minskoff, E.H., Sautter, S.W., Steidle, E.F., Baker, D.P., Bailey, M.B., & Echols, L.D. (1987). Needs of learning disabled adults. *Journal of Learning Disabilities, 20*(1), 43–52.

Kissire, P., & Kissire, W. (1996, March). Speech presented at the Learning Disabilities International Conference, Washington, DC.

Krantz, J. (1996). My life with dyslexia. *Linkages, 3*(1), 12–13.

Latham, P.S., & Latham, P.A. (1997). Legal rights of adults with learning disabilities in employment. In P. Gerber & D. Brown (Eds.), *Learning disabilities and employment* (pp. 39–55). Austin, TX: PRO-ED.

Latham, P.S., & Latham, P.A. (1998). Specific learning disabilities: A civil rights issue. In K. Lens, N. Sturomski, & M.A. Corley (Eds.), *Serving adults with learning disabilities: Implications for effective practice* (pp. 45–61). Washington, DC: National Adult Literacy and Learning Disabilities Center.

Lee, C.M., & Jackson, R.F. (1992). *Faking it: A look into the mind of a creative learner.* Portsmouth, NH: Boynton/Cook.

Mangrum, C.T., & Strichart, S.S. (Eds.). (1997). *Peterson's colleges with programs for students with learning disabilities* (5th ed.). Princeton, NJ: Peterson's Guides.

Minskoff, E.H. (1994). Post-secondary education and vocational training: Keys to success for adults with learning disabilities. In P. Gerber & H. Reiff (Eds.), *Learning disabilities in adulthood: Persisting problems and evolving issues* (pp. 111–120). Austin: PRO-ED.

Minskoff, E.H., Sautter, S.W., Hoffman, F.J., & Hawks, R. (1987). Employer attitudes toward hiring the learning disabled. *Journal of Learning Disabilities, 20*(1), 53–57.

Nadeau, K.G. (1995). *A comprehensive guide to attention deficit disorder in adults.* New York: Brunner/Mazel.

Nadeau, K.G. (1996). *Adventures in fast forward: Life, love, and work for the ADD adult.* New York: Brunner/Mazel.

National Joint Committee on Learning Disabilities. (1999, January). *Learning disabilities: Issues in Higher Education:* [Online] Available: http://www.ldonline.org/NJCLD/higher.ed.html.

Osman, B.B. (1997). *Learning disabilities and ADHD: A family guide to living and learning together.* New York: John Wiley & Sons.

Payne, N. (1997). Job accommodations: What works and why. In P.J.Gerber & D.S. Brown (Eds.), *Learning disabilities and employment.* (pp. 255–274). Austin, TX: PRO-ED.

Podhajski, B. (1996). Literacy and learning disabilities: Shared opportunities and challenges. *Linkages 3*(1), 4–5.

Posthill, S., & Roffman, A. (1990). Issues of money management for the learning disabled adolescent in transition to adulthood. *Academic Therapy 25*(3), 321–329.

Posthill, S., & Roffman, A. (1991). The impact of a transitional training program for young adults with learning disabilities. *Journal of Learning Disabilities, 24*(3), 619–629.

Quinn, P.O. (1994). *ADD and the college student.* New York: Magination Press.

Rehabilitation Act of 1973, PL 93-112, 29 U.S.C. §§ 701 *et seq.*

Rehabilitation Services Administration. (1985, January 24). *Program policy directive.* Washington, DC: U.S. Office of Special Education and Rehabilitation Services.

Reiff, H.B., & Gerber, P.J. (1994). Social/emotional daily living issues for adults with learning disabilities. In P.J. Gerber & H.B. Reiff (Eds.), *Learning disabilities in adulthood: Persisting problems and evolving issues* (pp. 72–81). Austin, TX: PRO-ED.

Reiff, H.B., Gerber, P.J., & Ginsberg, R. (1997). *Exceeding expectations: Highly successful adults with learning disabilities.* Austin, TX: PRO-ED.

Reisman, E.S., & Reisman, J. (1993). Supervision of employees with moderate special needs. *Journal of Learning Disabilities, 26*(3), 199–206.

Reisman, E.S. (1993). *Guidelines for supervising employees with learning disabilities.* (Available from E. Reisman, Threshold, Lesley College, 29 Everett Street, Cambridge, MA 02138-2790)

Roffman, A. (1997). Transition to work. *Linkages, 4*(1), 13–14.

Roffman, A., Herzog, J., & Wershba, P. (1994). Helping young adults understand their learning disabilities. *Journal of Learning Disabilities, 27*(7), 413–419.

Siegel, E. (1974). *The exceptional child grows up.* New York: E.P. Dutton.

Silver, L.B. (1999). *Attention-deficit/hyperactivity disorder.* Washington, DC: American Psychiatric Press.

Simpson, E. (1979). *Reversals: A personal account of victory over dyslexia.* Boston: Houghton Mifflin.

Smith, S.L. (1991). *Succeeding against the odds.* Los Angeles: Jeremy P. Tarcher.

Solden, S. (1995). *Women with attention deficit disorder.* Grass Valley, CA: Underwood Books.

Sylvester, H., & Sylvester, J. (1996, March). Speech presented at the Learning Disabilities International Conference, Washington, DC.

Vogel, S.A. (1997). *The college student with a learning disability: A handbook* (6th ed.). Lake Forest, IL: Author.

Wagner, M. (1992). Analytic overview: NLTS design and longitudinal analysis aproach. What happens next? *Trends in postschool outcomes of youth with disabilities: The second comprehensive report from the National Longitudinal Transition Study of Special Education Students.* Menlo Park, CA: SRI International.

Wechsler, D. (1997). *Wechsler Adult Intelligence Scale* (3rd ed.). San Antonio: Psychological Corporation.

Weltner, Linda. (1998, Feb. 5). Ever so humble. *Boston Globe*, p. F2.

White, W.J. (1992). The postschool adjustment of persons with learning disabilities: Current status and future projections. *Journal of Learning Disabilities, 25*(7), 448–456.

Whiteman, T.A., & Novotni, M. (1995). *Adult ADD*. Colorado Springs, CO: Pinon Press.

Woodcock, R.W., & Johnson, M.B. (1989). *Woodcock-Johnson psycho-educational battery* (Rev. ed.). Itasca, IL: Riverside Publishing.

Yuan, F. (1994). Moving toward self-acceptance: A course for students with learning disabilities. *Intervention in School and Clinic, 29*(5), 301–309.

# Resources

## ORGANIZATIONS

ADDult Support Network
2620 Ivy Place
Toledo, Ohio 43613
An organization affiliated with ADDA; publishes a newsletter and other
  publications

Association of Higher Education and Disability (AHEAD)
Post Office Box 21192
Columbus, Ohio 43321
(614) 488-4972
E-mail: ahead@postbox.acs.ohio-state.edu
An international organization of professionals committed to full partici-
  pation in higher education for people with disabilities; provides training,
  publications, and conferences

Children and Adults with Attention Deficit Disorder (C.H.A.D.D.)
8181 Professional Place, Suite 201
Landover, Maryland 20785
(800) 233-4050
E-mail: national@chadd.ord
World Wide Web site: http://www.chadd.org
A national, nonprofit parent-based organization; provides information;
  conducts conferences and support groups

Council for Learning Disabilities (CLD)
Post Office Box 40303
Overland Park, Kansas 66204
(913) 492-8755
A national organization; assists professionals in LD field

Division for Learning Disabilities (DLD)
Council for Exceptional Children (CEC)
1920 Association Drive
Reston, Virginia 20191-1589
(800) 328-0272
World Wide Web site: http://www.bgsu.edu/colleges/edhd/programs/
  DLD

One of 17 specialty divisions in CEC, a nonprofit organization that provides
  information and conducts conferences.

ERIC Clearinghouse on Adult, Career, and Vocational Education
Ohio State University
1900 Kenny Road
Columbus, Ohio 43210-1090
(800) 848-4815
E-mail: ericacve@magnus.acs.ohio_state.edu
A clearinghouse offering publications, information, and referrals related to
  adult literacy

Equal Employment Opportunity Commission (EEOC)
1801 L Street NW
Washington, DC 20507
(800) 669-4000
World Wide Web site: http://www.eeoc.gov
Key federal agency for implementation of the employment section of the
  Americans with Disabilities Act of 1990

HEATH Resource Center
1 Dupont Circle NW, Suite 800
Washington, DC 20036-1193
(800) 544-3284
E-mail: heath@ace.nche.edu
World Wide Web site: http://www.acenet.edu/about/programs/Access&
  Equity/HEATH/newsletter/home.html
A national clearinghouse for information on postsecondary options for
  individuals with disabilities; offers publications relevant to LD along with
  other disabilities

International Dyslexia Association
8600 LaSalle Road
Chester Building, Suite 382
Baltimore, Maryland 21286
(410) 296-0232
E-mail: info@interdys.org
World Wide Web site: http://www.interdys.org
An international nonprofit organization with state chapters; offers training
  and provides publications regarding dyslexia

Job Accommodation Network (JAN)
West Virginia University
Post Office Box 6080
Morgantown, West Virginia 26506-6080
(800) 526-7234
E-mail: jan@jan.icdi.wvu.edu

World Wide Web site: http://janweb.icdi.wvu.edu
Free service providing information regarding work accommodations, the
    ADA, and the Rehabilitation Act of 1973 to employers, rehabilitation
    professionals, and people with disabilities

Learning Disabilities Association of America, Inc. (LDA)
4156 Library Road
Pittsburgh, Pennsylvania 15234
(412) 341-1515
E-mail: ldanatl@usaor.net
World Wide Web site: http://www.ldanet.org
A national nonprofit organization with state chapters; provides information
    regarding LD to parents, professionals, and individuals with LD and
    conducts conferences locally and nationally

National Association for Adults with Special Learning Needs (NAASLN)
808 17th Street NW, Suite 200
Washington, DC 20006
(202) 223-9669
E-mail: 75250.1273@compuserve.com
An international coalition of professionals, advocates, and consumers of
    lifelong learning for adults with special learning needs; publishes news-
    letter and holds annual conferences

National Attention Deficit Disorders Association (ADDA)
Post Office Box 1303
Northbrook, Illinois 60065-1303
E-mail: mail@add.org
World Wide Web site: http://www.add.org
A national organization focusing on ADHD

National Center for Family Literacy
Waterfront Plaza, Suite 200
325 West Main Street
Louisville, Kentucky 40202-4251
(502) 584-1133
World Wide Web site: http://www.famlit.org
Provides information related to family literacy

National Center for Law and Learning Disabilities (NCLLD)
Post Office Box 368
Cabin John, Maryland 20818
(301) 469-830
Provides information and education concerning the law, learning disabil-
    ities, and attention-deficit/hyperactivity disorder

National Center for Learning Disabilities (NCLD)
381 Park Avenue South, Suite 1401
New York, New York 10016
(888) 575-7373
World Wide Web site: http://www.ncld.org
A national nonprofit organization that offers a free information and referral
service, conducts educational programs, raises public awareness about
LD, and advocates for relevant legislation

President's Committee on Employment of People with Disabilities
1331 F Street NW, Suite 300
Washington, DC 20004
(202) 376-6200
E-mail: info@pcepd.gov
World Wide Web site: http://www.50.pced.gov/pcepd
Provides information, training, and technical assistence to employers,
service providers,and individuals with disabilities on the ADA and
employment issues; sponsers job fairs

Rebus Institute
1499 Bayshore Boulevard, Suite 146
Burlingame, California 94010
(415) 697-7424
A national nonprofit organization devoted to the study of adult issues related
to LD and ADHD; conducts annual conference; publishes newsletter

Vocational Rehabilitation Agencies
U.S. Department of Education
Office of Special Education and Rehabilitative Services (OSERS)
Switzer Building
330 C Street SW
Washington, DC 20202
(202) 205-5465
World Wide Web site: http://ed.gov/office/osers
An agency that provides job training, counseling, financial assistance, and
employment placement to individuals who meet eligibility criteria


## NEWSLETTERS

ADDendum
c/o CPS
5041A Backlick Road
Annandale, Virginia 22003
For adults with ADHD

ADDult News
2620 Ivy Place
Toledo, Ohio 43613
(A quarterly newsletter)

The ADHD Challenge
Post Office Box 2277
Peabody, Massachusetts 01960
(888) 239-4737
National Attention Deficit Disorders Association Newsletter

LDA Newsbriefs
Learning Disabilities Association of America, Inc. (LDA)
4156 Library Road
Pittsburgh, Pennsylvania 15234
(412) 341-1515

The DLD Times Newsletter
The Council for Exceptional Children
1920 Association Drive
Reston,Virginia 20919-5989
(888) 232-7733
World Wide Web site: http://www.cec.sped.ord


## OTHER RESOURCES

Center for Applied Technology (CAST)
World Wide Web site: http://www.cast.ord
Provides information on universal design

Directory of National Disability Organizations and Agencies
World Wide Web site: http://www.pacer.org/natl/yellowna.htm
A list of national disability organizations and agendas and their contact
 information

Division of Adult Education and Literacy
U.S. Department of Education
World Wide Web site: http://www.ed.gov/offices/OVAE
    Site focusing on literacy programs for adults

GED Hotline
Post Office Box 81826
Lincoln, Nebraska 68501
(800) 626-9433

24-hour service that provides information on local GED classes and testing services; offers an accommodations guide for people with LD

LD List
e-mail to majordomo@curry.edu: "subscribe ld-list (your name)"
A listserv; offers an opportunity for people with LD to engage in general discussion of LD issues

LD Online
World Wide Web site: http://www.ldonline.ord
Covers all aspects of LD; offers publications, chats with experts, bulletin boards, and an events calendar

LD Pride
World Wide Web site: http://www.byoc.com/homepage/137233/ldpage 1.htm
New website designed to build a community of adults with LD

National Institute of Health (NIH)
World Wide Web site: http://www.nih.gov
Features the work of the NIH, including information on LD and related items

Office of Special Education and Rehabilitative Services (OSERS)
U.S. Department of Education
World Wide Web site: http://www.ed.gov/offices/OSERS
Provides information about the Individuals with Disabilities Education Act of 1990, employment, and counseling of people with disabilities

Recording for the Blind and Dyslexic (RFB&D)
20 Roszel Road
Princeton, New Jersey 08540
(609) 452-0606
A national nonprofit organization; provides taped educational books on loan to people with LD and others

# Index